BY ALLEN LACY

Home Ground: A Gardener's Miscellany

Farther Afield: A Gardener's Excursions

FARTHER AFIELD

FARTHER AFIELD

A Gardener's Excursions

by Allen Lacy

Farrar Straus Giroux

NEW YORK

Copyright © 1981, 1982, 1983, 1984,
1985, 1986 by Allen Lacy
All rights reserved
Published simultaneously in Canada
by Collins Publishers, Toronto
Printed in the United States of America
First edition, 1986

Library of Congress Cataloging-in-Publication Data
Lacy, Allen.
Farther afield.
Includes index.
1. Gardening—Essays.   I. Title.
SB455.3.L325   1986   635.9   86-1467

Grateful acknowledgment is made to *The Wall Street Journal,* where
the majority of the chapters in this book first appeared, in slightly
different form. Parts of the text also appeared in *American Horticulturist,*
American Photographer, Connoisseur, Garden Design,
and *Organic Gardening.* "Dear Thompson & Morgan," "A Craze for Hostas,"
"Mr. Shaw's Garden," and "The Disappearing World of Peter Raven"
were first published by *Horticulture*

For

Martha Blake-Adams & Carol Hall

two friends who have stayed the course

And in memory of William K. Stars

who left us far too soon

Preface

This book deals with a gardener's excursions, some of them long and complicated in itinerary, some of them so short as to be completed in a minute or two, without ever leaving my premises. (A few minutes ago, I went out to pick up the morning paper, discovering that some zephyranthes or rain lilies, planted a year ago and then forgotten, had just popped up, displaying their cheerful pink blossoms, despite a terrible drought this year and nothing resembling rain in over two weeks. It was a short excursion, but a pleasant one.) *Webster III's* first definition of "excursion" reads: "A going out or forth as from a place of confinement." That covers a wide range indeed, anything from escaping the burden of all those newspapers to read and the dishes to do on Sunday morning all the way to leaving the States. Webster further details this definition with "for recreation" and "with the intention of returning to the starting point." In every way this definition seems to cover the essays in this book. I've traveled some, I've always made it home, and I've generally been refreshed by what I've seen and by the people I've met, some of whom appear quite prominently in these pages.

There is a framework hidden behind the pieces that make up this book, which I want to own up to immediately, lest the reader conclude that I have traveled rather freely and at random through several parts of the world at my own will, discovering in the process such things as the fact that there's an oasis of tranquillity in Central America, a country where the big story is not insurrection or oppression but petunias and impatiens. I have been richly gifted over the past several years to have the support of several editors who haven't minded sending me places, so I gladly mention them here: Raymond Sokolov of *The Wall Street Journal*; Thomas C. Cooper and Roger Swain of *Horticulture*; Jack Ruttle of *Organic Gardening*; Barbara Ellis of *American Horticulturist*; Sean Callahan of *American Photographer*; and Joan Downs of *Connoisseur*. There's one other editor who deserves a good bit more than mention: Pat Strachan of Farrar, Straus and Giroux. Constantly patient and supportive, she has encouraged me in every way possible to turn an assortment of fugitive pieces and essays into more permanent form.

There are other people to thank. I am a writer only as a sideline, and writing about gardening is a subspecialty. Primarily I am a teacher, a college professor of philosophy. I must express gratitude to students who have borne with me when, in the midst of a discussion of Plato's *Republic*, I have suddenly launched into a description of a seed farm in Costa Rica. I also would like to say some good words about my colleagues at Stockton State College, who have never been so peckish as to suggest that someone in their midst whose recent writings dealt with dahlias instead of Descartes was an embarrassment. I should also express my gratitude toward the Research and Professional Development Committee at my college for the financial and intellectual support it has provided to keep some recent summers free for writing. And finally, I must again confess that my wife, Hella, did a great deal of the actual gardening at my house while I engaged in the strange and ironical pursuit that one of my sons calls "gardening at the typewriter."

My first book on gardening was dedicated to my family—my wife, Hella, and my two sons, Paul and Michael. This book is dedicated to two excellent friends of long-standing, and for good reason, and to the memory of a teacher at Duke University, who is missed by his many friends and former students. But the family has continued to play an important part in my writing life. Michael, for one, had the wit to coin the phrase about gardening at the typewriter, meaning that the chickweed was flourishing and the artemesia languishing while I was sitting at the word processor finishing a book. He—and Hella and

Paul as well—also had the grace not to use the phrase, despite its aptness, more than once or twice.

The world of horticulture is very large. I have explored only some parts of it here. There will be, I hope, more excursions to come.

New Jersey
November 1985

Contents

Contents

Contents

Contents

I. BRINGING ON

THE NEW

Claude Hope, the Seed
King of Costa Rica

May 8, 1982   *Dulce Nombre, Costa Rica*
The seed that brought me here was planted in my mind a year
ago by a biologist who had a long-standing love affair with Costa
Rica, a passion quite common among biologists because of the
extraordinary diversity of this Central American country's flora
and fauna. He had just returned from here, and he was waxing
ecstatic over his visit to Linda Vista, a flower-seed farm just
outside Cartago. "The place will knock you over," he said. "Can
you imagine entire greenhouses full of petunias and impatiens
being pollinated by hand, one blossom at a time, by beautiful
young women with soft, shy smiles? Whenever you buy bedding
plants, chances are more than fair that the seed came originally
from Claude Hope's *finca* in Costa Rica."

It was late April. I had just filled the flower boxes on the
deck with White Cascade petunias and planted two dozen white
impatiens, a hybrid strain called Super Elfin, in their usual spot,
a shady bed beneath a cedar tree. I had bought them at a nearby
garden center, already blooming in their market packs. I knew
that the garden center had gotten them from a wholesale grower
out in the country somewhere, but I had never wondered where
the seed from which they grew had originated. A Costa Rican
connection in my garden had never occurred to me, but that
evening I sat on our deck sipping gin and tonic, swatting the
first mosquitoes of the season, pretending it was a little warmer

[3]

than it was, and trying to imagine beautiful young women with soft, shy smiles spreading pollen among my impatiens.

Conversations sometimes repeat themselves. Two weeks ago my biologist friend was again waxing ecstatic. "You know, you really ought to get down to Costa Rica to see a place called Linda Vista, which is run by Claude Hope, an expatriate Texan. Can you imagine whole greenhouses . . ."

"Whole greenhouses where lovely women hum melodies by Mozart as they assist petunias with their reproductive processes," I interrupted. But a trip to Costa Rica suddenly sounded like a splendid and impulsive thing to do. April had been cold and snowy and damp. I badly needed to look at some hibiscus. "I'll go, as soon as I can," I said. "Can you put me in touch with Mr. Hope?"

And so, after a couple of phone calls between New Jersey and Central America, I flew from Philadelphia to Miami and caught the afternoon flight to San José on LACSA, the airline owned by the Costa Rican government. We flew over Cuba, instead of making the prudent detour American airplanes make, and then the sea disappeared from sight and a couple of hours later we descended through immense, anvil-shaped clouds to land at the San José airport, where I was met just outside customs by Claude Hope, a tall and courtly man in his late seventies. His bearing was military, his manner amiable but direct. We shook hands, and before I could protest he lifted my heavy suitcase and set out for his Toyota diesel pickup at a pace twice my own. "We'd better get a move on," he said. "There's a new president being inaugurated today, the city is filled with diplomats and politicians and parades, and the traffic is bound to be fierce."

We took a back road into San José and then the main highway across the Continental Divide to the province of Cartago, exchanging the usual scraps of personal history as he expertly guided his Japanese pickup to dodge rocks in the road and the occasional bus headed toward us on our side of the highway. Claude Hope couldn't remember a time when he wasn't fascinated by flowers, even though very few of them grew at the dairy farm near the west Texas town of Sweetwater where he grew up. Just before the Depression, he graduated from Texas Tech, one of four students in the college's first class in ornamental horticulture. He worked briefly for the U.S. Department of Agriculture in Arizona, then moved to the department's experimental station at Glen Dale, Maryland, where he remained, except for a period of graduate study at Michigan State College, until the outbreak of World War II.

The day after Pearl Harbor, Hope was commissioned in the U.S. Army and was soon assigned to deal with one of the country's most desperate military problems—a severe shortage of quinine to support combat troops in malaria-infested theaters of war. When the Germans invaded Holland in 1939, they seized most of the world's supply of processed quinine, stored in warehouses in Rotterdam. Early in 1942 the Japanese captured an important quinine factory in Manila as well as the extensive plantations of *Cinchona ledgeriana* in Java which supplied the crude bark from which the valuable alkaloids in quinine were refined. The last American plane to depart from the Philippines, a B-17 Flying Fortress, carried precious cargo—four million cinchona seeds that Colonel Arthur Fischer, an intelligence officer, had rescued from a plantation on Mindanao to bring back to the States.

After the seeds germinated in Glen Dale, the army ordered Hope to go to Costa Rica to set up a nursery and establish a cinchona plantation on ten thousand acres of leased land in the jungles near Serrapiquí, north of the volcanic ridge above San José. The site was poorly chosen, and the plantation failed (a failure that was less than catastrophic, thanks to the development of synthetic anti-malarial compounds to replace quinine), but when the war ended, Hope was determined to stay in Costa Rica. He had learned fluent Spanish, and he had come to love the country for its lush vegetation and profusion of tropical plants, its dramatic scenery of jungles and volcanoes. Furthermore, he had a hunch that the climate of the Meseta Central, the high tableland around San José, would be highly suitable for commercial hybridization and large-scale production of annual flower seed for sale to wholesale customers in the U.S. and in Europe. There was a dry season ("summer," lasting from December to early May) and a rainy season ("winter," lasting from mid-May through November), but almost no variation in either day length or temperature throughout the year, no matter what the season. "I knew I could get three or four separate crops of seed harvested in twelve months' time here," Hope recalled. "This meant two things: rapid progress in developing hybrids of petunias and other ornamental annuals, and very efficient land use in producing them on a commercial scale. Besides, labor costs were reasonable, and Costa Rica is unusual among Latin American countries, in that revolutions are few and far between, there's a disposition here toward stability and democracy, public education is of a fairly high order, and there's remarkably little social unrest."

By the time we had reached this stage in Claude Hope's reminiscences about his career, we had passed through the provincial capital of Cartago and arrived at the village of Dulce Nombre, where the larger of the two farms making up Linda Vista is located. The road grew worse and worse, pocked with potholes, some of which would be perfectly at home on the moon, and strewn with formidable boulders. But despite the calamitous state of its main thoroughfare, the village had a certain charm. The houses, most of them made of concrete block and roofed with corrugated metal, were brightly painted in so many different colors that it seemed possible that a paint salesman had come through one day and sold every shade and hue he had in stock. Each house had its small front garden, thickly planted in hibiscus, oleanders, allamandas, oranges, bougainvillea, and other exotic plants I couldn't identify. Near nightfall—which in the tropics descends abruptly, with no lingering twilight—the air was fragrant with jasmine and redolent with the smell of cooking fat. Unlike their Yankee counterparts, the chickens of Dulce Nombre ran free, squawking and taking refuge behind boulders as our pickup truck clattered its tooth-jarring way through the village.

Claude Hope honked his horn at the high and wide metal gates guarding the entrance to Linda Vista. A watchman carrying a walkie-talkie and accompanied by a German shepherd that looked at me as if I were Alpo appeared and opened the gates. We drove in the gathering darkness through a maze of deserted, starkly functional greenhouses and sheds, then up a winding driveway to the bungalow Hope designed some years ago with an eye toward convenience in putting up his frequent guests—

people in the seed business from the U.S., Great Britain, Western Europe, and Japan. A long central room which doubles as a living room and a library divides the kitchen and laundry and Hope's own quarters from a pair of rooms for visitors. The living room is separated from the glassed-in dining room by a heavy iron gate which can be locked at night. A similar gate secures the carport. "I got a little cautious about security a couple of years ago," my host explained, "after burglars broke in one night while I was asleep, tied me to a chair, pulled out the telephone, and thoroughly ransacked the place, out of a quite mistaken notion that I kept the Linda Vista payroll here."

Soon after our arrival, the cook had dinner on the table. Far in the distance, the cloud cover lifted momentarily, and high on a mountainside across the valley a cluster of twinkling lights appeared. "That's the village of Tierra Blanca on the slopes of the volcano Irazú," said Hope. "A pretty sight this time of night. But how they came up with that name I'll never figure out, since the earth up there is either chocolate-brown or else as red as any dirt you ever saw in east Texas."

"Did you say *volcano*?" I asked. Ever since childhood when I watched too many serials at Saturday-afternoon picture shows, I've had a recurrent nightmare in which I'm trapped in the path of flowing hot lava. Hope reassured me. Irazú has behaved itself since 1963, when it rained down ash over most of the Meseta Central, cut the main road between San José and Cartago with molten lava, caused some terrible flooding by blocking usually tame rivers, and gave the country some highly spectacular sunsets for several months.

While Hope drove the cook home, I browsed in his library to find something to read in bed. The evidence was that he had keen curiosity about many things and an extremely well-furnished mind, but I rejected Euripides, Goethe, and George Orwell, choosing instead a book on hybridizing made simple. I knew vaguely what an F_1 hybrid was, but wanted to make sure.

Over a couple of brandies, my host explained his usual routine: up by four at the latest, he gets his own breakfast and goes to the office to tend to his correspondence before Linda Vista comes to life with the arrival of the work force—eight hundred to a thousand employees, depending on the season. During my visit, the schedule would change a bit, in that the cook would fix breakfast for us both at seven.

May 9

I was up before dawn, but not before Hope, whose truck had already disappeared from the carport. As the sun rose abruptly, I wandered about the bungalow grounds, admiring some handsome specimens of datura, ficus, cobaea, and *Monstera deliciosa*—three colonies of it, eight feet high and perhaps twenty feet wide. At six, just as Hope pulled into the driveway, a series of alarming explosions sounded from the village below. Again, he reassured me. "It's not a revolution brewing. The parish priest calls the faithful to early Mass by setting off some very sizable firecrackers. It's a local tradition."

After breakfast, he suggested a drive to the top of Irazú. We would have to leave right away, since the rainy season was near and clouds would roll in around noon. He grabbed a handful of plastic bags from the kitchen to collect specimens of any interesting plants we might run across, and we were off.

Irazú lies only a few kilometers from Dulce Nombre, but the road twists and turns so many times as it makes its way to the peak that it takes a good two hours to reach it. It took us a good deal longer because we made so many stops en route. We watched part of a soccer game in a tiny hamlet on the volcano's lower slope, then drove past a great many newly planted potato fields where the fresh-plowed earth was as dark and gleaming as milk chocolate. We paused often to admire a vista or to stop at farmhouses beside the road to ask for cuttings from homely looking naturalized stands of petunias that he thought might carry genes for resistance to the *Botrytis* blight that makes some petunias a sorry sight near the end of their season. He pointed out to me in particular a native shrubby perennial in the lobelia family, *Centropogon solanifolius*, which he believed might be improved for garden use by careful breeding and selection. Apologizing that his vision for slight differences of color at a distance had weakened a bit, he mentioned that most centropogons were a muddy reddish-orange and asked me to keep an eye out for variations—clearer reds or golden yellows;

by the time we were halfway up Irazú, a dozen or more promising cuttings were in plastic collecting bags in the glove compartment.

The last several kilometers to the top of the dormant volcano possessed a strange and wonderful beauty. Clouds and banks of mist drifted in and out, now hiding, now revealing the valley far below. The potato fields gave out, and we entered a landscape of rolling pastureland. Cows and oxen grazed on lush, emerald grass beneath ancient and handsome live oaks whose branches abounded with teeming plant life—huge candelabras of flaming orange mistletoe, mosses and algae and lichens, orchids, and bromeliads of many sizes and colors. The pastures were fenced with strands of barbed wire attached to rows of living fence posts—tree limbs which had rooted in the rich red volcanic soil and which, like the oak trees, supported a variety of epiphytic plants. Along the roadside, which grew steeper as we neared the crater, there were thick stands of gunnera or "poor man's umbrella," so called because its enormous leaves can be broken off and held overhead for protection in a sudden, unexpected downpour.

The altimeter on the dashboard passed 11,000 feet, and we were in the lunar landscape of ash and sulfurous mist overlooking the huge crater—round and flat and slightly tilted. Claude Hope announced that he needed to stretch his legs after almost three hours of confinement behind the wheel, and set out across the volcanic plain, taking a long constitutional in a brisk military stride. (His employees call him El Capitán, in honor of his army service during the war at the cinchona plantation near Serrapiquí.) I couldn't keep up. I was chilled by the rapidly gathering mist and weakened by the oxygen-thin air, and the pumice underfoot was cutting the rubber soles of my sneakers to shreds.

Back at Linda Vista, Hope left the cuttings in a greenhouse devoted entirely to propagation. Two employees are charged with the task of looking for the plastic bags in the place where he customarily deposits them after a collecting trip to the countryside and then planting them in mist propagators.

Hope gave me a quick tour of his farm, showing me greenhouse after greenhouse devoted to the production of petunias, geraniums, snapdragons, and impatiens. Each mother plant grew in its own black plastic bag filled with sterilized rice hulls, fed and watered through thin tubes in a system of drip irrigation. I was particularly impressed by the ingenious system of harvesting impatiens seed. The seed capsules of impatiens explode when they ripen, and so these plants are arranged on steeply tiered benches draped with nylon film. Seeds falling on the plastic are washed toward a drain of nylon mesh that allows water to escape but not the seeds, which can be easily gathered for cleaning.

Hope said he needed to look at the petunia field, so we climbed back in his truck and drove past a high mound of discarded rice hulls to a bridge spanning a small stream, where I glimpsed something so wonderful that I asked him to stop the truck so I could get a closer look. It was a hollow, lush with tropical vegetation: enormous castor beans, bamboo with trunks as thick as my arm, elephant ears, and a steep cliff covered from top to bottom with a cascade of naturalized impatiens. Blossoms in a dozen colors were radiant in the bright sunlight and reflected more somberly in the still pool at the base of the cliff. It looked so much like an Henri Rousseau painting that I half expected to see a tiger crouching deep in the bamboo thicket, staring out at me with sober and appraising eyes.

We drove on, past rows and rows of the vine *Cobaea scandens* planted on high fences. The flowers, Hope said, are pollinated by bats, and most of the seeds end up in Europe, where these handsome vines are more favored than in the United States. The petunias, perhaps a hundred cultivars, including many hybridized by rival breeders, are planted in neat, trapezoidal patches. They aren't used for seed production— petunias do not set seed well in the open, and these, being F_1 hybrids, would not breed true anyway—but for observation, particularly for comparing the cultivars' resistances to *Botrytis*. Hope took out a notebook and scribbled down a few comments as he moved from one patch to the next, sometimes shaking his head in dismay, sometimes expressing approval.

"Here's one that seems to be entirely immune," he said.

"Let's see what it is." He dug into the earth, pulled out a metal tag, and read it. "Good. It's one of ours—Yellow Sun."

"You bury a label for every patch?" I asked.

"Yes, and always in the left-hand corner so we can find it easily."

Confused, I asked exactly how one determined which was the left-hand corner of a trapezoid.

"Well, yes, I had to make up a definition for that. It's the left-hand corner closest to you as you stand facing a petunia patch as you look in the direction water will flow in a heavy rainstorm. Since all our fields slope somewhat, it works fine." He handed me the label. "We make all our own labels here out of thin aluminum sheeting. You can write on them with lead pencil, and once they've been wet the writing won't wear off. But we can scrub it clean with bleach and use the same label over and over. It's something we developed here years ago. You'd be amazed how much money a business can save by keeping an eye out for the small details."

May 10

Linda Vista is a vast and complicated place—over two hundred acres, forty-five of them under roof. Yesterday it reminded me of a ghost town, but one so neatly tended that its inhabitants seemed to have left suddenly, perhaps in flight from an erupting volcano. But this Monday morning at six, a whistle blew, a guard flung open the gates, and more than eight hundred employees streamed in, some on foot, some in jitneys from other villages than Dulce Nombre, some on bicycles. In the main offices, phones began ringing and typewriters clattering as the field and greenhouse workers fanned out over the farm to start their chores. A truckful of young men headed for a newly plowed field near the petunia test patches to set out celery plants, one of Linda Vista's cash crops for the San José market. The farm tries to be self-sufficient. It has its own machine shop, concrete shop for manufacturing greenhouse benches, and garage for repairing the sizable fleet of vehicles used in day-to-day operations.

At breakfast, before he took me to see how petunia hybrids are made, Hope gave me a refresher course in hybridization.

The petunias he produces are F_1 hybrids, meaning that they result from crosses between two genetically stable and inbred lines, neither of which is closely related to the other. Therefore, except for the outdoor petunia field and some flats of petunias in a greenhouse where purity tests are conducted to make sure that a batch of seed is true to name, most of the petunias visible at Linda Vista are the inbred lines, not the final product that will appear in American garden centers several months after the seed crop has been shipped north to brokers and mail-order seed companies.

An F_1 hybrid must be absolutely predictable. Any surprise in a batch of seed is very bad news for the grower. Should a double pink petunia appear in a market pack of white grandi-floras, Hope's customers would have conniptions. To insure predictability, all of the contingent elements of hybridization must be rigidly controlled. Knowledge—some of which dates back to Gregor Mendel and his peas—makes control possible. Crossing a red inbred petunia with a rose inbred petunia will always produce a deep rose in the F_1 progeny—unless there has been self-pollination in the seed parent. To prevent this possibility, the anthers and corollas of the plants to be pollinated are removed three days before their stigmas become receptive to pollen. The task is tedious, but absolutely necessary.

At a petunia greenhouse I watched petunias being emasculated. At one bench a pair of young women moved swiftly down either side, removing petals and anthers. When they finished, it looked as though an insect horde had munched its way the length of the bench, dining on flowers but eschewing leaves. At another bench, workers—some of them with soft, shy smiles—applied pollen to blossoms that had already been emasculated. Each worker carried a small glass vial of pollen and a pollen applicator, an implement invented and manufactured at Linda Vista. It's a tiny, bell-shaped piece of plastic sponge attached to a wire. "It works better for some reason than the old brushes of camel's hair or human hair," Hope said. "I don't know exactly why. Also, it wastes less pollen, which is very precious stuff."

The labeled vials of pollen are kept until needed in ice chests at a central desk. A clerk brings the vials to the women doing the pollinating and checks their labels against the sign on the bench which indicates the cross to be made. Hope explained the reasons for this intricate system of checks and double-checks. "We can't run the risk of a worker accidentally getting lost and pollinating the wrong bench. There's too much at stake, both money and reputation. Okay, let's go see where the pollen comes from."

We crossed to an adjacent building. In the doorway a woman sat at a small table, a pair of nail clippers in one hand, a mound of seed to her left, and another mound to her right. She would pick up a seed from the right-hand mound, nick it slightly with her clippers, then drop it on the left. "She's scarifying geranium seed to improve germination," Hope said. I felt like a lucky person, not to have pursued a career in geranium-seed scarification. Inside the building, there was much din and hurly-burly. Machinery chattered, exhaust fans roared, radios played, and women laughed and joked as they extracted pollen from petunia blossoms, freshly harvested and brought inside in large plastic sacks (always the same sack for the same inbred line, so as to avoid contamination and nasty surprises in the seed crop). The workers—many of them older than the emasculators and pollinators in the greenhouse—sat or stood around wooden tables covered with metal or plastic sheeting, tearing the blossoms apart and removing the anthers, screening and sieving them repeatedly to separate the pollen grains. Once a sack of blossoms had been picked over, the shredded petals were carted outside to a waiting truck headed for the farm dump. Linda Vista produces the prettiest garbage I'd ever seen. After the pollen is collected and sieved, it is taken to another, somewhat quieter room to be given a final cleaning in a stainless-steel bowl. Finally, it is placed in labeled vials and stored in a walk-in freezer. A gram of pollen, Hope told me, will normally pollinate ten plants during their entire season of bloom, and depending on the type, it takes anywhere from ten to thirty plants to produce a gram of pollen. Petunia-seed capsules mature thirty days after pollination. An average capsule contains three hundred seeds so tiny that a kilogram contains ten million. I can't fathom these figures except in personal terms.

I don't plant more than a dozen petunias a year. A single capsule from Linda Vista, given perfect germination, would last me until the year 2007.

A crackling voice on the walkie-talkie Hope carries with him through the workday summoned him to his office to take a call from the States. Left to myself, I wandered through the busy maze of sheds and greenhouses to a hillside test field planted entirely in impatiens, perhaps three acres of them. It may just have been the loveliest sight I will ever see, a crazy quilt of crimson and cerise and scarlet and clear pink and hot tangerine and white, colors so dazzling in the clear morning light of the tropical highlands that they almost pained the eye they delighted. Above the lush green mountains to the south, towering cumulus clouds billowed upward, announcing that the rainy season was at hand. Two young men, who moved with an admirable grace, were digging up some impatiens plants that had been marked with stakes and fluttering white tags to indicate some characteristic or other that was worth close observation. They put them, each with its clump of earth, on a wooden pallet, which they then carried off to a greenhouse at the far end of the field.

I walked down to the hollow with its stream, its bamboo, and its hint of tigers, then up the road past the rows of *Cobaea scandens* and the petunia field, discovering several roofed sheds, open at each end, where coleus plants were in full flower, apparently to be pollinated by bees rather than greenhouse workers. I also found a small field of delphiniums, so dwarf that they wouldn't require staking, but with magnificently full flower heads in wonderful delphinium colors of steely blue, rich purple, deep rose, and unsullied white. Out of a thousand plants, three dozen were tagged for keeping and for further observation. Four workers were yanking up the remainder—any one of which I would be delighted to have in my own garden—for the discard heap. In Dulce Nombre, it seemed, a new race of delphiniums was coming into being, to grace us all in future years.

At eleven the whistle blew to announce the workers' break for lunch. I went back to the bungalow to wait for Hope's appearance, mulling over what I had seen thus far at Linda

Vista. I was strongly reminded of Plato's ideal republic, where a philosopher-king and a class of carefully selected guardians rule over all the processes of government and society to assure the good of the whole, the common weal. Plato believed that a perfect state might be achieved by establishing an entirely rational system, administered by elderly wise men and supported by the orderly and entirely specialized labor of the great mass of workers, who perform their appointed tasks with no more need to understand them than someone who dabs pollen on a petunia blossom needs to understand the science of genetics. Plato's ideal is a conservative ideal, of course: change and variation are more likely to produce ill than good, and so the same things are done day after day in the same manner in order to achieve the same result as in the past. One inbred line crossed with another inbred line will always produce the same uniform progeny—if the guardians insure that the pollen is collected and labeled with exquisite care and that the seed parent is emasculated at precisely the right time. I didn't know anything about Claude Hope's political views, but I did recognize that in his line of work he was essentially compelled to repeat the past, to see to it that the same crosses were repeated without variation in order to preserve lovely things. It struck me that if Plato were writing the *Republic* today he might well equip his philosopher-king with a walkie-talkie and a pickup truck.

When Hope returned for lunch, the conversation turned to the history of Linda Vista. He got started in the seed business in 1946, when he co-founded Pan-American Seed Company and with only six employees set up a farm in the Costa Rican town of Turrialba to produce petunia seed. His first real success was the seed of Comanche, the first red hybrid and a cultivar that still sells well today, although over the years it's been gradually improved through a little genetic tinkering. Late in 1950 he bought a farm five kilometers from Dulce Nombre, now used largely for the open pollination of ornamental asparagus. Disastrous weather—high winds and untypical heavy rains during the dry season—almost put him out of business, but he hunkered down and managed to survive. By 1954 he was able to lease a second farm, part of his current holdings in Dulce Nombre. He almost lost his lease four years later but was able to buy the property when the owner was killed in a dispute with a neighbor over a fence line.

Claude Hope might be a modern-day horticultural philosopher-king, but I was wrong about his being compelled endlessly to repeat the past. Musing about the future of the flower-seed business, Hope said that there was much that disturbed him. He hated to see the conglomerates gobbling up one seed house after another. He hated to see people who inherited businesses started by their grandfathers being replaced by corporate managers for whom a seed is a product just like any other—wing nuts or transistors or aerosol cans of shaving cream. "You wouldn't believe how ignorant some of these people in so-called top management are," he complained. "More and more, they order seed and expect delivery the day before yesterday. Snapdragons are a good example. It takes a minimum of six months to produce snapdragon seed from the time the parent plants are started until the crop is harvested, and what's more, the seeds need considerable time for after-ripening before they will show a decent percent and rate of germination. I've got an amazing number of customers who order snapdragon seed in May for delivery in October. You can figure that one out for yourself."

He had some especially sharp words for corporate managers in charge of marketing. "I'm not at all sure that it's a healthy thing to have encouraged gardeners to expect to get their bedding plants already in bloom in market packs. The fact is that a lot of things that look good in the market pack look downright sorry when they're established in the garden. I try to make both retailers and their customers happy by breeding toward annuals that look good in both places, but we should have educated the public a little. Take pansies. There's no getting round it, a pansy that's been transplanted in full bloom never performs nearly as well as one that's set out when it's quite small, with only four to six true leaves, but I'll bet you'd be hard put to find small pansy plants like that for sale nowadays. I blame the market people for this bad state of affairs, for not recognizing that gardeners are perfectly willing to wait for flowers if they know they'll get a better result that way. After all, people plant tulip bulbs in the fall, and they don't seem to mind waiting until April or May to see them bloom. Also, these marketing people are a trifle shy on imagination. They rely on surveys to tell them what will sell and what they should order. Well, there's no such thing as a marketing survey that isn't based purely on history, on what has sold in the past. A survey can't tell you what people might buy in the future, if it happened to be available. So the hybridizer, the seedsman who's got his eye cocked toward the future, has got to take risks, to use his imagination to dream up something new, and then work his tail off trying to make it a reality."

"Such as what?" I asked, and he trotted out some of his own current dreams, most of which turned out to be vegetables rather than flowers. He thought it would be dandy to have an edible pepper with several different colors of fruit on the same plant—red and yellow and white and purple. It would be festive in the garden, and it would give a new look to salads. He believed that some of the new semi-hot peppers could be improved by giving them their own distinctive size and shape to separate them from sweet peppers and from their more ferocious kin, perhaps by making them round and about the size of a tennis ball. And he saw a crying need for a Patio-type tomato with genuine, old-fashioned tomato flavor and an indeterminate pattern of growth so it would last the season. It might even be feasible for such a tomato to produce bright yellow flowers large enough to make the plant attractive as well as tasty in its fruit.

"I've been brooding a lot about that tomato lately," he said. "It would be a damn fine tomato for the home garden, although it wouldn't make the large farmer stand up and cheer. I've already made some crosses, and I'm pretty sure I have all the genetic material I need right here at Linda Vista to make it work as an F_1 hybrid."

A leading question occurred to me, and by then I felt comfortable enough with Costa Rica's undisputed seed king to ask it: "If you could produce that tomato you're talking about either as a purebred strain that would come true from seed year after year, so that home gardeners could simply save the seed in order to have it, or as an F_1 hybrid that would not breed true, which would you choose?"

He caught my insinuation and disarmed my question with

a smile. "Well, hybrid vigor is not exactly a myth, you know. But I'd have to say that if I were a home gardener I'd prefer something good that came true from seed, though of course I'd have to be careful not to contaminate the line by having other tomatoes around. But as someone in the business of producing seed to sell, I'd be a damned fool not to choose the F_1 hybrid to get a good return on my investment."

May 11

We rose at four, got our own breakfast, and met Fernando Villalta, Hope's assistant in business matters as well as in certain breeding projects, at the main entrance to Linda Vista, and the three of us set out for a meeting between some officials of the USDA Division of Plant Inspection and Quarantine and a group of Costa Ricans who grow cut flowers and foliage plants for export to the U.S. At breakfast, Hope had told me something about Fernando Villalta, who had returned the night before from a business trip to the States. First working for Hope in the fields as a boy, Villalta displayed determination, ambition, and drive, as well as keen intelligence. He picked up English with ease and was promoted from field hand to higher and higher positions of responsibility. It was clear that Villalta now has an intimate and detailed knowledge of Linda Vista's operations and that the farm's future and his own are strongly wedded to one another. One crucial task for philosopher-kings is to see to it that there's another generation of philosopher-kings being trained and nurtured.

On the way to the meeting, which was scheduled to take place at nine at a commercial nursery in Alajuela, on the other side of San José, I listened to Hope and Villalta talk business. I learned that their four top crops are impatiens, petunias, geraniums, and coleus, in that order. Linda Vista produces, by volume, seed for an estimated seventeen to eighteen percent of all bedding plants sold in Europe and North America. On a dollar basis, it has a forty percent share of the market because it specializes in the higher-priced seed like impatiens.

The meeting was conducted in Spanish, except for the phrase "hitchhiking insects," which came up repeatedly. I caught enough of the conversation, an exploration of the possibility of a Costa

Rican growers' cooperative paying a USDA plant inspector to clear its merchandise before exporting it to the States, to feel a little thankful to the high-school Spanish teacher who insisted that I master idioms and irregular verbs.

After the meeting, we took another jaunt, on an errand of my own, to Atenas, a village south of Alajuela. I had brought with me a half-dozen vials containing hundreds of tiny orchid plantlets. The species, *Cattleya skinneri*, just happens to be the national flower of Costa Rica. It also happens to be virtually extinct in the wild, thanks to marauders who have gathered them and sold them in the markets of San José for decades. A friend who is a professional orchid grower in my home town had several specimens of this rare plant and had reproduced them by tissue culture, asking me to deliver them to Harold May, a retired nurseryman from Pennsylvania now living just outside Atenas in a splendid new villa. May wanted to reestablish the orchids on a protected piece of ground. The heliconias in his garden were lovely, but I admired them from the wide verandah of his house after he mentioned having seen a fer-de-lance that morning. When we finished having some iced tea and a chat, Claude Hope had another plastic bag full of cuttings from a fuzzy, gray-green, thick-leaved species of coleus Harold May grew. It's not especially ornamental, but it's edible and spicy, being kin to one of the several plants that goes under the name of oregano. Hope, I felt sure, would take it in hand, teach it new tricks, and enliven the future salad bowls of the world.

May 12
Spending one's life hybridizing and improving plants is a noble but largely uncelebrated vocation. Claude Hope, who has given us the Wizard strain of coleus, a host of petunias including Comanche and Yellow Sun, and too many different impatiens to list, runs no risk of being mobbed by fans, as happens with even third-rate rock singers. Most people, asked to name three hybridizers, would draw a blank right after Luther Burbank.

I asked Hope what he would have done with his life if he hadn't entered the flower-seed trade. He looked puzzled. "I don't know. I can't imagine running a hardware store or a bank. If I hadn't stayed in Costa Rica after the war, I would probably have gone back to the USDA and retired ten years ago after spending my days as a bureaucratic hack. Now, let's see. This is your last morning here. Why don't we spend it looking at the results of some recent work in breeding, some things that have almost gotten to what I had in mind when I started working on them?"

Hope's reputation rests on annual ornamentals, so I was surprised when he drove me to a distant field filled with row after row of amaryllis, a bright array of deep reds, clear whites, and peppermint stripes, most of them quite short, their large, flat-cupped flowers borne just above the dark green foliage. "These ought to be fine for southern California and the rest of the Sun Belt," he explained. "I've bred them to be bedding plants, with fairly short stems of a uniform height, to look good in a mass. Look closely and you'll see that most of them have eight buds instead of the usual four or six. The buds open two at a time, on opposite sides of the flower cluster, and they stay in bloom for quite some time. It won't be long before I introduce these amaryllises for marketing." He picked a ripe seed pod and gave it to me. "Here, try it yourself. It will be years before it blooms, but keep it as a memento of the days you spent in Dulce Nombre."

We next walked through several greenhouses I had somehow missed in my wanderings around Linda Vista. We inspected some flowering maples or abutilons with enormous flowers in rich shades of gold and crimson, as well as some flowering purslanes that Hope said would likely appear on the market in the late 1980s. In the gerbera house, over one hundred benches were devoted to this most elegant of daisies. The house was shaded, but it glowed with color. I admired especially a delicate lavender gerbera as lacy and fringed as a Fuji chrysanthemum. But Hope took off his pith helmet, stood with his arms crossed, and shook his head. "I'm disappointed," he announced. "Look, I came through here last week and put tags on the plants that looked good prospects for further breeding. I tagged under one hundred, out of several thousands. We should have made much more progress on these things by now. Something else has to be done; when it comes to gerberas, the plant breeders in Japan are still out in front." The gerberas all looked marvelous to me, so I just took Hope's word for the fact that they were congenitally unfit.

In yet another house, there was yet another marvelous sight: impatiens unlike any I had seen growing in the field, the results of Claude Hope's work with the New Guinea species discovered and introduced a couple of decades back. These were tall and dense and shrubby, and so smothered with two-inch blossoms that from ten feet away they looked like Easter azaleas from a florist shop. Hope looked pleased. "Excellent progress here," he said. I couldn't speak. There was something magical, that radiant flood of color that seemed to glow from the flowers themselves.

"It's nothing like Kansas," I said, but Hope was already far off across the greenhouse.

Dear Thompson & Morgan

Gardeners and especially gardeners who also write about gardening get a lot of peculiar mail about the latest horticultural gimcracks and doodads and the newest thing in miracle plants. Usually I just consign such mail to the wastebasket, but on that spring day when I got a form letter from Bruce J. Sangster, president of the American branch of Thompson & Morgan, the venerable British seed company, I found myself vexed. Mr. Sangster announced a "historical breakthrough"—a newly hybridized yellow geranium that could be mine for just $24 a pair. Living with a couple of yellow geraniums, it struck me, must be a bit like eating blue ice cream. I expressed myself vigorously on this issue to several people, Mr. Sangster included. It was a cranky thing to do, but early spring is a cranky time of year, and I allowed myself to overlook a salient fact about gardening: it's a matter of passion and prejudice, and probably there were a great many other gardeners, people of discrimination and taste, who would love to have a yellow geranium.

The upshot, a few days later, was a phone call from Sangster himself. He didn't at all seem to mind my aversion to the very idea of yellow geraniums. In fact, sounding downright jolly about it, he invited me to pay him a visit at his office in Lakewood, New Jersey, which happens to be an hour's drive from my house. I accepted on the spot. I had never visited a seed company. And that yellow geranium notwithstanding, I have always felt special affection toward Thompson & Morgan, purely because of its catalog, which sends out a flattering message about the gardeners who are its customers.

According to this catalog, we are a discriminating lot. If we are in the market for primulas, we enjoy having sixty-three sorts to choose among; for dianthus, forty-eight; for sweet peas, forty-two. We also seek out the rare and the unusual, appreciating the chance to grow as a houseplant the African baobab tree (*Adansonia digitata*). We are extremely patient. We will wait two years for our *Cardiocrinum* to come up, three for our rare *Lathraea clandestina*, a purple-flowered parasitic plant whose seeds must be planted in nicks in the roots of willows growing beside ponds. (Well, some of us will wait, at least, but I must confess that I get a little impatient with any seed that hasn't shown its cotyledons within a week.) We appreciate precise information about how to germinate such plants as *Clematis* ("stratify in freezer for 3 weeks"), *Lapageria* ("soak 3 days, changing water 3–5 times a day"), and *Callistemon citrinus* ("sow on kitchen towel in a saucer and keep moist").

A few of us like to keep things easy and uncomplicated. Here, too, Thompson & Morgan is accommodating. For gardeners who don't want the bother and fretful uncertainty of starting plants inside and then transplanting them, it has a special line it calls the Simplicity series—almost fifty fairly foolproof varieties which can all be sown directly in the ground, germinate easily and quickly, and go on to flower where they are sown. And in the case of a number of especially desirable items which also happen to be difficult to germinate, Thompson & Morgan sells them as Plantlettes—its trademarked term for plants which are pre-germinated under sterile and controlled conditions in its laboratories and then shipped to customers in sealed petri dishes.

Finally, Thompson & Morgan seems to know that every true gardener resents being prodded or nudged, that we just want the facts, along with a good many color pictures to help us make up our minds and our seed lists, and so its catalog studiously avoids hyped-up prose about this or that new and amazing vegetable wonder we all must grow and grow right away. In its pages, you can find an occasional exclamation point, but they are as scarce as the cashews in a can of mixed nuts.

❀   ❀   ❀

I drove to Lakewood with keen anticipation, expecting to see the Rolls Royce of the seed trade. After all, many of the catalog offerings are distinctly pricey. (Just three seeds of *Pachypodium lamierei*, the Madagascar palm, cost $3.95.) But Thompson & Morgan's American branch, which has since moved to Jackson, New Jersey, to quarters more befitting its status, proved to be unprepossessing, to put it gently. The tiny store was nestled between a delicatessen and a Radio Shack. The brightly colored packages of seeds on metal racks in the vestibule of the shop were cheering, but the back rooms were cramped and dreary.

Bruce Sangster greeted me warmly in his windowless office, possibly once a closet, and then suggested that we repair to Winkelmann's, a German restaurant of some reputation near Toms River. A half hour later, over hot potato salad and a fine platter of bratwurst, Sangster briefed me on the long history of Thompson & Morgan and its present ambitions to capture the same market that it has in Great Britain—gardeners who are determined to grow from seed the rare, the unusual, and the very best recent hybrids.

There's no Thompson at Thompson & Morgan and no Morgan either—but there are three Sangsters. William Thompson, originally a baker and confectioner whose shop was on Tavern Street in Ipswich, East Anglia, began selling seeds as a sideline in the early 1850s. The sideline quickly became his main business, and Mr. Thompson, who was widely known as the "Baker-Botanist of Ipswich," became highly respected in British scientific and horticultural circles and corresponded on occasion with both Charles Darwin and Sir Joseph Hooker, director of the Royal Gardens at Kew. When he was fifty-three, a special issue of *The Botanical Magazine* was dedicated to him, honoring him for his service to botany. Near the end of his life, the Royal Horticultural Society invested him with the Victorian Medal of Honour, its highest accolade.

This baker-botanist sought out seeds from all over the world, but he took a special interest in the flora of Texas, California, and the Rocky Mountains. Thompson sowed these seeds in a garden behind his bakery and later on a small farm called

Haslemere Nurseries, and sold the seeds he produced through a mail-order catalog.

And Morgan?

"Yes, that would be John Morgan," Sangster said. "No one is exactly sure when he entered the firm as a partner. The company has moved four times and our archives are far from complete. The best guess is that he came in just before the turn of the century, a few years before William Thompson died at the age of eighty in 1903. My grandfather, Joseph Sangster, became a partner in 1913 and assumed full ownership of the firm when Mr. Morgan died in 1921."

Since then, there's been a succession of Sangsters. Joseph Sangster's son J. Murray Sangster joined Thompson & Morgan in 1933 and ran the business from the time of his father's death in 1952 until his retirement in 1974, when he turned it over to his two sons. Keith Sangster, the elder of the two brothers, now in his early forties, is in charge of the company's operations at its headquarters in Ipswich. Bruce watches the store in Jackson. His grandfather began mailing out catalogs here in 1937, with prices given in dollars. Even before the American branch officially opened, T & M was sending twenty thousand catalogs to the U.S. each year and receiving about ten thousand orders as a result. Some Anglophiles still insist on ordering directly from Ipswich, even though the seeds are the same.

By the time lunch was over, Bruce Sangster had invited me on his brother's behalf to visit Ipswich the next time I got to England. With a sabbatical coming up, I could say I would be there in September. I still wanted to see where seeds come from.

One crisp afternoon the following September, I walked up a hillside just outside Ipswich to T & M's headquarters, two low and sprawling brick buildings deliberately designed to resemble the almshouses that are typical of the East Anglian countryside. The narrow road leading upward past the company's front gate had no shoulders whatsoever and was filled with lorries racing in each direction at perilous rates of speed, so I walked through the stubble of a newly mown field.

Minutes after I presented myself to the receptionist, Keith

Sangster appeared and shook my hand with an enthusiasm that made it clear that cordiality to total strangers runs in the Sangster family. He was also frightfully sorry. He had thought I would be arriving tomorrow, and he was in the middle of a staff conference that would continue until early evening. He asked if I'd like to look around the place, wander around the warehouse, and walk through the small field out back where the company grew some of its seeds, including a fine light blue salvia, *S. patens*, and a highly amusing plant called *Ecballium elaterium* or squirting cucumber. I might like to visit the Customer Service Department. Pamela Shepherd would be there, and she would be delighted to show me some old seed catalogs from the nineteenth century and to let me read some recent correspondence from customers. As for tomorrow, Sangster and his chief buyer, David Tostevin, had blocked out most of the day to satisfy my curiosity about Thompson & Morgan—past, present, and future.

In the mood for a little horticultural amusement, I made a beeline for the squirting cucumbers, whose peculiarities were explained to me by a young man out in the field who was harvesting some salvia seeds. "It's a joke plant, really," he said, pointing to a patch of low, cucumber-like plants bearing a heavy crop of bristly green fruits the shape of footballs and the size of small grapes. "In late August, the water pressure builds up inside these things so much that anyone—a small child usually—can squeeze them and the pulp and seeds fly out for an amazing distance at a terrific rate of speed. Now, when they're really ripe . . . well, just touch a plant."

I touched a plant. Half a dozen ripe fruits flew in every direction, falling to the ground ten or more feet away. I touched another plant. I forced myself to stop. Such amusement probably wasn't seemly in a grown man, and besides, if I allowed myself more of it, T & M probably wouldn't have seeds for next year's catalog.

The warehouse at T & M reeks and screams of fertility. Ripe seeds, billions and billions of them. Seeds of all sizes, from the faint dust of petunia seeds to the hefty bulk of lima beans. Seeds smoothly rounded, seeds with sharp hooks on the ends. In the dry-storage room, 50-kilo bags of seeds in bulk from Holland, Greece, Japan, Israel; seeds from Sakata's Reliable

Seeds in Yokohama, from Ball Seed in West Chicago, from Flamingo Enterprises in East Mowha, Australia. Seeds from the four corners of the world, four thousand different kinds, gathered here for their brief season, before being dispatched to those who will grow them in Liverpool and London, in Bonn and Brussels, in New Haven and Nashville.

But on the first day of my visit there was more in the air than fertility. Bette Midler was belting it out from a blaring radio near the commissary at the rear of the warehouse. Seven women attended the humming and clattering carousel machines that spewed metal-foil seed packets into picture packets for the four hundred most popular items T & M sells. The odor of glue permeated the air above the long tables in the middle of the warehouse, where other workers sealed by hand the packages of the less popular seeds, the novelties and rarities that added to the eight million packets that had to be ready for shipment to the retail trade by early October. The air was delicious with the overpowering scent of fenugreek.

In the Customer Service Department, which resembles a library, Pamela Shepherd offered me a nice cup of tea and then went to get it, giving me the 1877 catalog of William Thompson, seedsman of Tavern Street. It was bound with blank pages at the back where Mr. Thompson kept his notes on a great many matters, including the fact that he had filled and shipped an order to a Mrs. Ransome of Sunnyside for gold-laced polyanthus, pyramidal mignonette, and *Collinsea violacea*. In a fine and spidery hand, he also noted that he meant to write to Kew for seeds of *Phlox divaricata*, *Oxalis arenaria*, and *Salvia farinacea* and recorded the recipe for a liquid guano especially suitable for roses.

As we sipped our tea, Pamela Shepherd told me about her work. Customers write in directly on their own with questions, or use special inquiry forms that are available at retail outlets. Or they telephone: yesterday there were 120 telephone calls in six hours' time. Sometimes customers come in person, a practice the company discourages. To give me some notion of the kinds of inquiries her department receives, Miss Shepherd handed me a thick pile of letters, a various lot. Some people wrote for advice: their asters had the blight, or some horrible insects were attacking their tomatoes. One wrote to complain that the primulas he bought—from another firm—had not germinated properly. Some people sent photographs of their hibiscus or their vegetable marrows. A woman in Brisbane sent a dried cosmos blossom, carefully pressed in tissue, pointed out that it had "the loveliest scallop in the edges of its petals," and said she'd send along some seed if T & M thought others might enjoy growing it. Some wrote simply to say, "God bless Thompson & Morgan."

Three people wrote several letters—long ones—within a single week. They didn't seem to be asking for advice. They didn't complain. They didn't really seem to be making any point. They simply wrote, as if seeking some understanding human contact in a lonely world. Every letter to Thompson & Morgan gets answered, and answered personally, even those that seem directed not to a seed company but to Miss Lonelyhearts.

In Keith Sangster's orderly jumble of an office—a jumble because his desk and several adjacent chairs were piled high with manuscripts and proofs for next year's catalog, orderly because he seemed to know exactly where to find what he wanted—my second day began with more tea and another letter. Sangster rummaged through the papers on his desk, found the letter, and said, "Here, read this. I fairly pounce on this kind of thing." The letter came airmail from a customer on the South Pacific island of Tarawa. "I enclose herewith," it read, "the outer cover of a package of *Passiflora quadrangularis* I ordered from you last year. It is NOT *P. quadrangularis*. Please send me a correctly labeled package, plus some apple squash for my garden."

Sangster explained why he fairly pounced. "The reason I've kept this letter is that *Passiflora* is a very muddled-up genus. From the looks of it, this chap may be an expert. I mean to send him some seeds of all the species we sell to see if there are any other mistakes he can sort out for us. It may even be that he's growing some species we don't offer and might become one of our suppliers. In the seed trade, information is the key commodity, and it's a two-way business. You know, of course, about our challenge contest for amateur gardeners?"

When I confessed ignorance, Sangster rummaged again and handed me a press release announcing that T & M would pay £12,000 to the first amateur gardener who finds, grows, or successfully breeds an improved flower or vegetable. According to the release, "Plant breeding is not just for boffins only, working in sterile laboratories, nor is it necessary to have acres of space. Many gardeners who have taken to breeding as a hobby only have the tiniest of back gardens. What is needed is an abundance of patience, good powers of observation, and the ability to know what to aim for." To encourage home gardeners to develop what it called "a hobby within a hobby," T & M was offering a free booklet called "Plant Breeding" and holding a contest that would last at least four years—and perhaps longer.

Any results?

"Oh no, it's too soon to tell. We've just got started on this thing, and there've only been about fifty entries thus far—a potato, a white aubrieta, a hardy fuchsia that's said to have all the attributes of the fancier tender sorts, among those I can recall. And of course there have been a good many letters from people telling us what they're working on. There's an American living in Kent who claims he's almost got a truly novel delphinium perfected with flowers that are red, white, and blue." Sangster paused in disbelief, giving me a chance to ask about his training and experience.

As a young man, Keith Sangster studied botany for a year, spent the next year working for his father, and then began a series of apprenticeships in Scotland and in Holland, where he hybridized and rogued pansies for a Dutch wholesale grower. Shortly thereafter, he returned to Ipswich, his father retired, his brother Bruce came aboard, and T & M hired a new buyer, David Tostevin. I would meet Tostevin somewhat later in the day, but Sangster wanted me to know in advance that Tostevin deserved much of the credit for what amounted to a brand-new T & M.

"In 1973, David came to us on loan from Unilever, where he was in charge of purchasing vegetable-oil seeds—linseed, soybeans, and so on. We bought up his contract in August of 1974, and from then on we more or less rewound the clock, setting up a modern purchasing department, something we badly needed. David's predecessor, a wonderful woman named Dorothy Monks, who is known all over England for her ability to identify a phenomenal number of seeds at a quick glance, kept many of the details of the warehouse operation in her head. It worked, but David put in computers for a new system of inventory control, solved a nasty problem we'd had with rodents, and instituted the picture packets which are now so important in our marketing.

"Now there's been a complete turnaround. For the past four years we've been monitored by the Ministry of Agriculture at Cambridge; they come here every fortnight and take random samples from dry-storage and packaged seed, test them, and we've had no rejections. We've also upgraded our lines, sold on quality rather than quantity, and here again David deserves much of the credit. It's getting very hard to find unusual seeds of high quality, and David does a great deal of travel—to Malaysia, Hong Kong, Taiwan, Japan, and the States, all of which he will be visiting in the next year or so."

Although David Tostevin is the chief seed hunter, the Sangster brothers are hardly stay-at-homes, and they sometimes turn up new treasures for future catalogs. Keith Sangster fairly glowed as he talked about his not entirely serendipitous discovery of a new and wonderful strain of Iceland poppies. Ruth Saltzman, a businesswoman who is president of White Swan, Ltd, a company which makes sundials and other garden ornaments and serves as T & M's distributor to retail outlets in the Western states, saw to it that Sangster couldn't miss those poppies, by having a huge bouquet of them delivered to his hotel room while he was on a business trip to Portland, Oregon.

The next day, when he met with Mrs. Saltzman, Keith Sangster told her, "Those are absolutely lovely flowers, you know, except for one thing—they don't exist. They simply can't."

Ruth Saltzman assured him that they could and did exist—extremely hardy and long-blooming biennials and often perennials, with blossoms up to eight inches across in their first flush of bloom, many of them double, in apricot and lavender and other sumptuous colors unknown in the genus previously. They were the product of over fifty years' work of careful hybridization by Erma Westcott, a dedicated amateur plant breeder, who raised them in her small home garden, gathered them each morning during their season, wrapped each blossom in tissue paper, and then took them by bus to several local florists who knew well how rare and extraordinary they were. Now grown frail and elderly, Mrs. Westcott, who thought of her poppies as ample recompense for the children she never had, feared that her work of many decades of painstaking hand pollination and careful selection would not survive her.

Ruth Saltzman took Keith Sangster to meet Erma Westcott, who cried with happiness when she realized that Thompson & Morgan would introduce her poppies—which according to her desire would be named the Oregon Rainbow strain of Iceland poppies—and that the company would ensure the hand pollination and constant roguing necessary to maintain their extraordinary beauty.

"We lost no time in buying up the entire stock of these wonderful plants, which are now being grown and increased in my father's garden," Sangster said, "and now we've got enough seed to introduce them. I wish she could have lived to see the reception her poppies got, but she died in 1982—a great pity, for hers may be one of the finest achievements in recent years by an amateur hybridizer."

Sangster was sorry I could not meet David Batty, who was out of town. Batty's specialty is ferreting out ingenious methods of germinating usually recalcitrant plants, such as *Lapageria*, the Chilean bellflower, a vine for cool greenhouses whose large blossoms of strawberry red or blush white seem to be unusually toothsome, judging from their picture in the catalog. "You'll read in our latest catalog to soak the seeds for three days, changing the water three to five times a day, and to expect germination within three months, at a temperature of 70°–75°. Well, Batty has experimented a bit further, and he's now able to get lapagerias to germinate almost as easily as chickweed. The trick is that after the three-day soak at the recommended temperature, he puts maybe two hundred seeds into a polyethylene roll—something like an egg roll in a Chinese restaurant—and then puts them in the fridge at 32° F. Six weeks later, every last one will have germinated. We'll be updating the information on lapagerias in future catalogs."

Sangster thought it was about time for me to drop in on David Tostevin, before the three of us went out for a pub lunch in Ipswich. But he had one more point to make. The plant-breeding contest for amateur gardeners is really just an extension of T & M's present practice of relying on gardeners, as well as wholesale growers, for much of the seeds it sells. In his words, seed production is often "cockhatted out." "In the United Kingdom and all over the world in fact there are a lot of very keen gardeners, sometimes retired, with large gardens, who help us out. The head gardener at a large estate in England has located for us a rare perennial sweet pea, a blue one that ought to attract much attention when we have enough seed to offer it. A doctor in Singapore, Dr. L. Tuck Lock, has provided the seeds for one of our forthcoming novelties, the Singapore Hybrid Episcias, which have exceptionally handsome foliage and flowers. Dozens and dozens of gardeners collect seed for us, and they are exceptionally committed and dedicated people."

In David Tostevin's office, I again thought of Miss Lonelyhearts, and I told him how struck I had been yesterday by the stacks of mail from people who just seemed to want a human contact as well as from people seeking practical advice about plants. He had his own story to tell, and as he told it, I refrained from commenting on his astonishing resemblance to Richard Burton. For several years he had been corresponding with a prisoner in a top-security prison on the Isle of Wight. The prisoner wasn't permitted to read, except for seed catalogs. He asked for a catalog. Tostevin sent him one, plus a few seeds for the four small pots he was allowed to have on his windowsill.

"I sent him seeds for some small and dainty things that first year, and I've kept it up ever since. He sows and waters the seed the first of April, and he keeps meticulous notes on germination and growth. Twice a year he writes extremely long letters about the plants in those four small pots. I've never encountered anyone who observed plants so precisely, except among professional botanists. But lately I've worried just a little. I don't know what crime he committed, nor if he's eligible for parole, and I'm not absolutely sure that I'd be keen to see him walk in my door."

I didn't bring up Richard Burton, but I did ask Tostevin if he was, perhaps, Welsh? He isn't. He was born on the island of Guernsey, where his great-grandfather had immigrated from Normandy. His family were farmers who raised iris, freesias, and tomatoes. He managed to get to England at the outbreak of World War II, joined the Royal Navy but was soon invalided because of chronic seasickness, and after the war discovered that he was fascinated by seeds, so he joined Unilever, where he rapidly rose through the ranks.

He first met Keith Sangster in 1972, and it was soybeans that brought them together. T & M had offered soybeans to British gardeners for the first time, and a vast number of them ordered, far outstripping the modest supply. Someone suggested that Sangster call Unilever, and Tostevin stepped into the breach with four tons. Two years later David Tostevin joined T & M. Now he can't imagine any other line of work.

About sixty other people were lunching at that pub. Keith Sangster, David Tostevin, and I shared a tiny round table with two sporting gentlemen. Two separate conversations took place, but to an eavesdropper it must have sounded like a single, oddly disjointed one that leaped from water fowl to nicotiana and back to retrievers. The two men left just as Sangster and Tostevin were summing up the three plants that most excited them as possible introductions over the next few years.

Sangster singled out something called *Schizopetalon walkeri.* "It's got flowers like white feathers and an almond scent so wonderful you want to put it in your mouth."

Tostevin favored a sedum, *S. caeruleum.* It spreads widely, its stems turn red in midsummer, it's highly drought-resistant, it probably will reseed itself, and when it blooms it's absolutely covered with tiny, deep-blue flowers.

The third plant? It is a fragrant, summer-blooming perennial sweet pea commonly called Lord Anson's pea, after the man who commanded *H.M.S. Centurion* on a voyage to South

America in 1744. The ship's cook collected it and brought it back to England. For many years this sweet pea (*Lathyrus nervosus*) was thought to have disappeared from cultivation, but recently a gardener offered Thompson & Morgan some seed. It will be offered in limited quantity in the 1986 catalog. Keith Sangster and David Tostevin were so excited by this one that they almost sang its praises in chorus.

Steichen's Delphiniums

Gardeners who live in climates where tall delphiniums grow well owe a tremendous debt to the French hybridizer Victor Lemoine, who brought them into being in the middle of the nineteenth century by crossing several species native to Siberia, and to subsequent breeders in Great Britain and northern California who by careful selection produced dozens of strains to delight the eye and gladden the gardener's heart.

It takes no ingenuity at all to praise delphiniums. Their spikes of blossoms, which can tower over six feet tall, are stately and elegant. Their wonderful colors—sky blue, royal blue, dark purple, mauve, lavender, and creamy ivory—never clash among themselves or with any other flower. Their petals have a silken sheen, and they're often iridescent.

That's the good news about tall delphiniums. The bad news is that except in New England, the coastal regions of the Pacific Northwest, and some parts of Alaska they are difficult to grow. Slugs adore them. If they're not carefully staked, they topple in wind or rain. They are subject to crown rot and other maladies. Even with the best of care, they are fickle, having so strong a tendency to disappear from one year to the next that some horticultural authorities class them as perennials, but advise treating them as annuals.

After a long history of disappointment, I've given up trying to keep tall delphiniums in my garden. But I do have delphiniums —a remarkable strain called Connecticut Yankee, which was introduced in 1965, when the seed industry acknowledged its merit by naming it an All-American Selection.

The Connecticut Yankee delphinium has proved itself over the past two decades, in my own and many other gardens. It isn't especially stately, and it doesn't tower, reaching no more than three feet. It's fairly bushy, and produces large numbers of stems which branch out from the base of the clump. The single flowers, up to two and a half inches across, have the same range of radiant color as other delphiniums. It doesn't require staking, and if cut back sharply after it blooms it will produce a second crop of flowers. Occasionally I lose plants in a harsh winter, but it's much less likely than its taller kin to pull a disappearing act, and it performs well in summer heat.

There's one other thing about the Connecticut Yankee delphinium. It was hybridized by Edward Steichen (1879–1973), earning him a niche in the history of American gardening that neatly complements his preeminent position in the history of photography. For many years I've pondered this little quirk of a fact, which is something like hearing that Albert Einstein wrote a symphony or invented a soufflé. By itself, the fact is intriguing, but puzzling. I've long been curious. How serious a gardener was Mr. Steichen? Was the Connecticut Yankee delphinium a one-time shot? Did it turn up in his garden by lucky accident, or was it the result of a careful program of hybridization?

Just recently I shared my curiosity in this matter with a photographer friend, who suggested a bit crisply that information about such things could often be obtained, provided that it was deliberately pursued. He suggested further that a likely person to talk to might be Joanna Steichen, Mr. Steichen's widow. I telephoned Mrs. Steichen and found her gracious and willing to talk about her late husband's horticultural labors, which were as much a part of his life as photography. Here is part of what I learned.

Edward Steichen was an ardent gardener all his life. Sometime before World War I, he became interested in genetics and took up plant breeding. He worked on cleomes, nicotianas, poppies, and sunflowers, among other things. But delphiniums were closest to his heart. From 1928 on, he raised five acres of them at his country home near West Redding, Connecticut. He hybridized many of the tall and spiky sorts, naming them for poets such as Paul Claudel.

The Connecticut Yankee delphinium was no fluke. Mr. Steichen had a precise goal in mind—large flowers on a bushy, fairly compact plant—and in the early 1960s, after achieving this goal in a strain that came true from seed generation after generation, he turned it over to Frank Reinelt, a well-known professional hybridizer in California, who brought it into production for introduction in 1965.

At the end of our conversation, Mrs. Steichen reminded me that she had met her husband only in 1959 and suggested that I call someone with earlier knowledge of his passion for delphiniums—Grace Mayer, former curator of photography at the Museum of Modern Art. Miss Mayer turned out to be another gracious soul, and an enthusiast for Edward Steichen as hybridizer as well as photographer. Years later, she still recalls what he said to her one summer's day sometime in the 1950s as the two of them pulled into the driveway of his country place in Connecticut. "This," he said proudly, "is where the blue begins."

"I will never forget the splendor of the sight," she said, "a vast field of delphiniums, every imaginable shade of blue, and to add to the beauty, bright golden sunflowers planted at the fringes of the field. Such a sight, once seen, burns itself into memory. And then of course there was also that famous flower show of his, which people still talk about, almost fifty years later."

His flower show?

"Yes, in 1936, from June 24 until July 1, Steichen staged a show of his delphiniums at the Museum of Modern Art, bringing in flower spikes by the truckload." Everyone who saw them was dazzled by their beauty. It was the first—and the last—flower show in the museum's history. The day after it opened, the New York *Herald Tribune* pronounced it "the most amazing exhibit of delphiniums we have ever seen in this country by one man, one woman, or all men and women put together."

After my conversation with Grace Mayer ended, I realized that it isn't so odd after all that a great photographer should also have been a great hybridizer. Both artists and plant breeders bring something new into being. They must have a vision to guide them in dealing with intractable materials. And if they succeed, they leave behind a great legacy to the rest of us.

No Steichens hang in my house. But I grow some out in my garden, having raised them from a package of seeds that cost less than a dollar. I put them right alongside Luther Burbank's Shasta daisies as fine examples of the contribution of the hybridizer's art to the American garden.

Cobia's Cacti

Since his firm sells only wholesale the plants it raises, chances are slim that even the most dedicated houseplant fancier has ever heard of B. L. ("Larry") Cobia of Winter Garden, Florida. Even though his complex of more than 275,000 square feet of greenhouses is open to the public, there's no sign identifying the company, which does business under the odd name the Garden of the Leprechauns (suggesting that Cobia is somehow involved with shamrocks), as well as under the more sober name of B. L. Cobia, Inc. One of Mr. Cobia's sons, Michael, the firm's business manager, is fond of congratulating visitors who do manage to find the place. He has pointed out to his father more than once that even the CIA has a sign in front of its headquarters in Langley, Virginia.

In the Cobia greenhouses a wide range of both flowering and foliage plants are propagated before being shipped to market or to other commercial greenhouses all over the country, where they will be grown on to maturity before they are sold at retail. Cryptanthus, dieffenbachias, fittonias, hoyas, philodendrons, and scheffleras are all raised at Cobia's, as at a large number of other greenhouse nurseries in the Orlando area. But what differentiates Larry Cobia from other plantsmen in Florida is his dedication to Christmas cactus. A fine houseplant to begin with, in his hands it has been transformed into one of the glories of countless winter windowsills, where Cobia's cacti are grown even if his name is not spoken.

Christmas cactus is not an especially apt name for these plants, which are botanically known as *Schlumbergera*, although they used to be called *Zygocactus* and are still discussed under that name in some books on houseplants. It's pretty much an accident if one actually is in bloom on Christmas Day. Holiday cactus would be a better term, since their season of bloom, which is determined by nighttime temperature and by day length, extends, according to the variety, from Halloween until Easter. Furthermore, the same plant, if kept in a hanging basket in a sunny window and turned a notch or two every couple of weeks, may bloom over a period of three months or so as it continues to set new buds. (In the uniform overhead light of a greenhouse, however, it would bloom all at once, for a couple of weeks.)

The Cobia breeding program for holiday cacti is complicated and has stretched over many years. He began with some eighty-five named cultivars, most of which were plagued by a short season of bloom and a limited range of color. Two things, apart from a mastery of the art and science of hybridization, were essential to his success. First, the existence of a legal system of plant patents, whereby he could retain control of propagation for seventeen years after any given cactus was named and introduced. Second, a particularly ingenious and admirably crafty scheme of breeding. Cobia maintains two separate lines of plants. One is diploid, the other tetraploid, meaning that it has twice the usual number of chromosomes. The offspring of these two lines, which are the plants from which selections are made for commercial introduction, are triploid—"mules," which cannot set seed. This scheme assures that no other breeder but Cobia, who keeps his breeding stock under tight surveillance, can stand on his shoulders to hybridize new cacti using the genetic material he has developed. If this policy sounds selfish, one should consider that over the years there have been only twenty-two introductions by Cobia, of which some ten are still protected by patent, meaning that they cannot be propagated vegetatively except under license. It takes, on average, seven years to develop a new cultivar, at a cost of around $75,000, since for every one that reaches the market tens of thousands of other seedlings have been rejected and destroyed by kerosene—a necessary safeguard since otherwise the Cobia garbage would be a gold mine for would-be competitors.

Cobia's holiday cacti aren't at all difficult to come by. Many florist shops start selling them in early November—small plants, with only three or four branches, but already in bud. They are also widely sold in the produce sections of grocery stores in several chains, typically in square plastic pots wrapped in plastic film. Generally there's a label with the plant's name— Lavender Doll and Peach Parfait, as well as more Christmasy names like Kris Kringle and White Christmas—and the patent notice and logo of the Garden of the Leprechauns. The selection of colors is wide: tangerine, salmon, white, blush pink, crimson, and even an apricot gold which is new in the *Schlumbergera* palette.

Ira Slade, whose Greenlife Nurseries in Griffin, Georgia, is a good mail-order source for the Cobia cacti (in case someone lives in some benighted locale), wrote an article about them a few years back in *Florist's Review*. According to him, these cacti were real toughies, even before Larry Cobia got his hands on them. They are exceedingly long-lived: Slade cites a woman in New England who has a Christmas cactus over eighty years old. Their care is simple. They should be watered thoroughly, but allowed to dry out between waterings. Water should be withheld entirely for a month beginning in mid-September, to help induce flowering. They should be fed with 20-20-20 liquid fertilizer right after the buds show and then again in early spring.

I can testify to Slade's commendation of the Christmas cactus as something to pass down to one's grandchildren. We have one—the old *Schlumbergera truncatus*, which has narrower leaves than Cobia's hybrids—which started its life with us as a rooted cutting my wife bought in a farmer's market in Harrisonburg, Virginia, in 1962. Now two feet high and almost three feet across, it covers itself in bloom for a week or so just before Thanksgiving, with sporadic blossoms appearing until Valentine's Day. In the last eight years, it has been joined by a dozen of Cobia's lovely creations, which lend interest and glowing color to every window we have that faces east. More will come, and I am eagerly awaiting 1990, when Larry Cobia has promised, somewhat mysteriously, holiday cactus blossoms that much resemble . . . well, he won't quite say, but he seems to have a great surprise for us all.

II. INTO MY
GARDEN

Clove Currant

One of the fascinations of gardening is that no matter how long one keeps at it, something new and surprising keeps turning up. Take, for example, the shrub I encountered this spring in my brother-in-law's back yard in Tullahoma, Tennessee. All around his neighborhood, garish forsythias were screaming for attention, but this shrub didn't scream. It simply beckoned for a closer look.

I had no idea what it was, but it was wonderful to behold— a bush some four feet tall and three feet across, with erect stems arising directly from the base, pale green foliage, and hundreds of soft primrose-yellow blossoms, much like those of winter jasmine, hanging in loose clusters all up and down the stem. Closer up, I discovered that it was beloved of bees and very fragrant and spicy.

Whatever it was, I had to have it, so I dug up several small suckers and brought them home to my garden in southern New Jersey. With a little help from *Gray's Manual of Botany* and *Hortus Third*, I've managed to identify it as *Ribes odoratum*, commonly known as Missouri currant, buffalo currant, and clove currant, an especially apt name, considering its heady perfume.

Many garden books don't even mention the clove currant, but from those that do I've gleaned the following bits of information. A native of the central United States from the Dakotas southward into Texas, it is quite hardy. The foliage is attractive in both summer and fall, when it turns a glowing scarlet. In

Jewels of the Plains, the late Claude Barr, an eminent authority on American native plants, asserted that *Ribes odoratum* "will grow and perform well in drier and more difficult garden situations than perhaps any other fruit bearer." He also judged its brownish-black fruits "very pleasant eating."

Others before me have fallen for the charms of the clove currant. In 1812, Thomas Jefferson gladly planted some rooted cuttings at Monticello; they had been sent to him by Bernard M'Mahon, a Philadelphia nurseryman who had acquired stock collected in Missouri by Lewis and Clark. In *Old Time Gardens* (1901), one of my favorite garden writers, Alice Morse Earle, said of it: "I do not see this sweet and sightly shrub in many modern gardens, and it is our loss. The crowding bees are goodly and cheerful, and the flowers are pleasant, but the perfume is of the sort you can truly say you love it; its aroma is like some of the liqueurs of the old monks."

Although I am strongly inclined to argue that every last forsythia bush in America should be ripped up and replaced with a clove currant, there are two obstacles. First, like most species of *Ribes*, the genus that contains gooseberries as well as currants, *R. odoratum* serves as an alternate host to white-pine blister rust disease, and growing it is restricted or even prohibited in some parts of the country. Second, it is extraordinarily rare in the commercial nursery trade.

I had thought that so winsome a plant would be easy to locate, elsewhere than in my brother-in-law's yard, but I was dead wrong. After discovering that the clove currant wasn't listed in any of the major mail-order nursery catalogs in my files, I turned to experts at the American Horticultural Society, the Arnold Arboretum, and the National Arboretum, who provided me with the names of some thirty nurseries specializing in uncommon plants. Except for discovering that Woodlanders, a highly regarded nursery in Aiken, S.C., offers *Ribes aureum*, a California native that somewhat resembles *R. odoratum*, my search for a commercial source for the clove currant was disheartening, as I made enough phone calls to gladden the heart of everyone who owns stock in AT&T.

Finally, with my twenty-ninth and thirtieth call, I hit pay dirt. We-Du Nurseries in Marion, North Carolina, doesn't list the clove currant at the moment, but they have it under propagation, and a limited number of plants will be available either this fall or next spring. And Emile Deckert of Carroll Gardens in Westminster, Maryland, who grows this flowering currant in his own home garden, has similar plans to propagate and offer it in the very near future, to customers who live where it isn't prohibited.

The plants sold by these two nurseries will obviously be small rooted cuttings which may not bloom for several years, but patience is every true gardener's keenest virtue. The clove currant's solid beauty and spicy fragrance make it well worth the wait.

Gaura

"Through a long Virginia summer . . . when daytime temperatures usually exceeded 90° F., only this and gaillardia flowered daily from June to October. It begins summer as a 2- to 3-foot, vase-shaped bush clad in downy 2–3-inch, spear-shaped leaves, sometimes maroon-speckled. Wiry pink wands rise above it, steadily elongating at the tip as lower flowers are neatly dropped until, by fall, it is shoulder high and still bearing flowers that look like flights of small, white butterflies, fading to pink." Thus write Pamela Harper and Frederick McGourty of a perennial native to Texas, a member of the evening-primrose family named *Gaura lindheimeri*, in *Perennials: How to Select, Grow & Enjoy.* It is an extremely fresh and lively volume which sets a very high standard for practical guides to horticulture and which is especially valuable for the 240 color photographs taken by Mrs. Harper, who has become one of America's best-known garden photographers since moving here from Great Britain a dozen or so years ago.

A few weeks ago I visited Pamela Harper's garden on a two-acre spit of sand projecting into the salty waters of a creek just off the Chesapeake Bay, in Virginia's Tidewater area. There I saw with admiring eyes several fine clumps of *Gaura lindheimeri*, which immediately leaped to the head of my long list of perennials to acquire as soon as possible. It is, quite simply, a marvelous plant—easy to grow, reliably hardy throughout the South and northward to coastal New England, tolerant of sandy soil (it resents any soil that isn't well drained), and a feast for the spirit. It manages the difficult trick of being so bold and commanding that it attracts attention all the way across the garden, while also seeming delicate and graceful, as its small flowers dance in the breeze on their tall and slender stems, which can reach seven feet high by the end of the growing season.

But a great mystery surrounds this very fetching native perennial: considering its many merits, why don't more of us grow it in our gardens? Linnaeus obviously thought highly of it, for the name of the genus comes from the Greek word for superb. So did his nineteenth-century American disciples who named the species to honor their colleague Ferdinand Jacob Lindheimer (1801–79), a German immigrant who immersed himself in studying the flora of Texas.

I'm not sure why this plant has been so badly overlooked despite its keen and obvious merits, but there are three or four possibilities. One is that many American gardeners feel more comfortable with common names than with scientific names for plants. *Gaura lindheimeri* is quite a mouthful, and the common name, bee blossom, lacks pizzazz and could describe hundreds of other plants. Another is that people who write about horticulture and dispense advice on gardening often follow in each other's tracks, repeating what their predecessors have written, and bee blossom has not had much in the way of a claque. The 1933 edition of Liberty Hyde Bailey's influential *The Standard Cyclopedia of Horticulture*, for example, claims of all the various species making up the genus that they "scarcely possess general garden value, although they are pleasant incidents in the hardy border for those who like native plants." Such praise is so faint as to be damning, certainly nothing to make you want to rush right out and track down a dozen or so gauras.

A third possibility, discovered when the roll of film I shot to show the glory of the gaura came back from the processor, is that gaura turns out to be decidedly unphotogenic. The individual blossoms came out okay, but a plant photographed from several feet away, so as to show the overall effect in the garden, looked something like a starving white larkspur close to its demise. Lots of us select plants on the basis of pictures in nursery catalogs. Who wants to order something that seems to be in mortal agony?

Finally, there's a simple fact about the state of horticulture in the country today. Two decades ago, almost out of nowhere, a great craze for houseplants seized America, one that still continues today as we peer out from our windows through a great jungle of hanging baskets full of asparagus ferns and hoyas and Swedish ivy. For the past three years, there's been a similar craze for perennials, if the garden center near my house is any indication. It still sells annual bedding plants like impatiens and petunias, yes, but it's also selling astilbes, brunneras, and stokesias, to customers increasingly inclined to plant things that come back from one year to the next and get better every year.

Gaura may be rare in commerce, but it can be found. Thompson & Morgan lists the seed. Holbrook Farm and Nursery offers small plants that if planted in the spring will probably bloom their first year.

There are a great many perennials to get to know, once past the basic things like phlox and Shasta daisies. Once *Eryngium giganteum*, or sea holly, comes, can *Gaura lindheimeri* be far behind?

Evening Primrose

It is one of the peculiarities of gardening in America that some of our best native annuals and perennials aren't appreciated until they've gone to England for an education. British plantsmen have long been keenly interested in selective breeding of North American plants. Generations ago they took the common field asters of New England, fussed over them for a while, and then transformed them into that glory of the fall garden on both sides of the Atlantic, the Michaelmas daisy. Much the same thing took place with our native columbines, lupines, penstemons, and phlox. More recently, the British have taken in hand the goldenrods of our fields and roadsides, gussied them up, and returned them to us via some of our more selective nurseries under their botanical name *Solidago*, giving us perennials not to be sneezed at, for two reasons: they don't really cause hay fever, and they brighten up the dullness of the late-summer garden.

Some American plants, however, are still much better known and appreciated by British gardeners than they are on these shores. An excellent case in point is *Oenothera*, a genus with many species, whose common name of evening primrose is misleading, because some species bloom during the day and none is a primrose. Walk up a street of any American suburb on the Fourth of July and your eyes will everywhere be assaulted by the salvia's red glare. You aren't very likely to be comforted and soothed by the sight of evening primroses, and that's a pity.

William Robinson, the most outstanding British garden writer of this century and last, had nothing but praise for evening primroses. In his influential book *The English Flower Garden* (1883), the fifteenth edition (1933) of which has just been reprinted for American readers, Robinson revealed his ongoing love affair with "these handsome plants of the plains and hills of America." He had a special affection for the showy evening primrose (*Oenothera speciosa*), whose blossoms range from white to pink, rather than the yellows and golds which are more typical of the genus.

I fully share Robinson's affection for this plant, although some other gardeners violently disagree, including one friend who briskly told me that if I dared say a single word on its behalf I deserved to have a picket line on my front sidewalk. I have a large clump, some twelve inches high and four feet across, in a corner of my yard, where it blooms nonstop for most of the summer.

From a distance, this evening primrose is a visual treat— a wide, low mound of softly glowing pink. Up close, the blossoms are wonderfully complicated and lovely to behold. Three inches or so across, each has four wide, overlapping petals, with an intricate pattern of deep rose veins leading out from the nectary and a halo of olive yellow at the center. The star-shaped, four-pointed pistil and the stamens protrude sharply and on a sunny day cast sharp shadows on the silken petals. The flowers get smaller as summer wears on, but they still give a welcome bit of pleasant color, and the plant is remarkably tolerant of drought.

There are only two problems with *Oenothera speciosa*. The first is that it's hardly available at all commercially, even though it's far from uncommon, considering the fact that it grows abundantly in the wild along the roadsides of Texas and the Midwest. No seed company, to my knowledge, offers it, and I've found only one nursery, Woodlanders, whose catalog offers it as a plant.

The second problem, the one that brought my friend to declare that I am virtually a public menace, is that the showy evening primrose has a great deal of gumption and muscle. Spreading rapidly by means of underground runners, it can soon engulf a garden. In *Jewels of the Plains* Claude Barr declared it a worthy garden perennial but also warned that it should be encircled with a metal band eight inches deep to keep it from roving.

Perhaps my critic is right: I have introduced into my garden a monster, something as bad as crabgrass. But then, if crabgrass produced huge pink blossoms for two months or more, I'm not sure I would mind it at all.

Prairie Gentian

Starting with what to call it, it's a perplexing plant. Its common names in English include blue marsh lily, Texas bluebell, and prairie gentian, the last name being preferable I think, since it is a member of the gentian family and certainly no lily. It's also known as catchfly gentian, tulip gentian, and Western blue gentian. In Mexico its name is *lira de San Pedro*—St. Peter's lyre—but I don't know why.

The short way through such a confusion of common names is to resort to the botanical or scientific name, but in the case of this flower the confusion continues, even with the Latin. Thompson & Morgan lists it as *Eustoma grandiflorus,* Geo. W. Park as *Lisianthus russellianus. Hortus Third,* the Bible of all who would rather appear in public with catsup-stained clothing than get a name wrong, supports Thompson & Morgan on *Eustoma,* but says the species name terminates in *-um,* not *-us,* and it must be correct.

Turning to the rather meager information about *Eustoma grandiflorum* in my gardening library, I get further confused. Some books say it likes a moist location, others that it almost rivals a cactus in drought tolerance. What's more, there's no agreement among various experts about how long the prairie gentian will stick around in my garden. It's an annual, a biennial, a hardy perennial, or a half-hardy perennial, depending on which authority I consult.

It would be tempting simply to forget all about the prairie gentian and grow something else instead, except for one thing:

it's a world-beater, a plant with an American past, an interlude in the Orient, and a future for discriminating gardeners throughout the temperate zone, especially considering some things that are taking place now in Costa Rica and in Maryland.

I noticed prairie gentian for the first time, under its divergent names, last year in the catalogs from Park and Thompson & Morgan. The pictures showed it to be winsome—graceful, wiry stems bearing fat and sassy buds which opened into large, goblet-shaped flowers in deep purple, creamy ivory, and soft and glowing pink. There was also impressive news about its virtues as a cut flower: it lasts up to a month in water. This year I bought several pots of lisianthus in different colors and stuck them out on our deck so we could enjoy, up close, the beauty of both the flowers and the blue-green foliage, which has a slight patina.

According to a recent article in the florist trade magazine *Greenhouse Management* by Mark Seung Moon Roh and Roger H. Lawson, even flower lovers who don't have gardens will increasingly be able to enjoy prairie gentians, as cut flowers from the florist. Drs. Roh and Lawson, who are horticulturists at the Florist and Nursery Crop Laboratory of the Beltsville Agricultural Research Center in Maryland, believe that lisianthus—the name likely to stick among professional growers—is a highly promising commercial plant, not only because of its long-lasting beauty but also because the cool temperatures it requires the first few months after germination are good news for greenhouse owners, who constantly fret over heating costs.

The Roh and Lawson article recites a bit of the history of the prairie gentian. A native wildflower of the American plains from Nebraska into Texas, it attracted, some sixty years ago, the attention of Japanese breeders who eventually extended its range of color and turned it into one of the most popular cut flowers sold in the Orient. It resettled itself in American soil, in six new forms, only around 1980.

Thanks to a quick telephone call to Dr. Roh in Beltsville, I've cleared up some further confusion. Prairie gentians are annuals in colder parts of the country, including Maryland. Where the climate is gentler, it's a perennial, but a fairly dicey one that might just as well be replanted from seed in very early spring. It requires a good supply of moisture during the four months following germination, a period of very slow growth indeed. But with the fourth set of leaves, it spurts into rapid growth and can withstand dry conditions. "It's an exciting plant, and a very pretty one," Roh told me. "But there's much we don't know, much basic research yet to be done."

Some of the research is now going on in the Costa Rican village of Dulce Nombre, as one of the best American hybridizers of the twentieth century turns his attention to lisianthus, eustoma, prairie gentian, or what you will. I mean Claude Hope, of course, the plant wizard of Linda Vista. We've exchanged numerous letters since I visited him. He believes that the prairie gentian, in its current stage of hybridization, has some flaws, such as sparse branching and slowness to come into bloom, and that the color range could be expanded still further. He's gone back to the original species, using collected seed from Texas. Astute hybridizers and seedsmen like Claude Hope don't make large promises until they know they have a solid achievement. In his last letter, however, Hope writes that he's very, very pleased with his progress. I suspect that we'll be hearing much more about prairie gentians as this century moves to an end.

Invasion of the Sumac

Ever since our first parents blew it and then beat it from Eden, every gardener has known that to balance every bright success there's a near-miss or an outright dismal failure. Near-misses and dismal failures come in many shapes and sizes, but the most embarrassing ones take place when we unwittingly invite some very ill-mannered and invasive plant or other into our yards and then watch in horror as it oversteps its bounds, making itself, like Sheridan Whiteside in *The Man Who Came to Dinner*, far too much at home. Most gardeners can list several such mistakes. My own list would take several hours to discuss, if listeners were willing to invest the time in someone else's recital of woes. For starters, there are spiderwort, ox-eye daisy, and old-fashioned tiger lilies, all of which immediately got out of hand, springing up in places where they were neither planted nor wanted. And I may well, in time, regret those pink evening primroses.

I did know better than to put in equisetum or horsetails. Even though they're genuine botanical curiosities, plants of such evolutionary antiquity as to call forth images of dinosaurs and pterodactyls in the vicinity, they're also such notorious spreaders that one friend of mine who grows them surrounds them with a metal barricade pushed eighteen inches deep into the ground. Bamboo is also nothing to trifle with. I grow it, but in an isolated corner of my garden, where thus far I've kept it under control, partly by cooking and eating those of its shoots which spring up where I don't want them. Spearmint was a calculated risk. It's one of the pushiest herbs on earth—but who could survive the hot afternoons of August without a pitcher of iced tea heavily laced with lots of lemon juice and fresh crushed mint leaves?

It is, alas, extremely simple to name the worst miscalculation I ever made as a gardener. Six or seven years ago, I let the glowing words of a mail-order nursery catalog persuade me that I had desperate need of the shrub *Rhus typhina* laciniata—the staghorn sumac. The catalog seduced me with its talk about the staghorn's subtle and haunting beauty. It also appealed to unimpeachable authority: the Royal Horticultural Society had given it a Garden Merit Award. But perhaps staghorn sumac simply behaves itself better in British gardens.

The staghorn sumac has its merits. It's a fast grower, to understate the matter. Its large, deeply cut, ferny leaves are handsome and bold from midspring into fall. In the winter its nobby, brittle branches are covered with the cinnamon-colored, velvety down that gives it its common name. Nevertheless, after several years of constant battle with it, I'm dogmatically of the opinion that it has no place whatsoever in the home garden and that any nursery that offers it to the public ought to write the words "Let the Buyer Beware" in its catalog before proceeding to celebrate its haunting and subtle beauties. This sumac, like most others in the genus, is an unrelentingly restless wanderer. It doesn't just spread from its center, like some other plants. It does that, but it also sends out underground stems that can meander thirty or forty feet from the mother colony before suddenly springing up in some unexpected spot. And it seems that once you've planted one staghorn on the premises you'll have many more, world without end. Two years after I planted mine, I concluded that it had to go, so I ripped it out—or so I thought. Its progeny are still with me. I hack them out wherever they pop up. I mutter curses at them, but they thrive on my dislike, proving the point that far from loving Mozart and doting on affectionate remarks addressed to them, plants don't give a fig for our esteem.

Despite some antipathy toward reaching for a chemical solution to every horticultural problem that comes along, in my effort to stem the staghorn tide I've resorted to a herbicide my friends in the nursery business swear by. But however effective it may be in sending chickweed and almost anything else to swift and certain doom, it barely daunts this monster whose far from subtle presence haunts my garden. The shoots die back, but within a month lusty new ones take their place.

But, on reflection, perhaps this plant serves some useful purpose after all. There are days when I want to exult over the fine bloom my clematis is having this season, or the splendid way the new perennial border is coming along, or the excellent growth made by a vitex tree after I removed it from a shaded spot and gave it a place in the sun—days when I want to hog the credit for the beauty of some of the plants I grow. Staghorn sumac keeps me humble.

Yucca

It's been a good many years now since the late Senator Everett Dirksen stumped the country to get us to make the marigold our national flower. He met some fearsome opposition from people who argued against the idea. I believe his opponents were right on target, inasmuch as the marigold originated south of the Rio Grande, lives but a season, depends on hybridizers to survive in its present form, and smells so rank that some people plant it next to their tomatoes to discourage insects. Some national emblem!

Our nation's failure to agree on a horticultural symbol of our identity doesn't seem to have led to any of the distresses of the present age. The debate has died, and I'm content to let it rest in peace. But in case it ever starts up again, I'd like to have my say well in advance of the need. If we must have a national flower, let's forget all about the marigold. The proper choice, obvious to all right-thinking persons, is the yucca, a genus with many species, some of which will thrive almost anywhere in the country.

To begin with, yuccas are uncommonly useful plants. Long before the first European colonists arrived, the Cherokee were making medicinal salves from yucca roots. The Navaho and Hopi dried and ate its fruits. Its very name probably came from the Taino tribes of the West Indies, one of very few such Indian plant names to be used in scientific botanical nomenclature. (Another is catalpa.)

A splendid recent field guide published by The University of

Texas Press, Campbell and Lynn Loughmiller's *Texas Wild-flowers* praises the yucca for its manifold benefits. "Ropes, sandals, mats, and baskets are made from the leaf fibers. The buds and flowers are eaten raw or boiled . . . A fermented drink is made from the fruits." Yucca root soap is also possible.

Neither bathing with yucca soap nor feasting on yucca buds vinaigrette, I leave these uses unexplored, but I do feel that any national flower should be useful. Nobody makes beer or sandals out of marigolds, which puts the yucca way ahead. But it should also be lovely, as yuccas are in any season. One species, *Yucca filamentosa*, is hardy from Florida to New Hampshire. This particular yucca dominates in my part of the world, in the coastal plain of southern New Jersey, growing in gardens and along roadsides and railroad tracks, where it has volunteered. It's exciting in late June when the sturdy flower stalks, which can tower up as high as eight feet, appear and branch out before bursting into spectacular clusters of creamy white blossoms, deliciously fragrant on a warm July night.

It's good to report here that the best British garden writers have long held our American yuccas in high esteem. Gertrude Jekyll, the leading theorist of the herbaceous border earlier in this century, used them lavishly as one of the staples in the gardens she designed. Vita Sackville-West often praised them for their bold and sculptural beauty.

But for a final word on the loveliness of yucca, here's what Alice Morse Earle had to say in *Old Time Gardens* about her childhood memories of them growing in Newburyport, Mass., at a garden called Indian Hill: "The tall columns of the Yucca or Adam's Needle stood like shafts of marble against the hedge trees of the Indian Hill garden. Their beautiful blooms are a miniature of those of the great Century Plant. In the daytime the Yucca's blossoms hang in scentless, greenish white bells, but at night these bells lift up their heads and expand with great stars of light and odor—a glorious plant. Around their spire of luminous bells circle pale night moths, lured by the rich fragrance. When I see those Yucca in bloom I fully believe that they are the grandest flowers of our gardens."

On Alice Morse Earle's testimony, I rest my case.

Coreopsis

For about a dozen years, a sign at the edge of a vacant field a few miles from my door has promised that a shopping center will be built there soon. It hasn't happened yet. The lettering on the sign is now so faded and wan that I suspect the owner, a real estate company located a couple of states away, may have forgotten its intentions. I hope no one nudges its corporate memory, for the twenty or so acres of rather poor and sandy soil in this field are one of the glories of the neighborhood, a token wild place in the midst of a suburbia that already seems to have more than its share of shopping centers, convenience stores, gas stations, doctors' offices, and fast food joints. Here sea gulls congregate in great numbers, especially when a coastal storm is brewing. Here grow a great many wildflowers, from late spring until early fall, when the field receives its annual mowing, right after the bright orange butterfly weeds, the blue chicory, and the tall white Queen Anne's lace have come to the end of their season. This field is lovely all during the summer, but especially in early June, when the coreopsis blooms, forming great sheets of gold so radiant that sunglasses are recommended.

I've sometimes been tempted to gather a few seeds of this coreopsis, which I take to be *Coreopsis grandiflora*, one of over one hundred species of the native perennials and annuals making up the genus, and plant them in some odd corner of my garden. But closer consideration and a little common sense lead me not into this particular temptation. The fact is that *C. grandiflora*, if that's what it is (it might be *C. lanceolata*), although lovely growing wild and seen from a distance, has some noteworthy demerits as a garden subject. Its stems cannot support the blossoms they bear, so the plant has floppy habits. Furthermore, the season of abundant bloom is brief, and when out of bloom the plant is coarse and unattractive.

That said, I must go on to sing the praises of another coreopsis that deserves attention, the threadleaf coreopsis (*C. verticillata*), a native of the Eastern coast from Maryland to Florida and westward to Arkansas. I grow two sorts, Golden Showers and Moonbeam, which are aptly named and wonderfully complement one another. Perennial catalogs describe them both as eighteen inches high and coming into bloom in June. Moonbeam is a lighter shade of yellow than Golden Showers and is said to bloom a month longer, but in my own garden both have thus far bloomed nonstop from early summer until the first frost of October. And these two are noticeably different in plant habit, Golden Showers standing so erect at twenty-two inches that it almost seems to have been corseted and staked, Moonbeam growing some five inches lower and spreading somewhat more loosely.

For their many solid virtues, I value these two plants as highly as any perennial I grow. In 1985's Northeastern drought, which had less plucky things gasping with thirst by early June, they held their own, permitting me to turn my attention and my garden hose to saving other plants. Their ferny, deeply cut, dark green foliage is attractive even before the first daisy-like blossoms appear.

It's one of the fundamental axioms of the history of gardening that every plant has its story, often in association with some person or other who brought it in from the wild, who carefully selected individual plants from which to cultivate a superior strain, or who deliberately hybridized it with other species in the same genus. So it must be with these two charming cultivars of *Coreopsis verticillata*, something I deduce from the fact that they go unmentioned in any of the garden books in my library from the 1950s and 1960s, and that *Wyman's Gardening Encyclopedia* (1977 ed.) somewhat dismisses the threadleaf coreopsis, praising its resistance to drought but terming its flowers "poor." It's obvious that someone fairly recently took this plant in hand, watched it with a sharp eye, selected superior specimens with some distinctive traits, and sent them into the marketplace, where they have spread quickly from one nursery to the next. I don't know his name, but I'd like to send him my thanks. Or her.

Hardy Fuchsias

Few sights are quite as fetching as a hanging basket filled with fuchsias, especially those whose branches have a graceful trailing habit instead of standing bolt upright. Only the incurably insensitive could fail to be enchanted by their fat and waxy buds and their pendant pink or magenta or white or crimson or two-toned blossoms, as perky as crinoline petticoats. These hybrids, among several tender Caribbean and Latin American species of a genus in the evening primrose family, have such beauty that they must be accounted as triumphs of the breeder's art.

The story of the fuchsia's origins is often told, with many a variation along the way. In one version, a British sailor named Thomas Hogg collected one species in Santo Domingo sometime near the end of the eighteenth century and brought it back as a gift for his mother, who stuck it in her window in Wapping. James Lee, a nurseryman who knew a good thing when he came across it, spied it in the window, bought cuttings, and a year later sold several hundred plants for a considerable sum, thus starting a vogue for fuchsias. It became a feverish craze after 1842, when a chance seedling appeared in the garden of a man named John Gulliver—a hybrid plant of unknown parentage which opened new horizons for breeders, in that its blossoms had a white calyx, something unknown before. In another version of the story, the first fuchsia to be grown in England was *Fuchsia magellanica* (about which more, a bit later), which arrived from coastal Chile in 1788.

Other stories are possible. According to Claire Shaver Haughton's *Green Immigrants: The Plants That Transformed America*, it was a sea captain named Firth, not Hogg, who brought that fuchsia, which he had collected in Chile, not Santo Domingo—but there was a nurseryman in New York named Thomas Hogg, who in 1873 imported some fuchsia seeds from Haiti which had some importance. Very confusing. And in *Green Thoughts: A Writer in the Garden*, Eleanor Perényi raises, with entire plausibility, the possibility that fuchsias were growing on Andalusian windowsills a very long time before Mrs. Hogg—or Mrs. Firth—had hers in Wapping. The credit for observing the first fuchsia generally goes to Father Charles Plumier, a Frenchman who botanized in Santo Domingo in the early eighteenth century and who ran across a plant with beautiful blue and red blossoms which he named for Leonhard Fuchs, a herbalist and professor of medicine at Tübingen University in the mid-sixteenth century. Perényi suspects that the genus must have been known by the Spanish, long before Father Plumier appeared on the scene: "It isn't conceivable that the brilliantly conspicuous fuchsia went unnoticed by some inquisitive Spanish friar . . ."

Whatever the early history of the fuchsia, its fortune in the nineteenth century is clear: it was the ornamental plant most characteristic of the Victorian era. Many new species were collected from Mexico all the way to Chile and introduced to Europe and Great Britain, and hundreds of hybrids among them produced by such breeders as Veitch in England and Lemoine of France, as gardeners competed with one another in flower shows, exhibiting their prized specimens of Try-Me-Oh! and Lady Heytesbury and other tender fuchsias.

Just before Mother's Day, when they arrive by the truckload from California and appear on sale at the local garden center, I suffer temptation to buy one or maybe five of these lovely fuchsias in hanging baskets. But I always resist. I don't have a basement to overwinter them in their dormant state, and I lack the patience to give them the twice-daily misting and daily watering they require to perform well where the summers are hot.

But for the past two years I have had fuchsias—not the tender sorts which must be brought inside during the winter, but some hardy kinds, which are known and grown by far too few

American gardeners. I saw my first hardy fuchsia in 1971, growing in the cloister garden of Chester Cathedral. I didn't know that it was hardy, only that it was a fair-sized shrub with small, two-toned red-and-purple blossoms produced in such profusion that they filled their corner of the cloister with radiance. Then three years ago I saw some similar fuchsias, a whole hedge of them, growing in the lee of one of the conservatories at the Royal Botanic Gardens at Kew. The royal botanists, whose word is beyond question, labeled them as cultivars of *Fuchsia magellanica*, a species indigenous to the woodlands of southern Chile. The label went on to say that they were winter-hardy and that their common name was lady's-eardrops. Lady's-eardrops immediately went to the head of my list of plants seen in England that I had to grow in my own garden, no matter what had to be dug up and discarded to make room for them. And my appetite for them was further whetted by Sacheverell Sitwell's wonderful descriptions in *Old Fashioned Flowers* of the hardy fuchsias that grow wild in Cornwall and Ireland and the Isle of Arran in Scotland, where "the hillsides are red with its peculiar and dropping fire, which, upon this scale of profusion, is as though it were falling slowly, like the descending fires of a rocket."

Locating hardy fuchsias in the United States is no easy task. After searching through an enormous number of catalogs, I found one place, Lamb Nurseries in Spokane, which offered them, some eight cultivars. I ordered all eight, setting them out in late April. I put seven of them in the fairly shady location recommended by the standard garden books. One I planted perversely in full sun, where it could be seen from our dining table. The plants were sturdy, but small, and I put them in my garden with mental reservations about how hardy they would turn out to be: "hardy" has a different meaning in different climates, and an Englishman's hardy plant often turns out to be an American's winter casualty.

The seven plants I put in the shade didn't do much at all, possibly because of competition for nutrients from the roots of the same trees that produced the shade. The one in full sun, however, thrived, soon becoming a bush three feet high and three feet wide, which was smothered with hundreds of tiny blossoms of amethyst and ruby produced over a long season from late May to early October.

After the first frost, I cut all the fuchsias back and mulched them lightly with pine needles. I fretted about them throughout the winter, deciding that if none survived I would just order new ones every year from Lamb. When the first days of spring arrived, I anxiously watched for a sign that any had made it through the winter. Only in late April was I rewarded with some lusty new shoots from the fuchsia that had been planted in full sun, as well as a seedling several feet away. Only one of those in the shade pulled through. It was weak and puny, but it quickly became vigorous when I transplated it to a sunny spot. The bloom season turned out to be later getting under way this year, probably because the plants I got from Lamb last year were already in active growth, but from late June until killing frost these fuchsias have been grand to behold—wonderful plants that more American gardeners should try.

Fritillaries

Let us now consider fritillaries.

Members of the lily family, the various species in the genus *Fritillaria* are far-flung geographically. Although the greater number of species are native to the rugged, rocky hillsides and low mountain slopes stretching eastward from Turkey to Afghanistan and Kashmir, others are found around the Mediterranean Basin and in northeastern Europe and the British Isles. A few species of this bulbous plant occur in the Orient, and others are native to California and Oregon.

There's good evidence in *The Bulb Book*, by Martyn Rix and Roger Phillips, that taken as a whole fritillaries are wonderful plants, possessed of great grace and charm. Occasionally their flowers are clear and pure in color, but the photographs Rix and Phillips provide show that most of the eighty-plus species making up this genus tend toward coloration that is muted, dappled, mottled in odd combinations—greenish-yellow stippled with chocolate polka dots, pale gold speckled with maroon, or soft green striped and bordered with dark tan.

I'd like to grow many different kinds of fritillaries, but only three species are readily available to American gardeners through mail-order nurseries—*Fritillaria meleagris, F. imperialis,* and *F. persica* cv. Adiyaman.

I don't grow *F. meleagris,* a native of Northern Europe whose common names include snake's-head lily and guinea-hen flower. Its graceful nodding flowers, oddly checkered in shades ranging from brownish-purple to dirty white, make wonderful spring adornments to grassy meadows, where if conditions are to its liking it will self-sow and multiply heartily, a dozen bulbs turning to hundreds in a few years. But this plant looks best in a naturalized setting, and I have no grassy meadow, my gardening being confined to a corner lot.

Of the two fritillaries I grow, the more spectacular is *F. imperialis*, the crown imperial, a plant with considerable history behind it as well as a commanding springtime presence in any garden. A native of southeastern Turkey, it was brought to Vienna from Constantinople sometime around 1576 by Augier Ghislain de Busbecq, who had been ambassador of Emperor Ferdinand I of Austria to the court of Suleiman the Magnificent.

Busbecq brought other Turkish plants to Europe, sharing credit with the Dutch botanist Clusius, who was for a time director of the imperial gardens in Vienna, for introducing the tulip, which in Holland in the early seventeenth century caused the strange episode of tulipomania, nearly ruining the Dutch economy as vast sums were spent for single bulbs of rare varieties in a frenzy of speculation. The madness belonged to the tulip, but the crown imperial also excited some attention. It spread rapidly from Austria to other European countries. It became a favorite subject for such botanical artists as J. P. de Tournefort and Pierre-Joseph Redouté. The English herbalist John Parkinson wrote of it in his influential *Paradisi in Sole* (1629): "For his stately beautifulness it deserveth the first place in this our Garden of delight."

Parkinson was dead right about the stately beauty. Well-grown, the crown imperial stands three feet high or higher, erect in posture, and it grows rapidly. At its base a whorl of cool and glossy leaves spirals up widely for a foot or more. Then in a great rush of growth the stem, which is dark green overlaid with a purple cast, rises above the foliage. The flowers, typically five, orange or yellow or red depending on the variety, open simultaneously, large blossoms which circle the stem like pendant bells. (Christian flower lore holds that fritillary blossoms once bloomed standing upright, that they maintained their proud position during the Crucifixion, and that their current habit of growth is the result of divine punishment.)

Above the flowers, there's an astonishing surprise, another

whorl of cool glossy leaves, like the leaves on top of a pineapple or something that Carmen Miranda might have sported on her head in a 1946 musical. Something about the crown imperial strikes me as hilarious, as well as elegant.

The other fritillary I grow is not so spectacular. *F. persica* has no topknot. Its tall flower spike, bearing twenty or more small blossoms of a dour shade of blackish-purple, rise above foliage that is somewhat coarse and unrefined. But its very sobriety makes it a good companion for its boisterous kin, the crown imperial.

Miniature Cyclamens

When it's cold and gray outdoors, among the cheeriest of indoor sights are potted cyclamens from the local florist. The color range of these undeniable beauties includes flamboyant crimsons and fuchsias, as well as more subtle pinks and lavenders, not forgetting whites as pristine and lovely as new-fallen snow. I've always loved the upswept, strongly reflexed petals of these plants, so perky and graceful and so strongly reminiscent of the shooting star. What's more, their heart-shaped leaves, as mottled as trout, are by themselves fetching enough to call up Gerard Manley Hopkins's joyous outcry, "Glory be to God for dappled things."

But I've always had more than my share of problems with the florist's cyclamen, which has been bred for generations as a derivative of *Cyclamen persicum,* a tender species native to the eastern Mediterranean. It's finicky about both temperature and moisture. It dislikes direct sunlight and temperatures of more than 68° F. during the day or less than 55° F. at night. Most books on houseplants offer the same, not very specific advice that it will bloom for two or three months provided that its soil is kept "moist, but not too moist."

Over the years, there's been a consistent pattern for me with these temperamental charmers. I've never been able to meet their needs. After much indecision over which color to get this time around, I'll bring one home. I've got high hopes, as usual, but the story has always had, until quite recently, the same sad denouement: a couple of weeks after acquiring the latest in my long line of cyclamens, I come downstairs for breakfast and discover that its flowers are sprawling, its buds dropping, and its leaves turning a sallow yellowish-brown.

But now there's a happy ending. Last year I bought no cyclamens. Someone gave us one just before Christmas, however, and it was still blooming, if looking a little peaked, when I threw it away after Memorial Day. This fall I bought four cyclamens, in four different colors. I liked them so much that I went out and got four more, in slightly different shades. And again, I expect them to stay in full flower well into summer.

I take no credit for my sudden success with these lovely plants, and nothing has changed in the treatment I've given them. What has changed are the cyclamens, thanks to the ingenuity of plant breeders, the problems that have beset greenhouse operators since the onset of the energy crisis, and the work of Dr. John Seeley, Professor Emeritus of Ornamental Horticulture at Cornell University, who realized several years ago that some new and richly promising kinds of cyclamen were becoming available from hybridizers in Holland, Switzerland, Germany, and Japan.

These new strains, developed by crossing the old florist's cyclamen with the much tinier and hardier species *C. purpurascens*, had a great deal to offer, and they appealed to Dr. Seeley's conviction that both the interest of the public and that of the floral industry would be well served by developing potted plants cheap enough to produce that they could be sold for under five dollars. The most immediately obvious feature of these new cyclamens was that they were small, less than half the size of the ones I used to buy and then torture to death. Being small, they didn't take up much greenhouse bench space. Many more could be grown in a given area than before, so there were considerable savings on energy. And although cyclamens used to take fifteen months or more to flower from seed, these new ones could be induced to flower in eight to nine months, so that seeds planted in mid-February might be sold in full bloom from Thanksgiving to Valentine's Day, a busy season for the nation's florists.

I'm not in the floral trade, so the economic benefits of growing these new, scaled-down cyclamens mean little to me. What does excite me is that these miniature versions of the genus are tough enough to survive my less than scrupulous care. They can take a little heat in their stride. They aren't as persnickety about being kept "moist but not too moist." There's still advice about keeping them out of direct sunlight, but mine seem to have no complaint thus far about their location in windows on the west side of the house. They bloom prolifically—and *long*. (In his technical publications on the matter, Professor Seeley has been conservative in estimating their season of bloom, but in a telephone conversation he told me he knew of instances where some had stayed in bloom one solid year.)

What's more, I like the cyclamens even better than the old *C. persicum*. They're grown in four-inch pots, not the six-inch ones their bigger brothers require. As a result, they easily fit on windowsills, four or five per sill. In my own kitchen, where I keep them, the sills are high enough that the plants are close to eye-level, so I can look at them in a new way, discovering the fascinations of their architectural structure. The round, flattened tuber of each cyclamen sits above the soil in its pot, each successive leaf and flower on its own individual stalk, all of them arranged in an intricate and attractive spiraling pattern that I suspect mathematicians would identify as exemplifying that most elegant of numerical arrangements, the Fibonacci series.

And cyclamens as houseplants, I now discover, are wonderfully suited for placement on windowsills in groups. If it's dark outside when I get home from work, the first thing I see is the bright rows of them in both kitchen windows, where they glow with the light from inside. And in the mornings, when the sun from the east touches the snowdrifts in the garden beyond the window, they become wonderfully translucent with subtle color.

I could raise these new, fairly undemanding, and really quite marvelous cyclamens from seed, I'm told. But techniques of propagation are somewhat complicated, I've got a lazy streak, and the greenhouse just down the street has been selling them lately for only $2.99. Unless its owners raise their prices quite a bit, I'll let them do the work. I'll have all their beauty—and a grateful heart for Professor Seeley.

Gloriosa Lilies

For about fifteen years, ever since I first saw them in a florist's shop and was bowled over by their spectacular form and color, I hankered to grow gloriosa lilies (*Gloriosa rothschildiana*). They're not really lilies, though they're close kin. I have no idea what they have to do with the Rothschilds, except perhaps that their large, deeply swept back blossoms of fiery red and yellow display unmistakable elegance and flair.

Twice, at intervals of about five years, I tried the gloriosas, putting their long pencil-shaped tan tubers in pots in late spring, covering them with four inches of rich, well-drained soil as all the garden books command, watering them well, and then waiting. I might as well have been Pozzo waiting for Mr. Godot, for at summer's end all I had to show for my effort was a pot of dirt. Gloriosas, I concluded, were congenital no-shows, or else I had unknowingly offended them by some horticultural malpractice or other.

Last year, the third time out, I succeeded. By midsummer, a very handsome pot of the things was flourishing on our deck, they were easy to grow, and I had identified the cause of my previous difficulties. Last year, the tubers I bought all had small pink eyes near one end, as they did not in my earlier experiences. An eyeless tuber of anything, be it a peony or a potato or a gloriosa lily, is not only blind but doomed never to grow.

I started them inside in mid-April, placing three tubers on their sides in a twelve-inch clay pot. Before covering them with the requisite four inches of soil, I thrust three bamboo stakes deep into the pot. Then I tied the stakes together at the top with inconspicuous florists' wire to form a tripod, and then wrapped the tripod with a spiral of wire to give the gloriosas the support they would eventually require.

Growth was rapid and dramatic, each tuber sending up a slender stalk which at first spurned the aid of the tripod's system of wires. But when the sixth set of leaves appeared, they underwent a fascinating change, the tip of each leaf changing to a tendril that uncurled like a long tongue until it encountered something—wire, bamboo stake, even another leaf—and then wrapped itself tightly around it. I followed all the standard advice, watering my gloriosas copiously, giving them sun but protection from wind, and applying liquid fertilizer every three weeks. (Some books said two, some said four, so in the absence of authoritative knowledge of my own I split the difference.)

Even if they hadn't bloomed, the gloriosas would have been attractive and fun to watch. The slightly waxen leaves are a pleasant shade of soft green, and the way they cling to all they touch, including each other, strikes me as very cheering and affectionate. But it's their blossoms that make these natives of tropical east Africa a summer feast and celebration for anyone who grows them. At the base of each flower, the stamens flare out in a wide circle, with no shyness whatsoever about proclaiming procreation. The six shiny petals above, twisted, crinkled, and swept back, gleam a bright golden yellow at their bases, then change to a glowing crimson edged with a thin band of golden yellow. Anyone with the least imagination will think of flames starting up; those with a better-developed sense of metaphor may be reminded of hot-air ballons, colorful and silky and gleaming in the bright light of a clear summer morning.

Those garden books agreed that, having had gloriosa lilies last year, there was no reason I shouldn't have them again this year, provided that as soon as they showed the first signs of dormancy when their season of bloom ended in September I nudged them along toward sleep by withholding water and then, once they had died back, brought them inside for storage in a cool dry place. They disagreed, however, on one point. Some said store them inside in their pots. Others recommended lifting them, with enormous caution not to damage their small pink eyes, and putting them in dry peat moss. I decided to follow this second piece of advice, since storage space is limited in our house.

I lifted the tubers at the right time, discovering to my satisfaction that the three little pencils of tubers had become long and fat cigars and that four smaller tubers had appeared in the pot. I stuck them in a paper bag on a shelf in the utility room (the farthest thing on the premises from a cool dry place), meaning to add dry peat moss for insulation and to transfer them to a cool closet. Then I forgot all about them, until they turned up early this April when I was rummaging for a ball of twine. The unorthodox storage didn't hurt them at all; they were as plump and firm as ever, and by mid-June they were again in bloom out on the deck, in a location that I thought protected them from the wind. But late one evening a sudden whirlwind, before a ferocious thunderstorm, wreaked havoc on the deck, lifting huge pots of hibiscus weighing more than fifty pounds and hurling them ten feet away. The next morning, I discovered the pot of gloriosa lilies resting by a mock orange next to the deck. The tendrils of the topmost leaves had already entwined themselves in the shrubbery, so I let them be.

That whirlwind, it turned out, produced a lovely bit of landscaping. The vines of this climbing "lily," this year, grew eight feet long—far too long to have been properly supported by the bamboo tripod that had been sufficient last year. They eventually covered half the mock orange, producing over sixty blossoms in two months and causing quite a few visitors to ask, "Good grief, Allen, what kind of shrub is *that?*"

Ailanthus

In Betty Smith's bestselling novel of a generation ago, it was the tree that grew in Brooklyn, but it also grows in London, Zurich, and almost everywhere else in the Temperate Zone. It may be better adapted to industrialized urban life than humans are. Pollution doesn't faze it, insects generally leave it alone, and it thrives without being fertilized or sprayed. People think of it primarily as a city tree, but in the dim interior of woodlands in Virginia and the Carolinas it competes so aggressively with more desirable trees that foresters curse it the same way they do Japanese honeysuckle. And except for Spanish broom, another toughie, it is often the only green plant to be seen in late summer along the parched roadsides of the sun-drenched plains of Castile. It is *Ailanthus altissima,* commonly known as the Chinese tree of heaven for its place of origin north of Peking and for the extraordinary speed with which its branches and their large ferny leaves push toward the sky.

The first European plant explorers who found it in China brought it back with them in the 1750s, together with the giant silk moth, *Samia cynthia,* whose caterpillars feed exclusively on its leaves. The hope was that moth and tree would contribute to the textile industry, but no method of unreeling the silk from the large cocoons was ever found. *Samia cynthia* didn't spread, but its host was quickly on the march. Reaching North American shores by 1784, it was despised by many. A. J. Downing, a well-known expert on orchards and ornamental trees, complained about it in 1852 in *Horticulturist*, the magazine he edited, with these words: "Its blossoms smell so disagreeably that my family are made ill by it; the vile tree comes up all over my garden; it has ruined my lawn for fifty feet around each tree." Shortly thereafter, the District of Columbia placed on the books an ordinance declaring its blossoms "nuisances injurious to health" and ordering fines for malefactors who allowed it to grow on their property. There was perhaps good reason for this legislation—and a lot of wishful thinking to boot, as a quick look around Washington's ailanthus-clogged streets today is sufficient to show.

Much can be said—and has been said—against the ailanthus. Its roots are poisonous. They also, like those of willows, invade water lines and sewer pipes. Its pollen causes hay fever, and some people break out in a painful rash after touching its leaves. Furthermore, the ailanthus reproduces itself so efficiently that if we didn't keep a sharp eye out we'd soon find ourselves living in a thicket of the stuff. A mature tree produces tens of thousands of light, winged fruits called samaras, and when they ripen in the fall the slightest breeze sends them whirling through the air hundreds of feet from their parent, spinning like tiny helicopters to reach their destinations. The seeds germinate easily, and they're not at all choosy about where they'll grow. They sprout in roof gutters, tiny cracks in sidewalks, and minuscule pockets of soil next to building foundations. As well as prodigiously seeding itself, the ailanthus is also a terrible colonizer, as bad as sumac or bamboo. Left to itself, a single ailanthus produces so many root suckers that it quickly becomes a grove.

These, however, are the venial sins of the ailanthus. Its mortal one is olfactory. The leaves have an unpleasant odor, and the blossoms of the male tree—the ailanthus, like the ginkgo and most hollies, comes in two sexes, although there are occasional bisexual anomalies—are renowned stinkers. Most garden writers keep things vague in describing this odor, using general adjectives like "objectionable" or, as in the case of A. J. Downing, "vile." I will be more specific: the male ailanthus in full flower smells like a cat box overdue for cleaning.

I don't grow ailanthus. If one of its samaras sailed into my yard and sprouted, I would rip it up instantly. Nevertheless, I rather admire it—from a proper distance. It is tough and resilient. It takes the worst that we can give it. It grows quickly, and its large leaves are really highly attractive. It survives and it endures, and it brings a touch of loveliness and green and ferny splendor to the wounded places of this earth, our slums and automobile graveyards and abandoned railways.

Not-So-Bouncing Bet

A friend, new to gardening, gave it to me last fall, saying she had gotten it from a neighbor who told her it was quite special. I thanked her, without saying what was on my mind, for I recognized it as *Saponaria officinalis*, whose common names include latherwort and soapwort (because its crushed leaves and roots produce a foam once used in the textile industry to clean fabrics, especially silk, after manufacture); London pride (because its fragrant blossoms somewhat mitigated the stench from that city's open sewers in the early days of the Industrial Revolution); world's wonder (because it is said to alleviate skin irritations from poison ivy and also syphilis); and bouncing bet. Claire Shaver Haughton's fascinating book *Green Immigrants* argues that this latter name, the commonest of its common names, arose because "the inflated calyx and scalloped petals of the flower suggested the rear view of a laundress, her numerous petticoats pinned up, and the wide ruff of her neck bobbing about as she scrubbed the clothes in a tub of suds." Perhaps she's right: common names sometimes show not just a poetic touch but some wild leaps into baffling metaphorical territory, as is witnessed in such names for plants as chicken gizzard and he-comes-home-drunk-but-she-loves-him-yet. I've always assumed, however, that this name comes from the way it bounces up everywhere in the garden once it gets a foothold; the robust fertility and relentless tendency to self-sow make this Eurasian perennial in the pink family, introduced to North America in early colonial times, one of our most common midsummer roadside wildflowers and also a garden pest. Years ago I extirpated all bouncing bet on my premises with a herbicide I reserve for desperate cases. But any gift plant is a token of the giver and therefore not to be despised, so I accepted my friend's bouncing bet and stuck it in a far corner of my garden, right between some aggressive English ivy and an equally pushy stand of bamboo that were on a collision course, thinking that it would have a brief season indeed, without my having to take direct measures.

Late this spring, I came close to rooting it out when I discovered that even for a bouncing bet it was extremely sturdy, having made a thick clump almost two and a half feet high and equally wide—considerably larger than usual, even though it was growing in poor soil under conditions of drought. Worrying that I had acquired some monster strain of this troublesome plant, I made a mental note to eradicate it right away, but then procrastination set in and I forgot. I'm glad I did, for yesterday I discovered the thing, now over three feet high and wide, in full and glorious bloom. It was bouncing bet, all right, but an unfamiliar sort, with clusters of soft pink double blossoms, instead of the usual single ones, all up and down the sturdy stems. The clusters look something like those of double geraniums or maybe like big powder puffs. The fragrance is intense, a little like allspice. This discovery sent me hightailing it to my small library of horticultural books, where I identified it as *Saponaria officinalis* flore-pleno, the varietal name meaning that its flowers are double. I was extremely pleased to learn that this particular form of bouncing bet, which has been in cultivation in England since the sixteenth century at least, is sterile, so it will stay in one place.

This fall I will rescue it from the encroaching tide of ivy and bamboo and give it a prominent place in the perennial border, after telling my friend that her neighbor was right about it being something quite special. I'll divide it next spring and pass on a small start of it to other gardening friends for their pleasure and delight. (Other gardeners will find it offered in the catalogs of both Wayside Gardens and the Andre Viette Farm and Nursery, whose addresses appear in the Appendix.)

Closely Watched Quinces

A member of the rose family, the graceful quince, which originated in Asia Minor, claims an illustrious history. Some scholars suggest that when he asked to be comforted with apples King Solomon probably had quinces in mind. The ancient Greeks made quince wine, and the Romans thought no banquet complete without boiled quinces on the menu, sometimes decorated with thorns to make them look like sea urchins.

The quince is widely grown today in Europe and Great Britain, and in the nineteenth century it was commonly found in American gardens and home orchards. Its owners keenly appreciated it for its deliciously fragrant, long-keeping autumn fruit, whose flesh is too tart to eat raw but which makes a tasty feast when stewed or turned into marmalade or jelly.

Today, however, the number of Americans who grow quinces is pitifully small. It would be unjustified to say that the quinceless life is not worth living, but I'm still willing to testify that the life of any gardener without one or two of these trees on his property can only be described as horticulturally deprived. (I should mention that the quince of which I write is the true quince or *Cydonia oblonga*, not the so-called flowering quince or *Chaenomeles*, a thorny spring-blooming shrub of Japanese origin, which Southern gardeners call Japonica bush and which produces occasional lumpy, misshapen fruits.)

I saw my first quinces, four mature specimens, in the herb garden at the Cloisters in Manhattan some years ago and immediately ordered one from a mail-order nursery. I planted it just outside the window above our kitchen sink, so we could follow its changes through the seasons. This year our quince flowered and bore fruit for the first time, in a fascinating succession of events. As in previous years, the tree broke its leaf buds in late April, producing handsome, oval leaves. Soft green on their upper surfaces, silvery and downy below, they made a fetching sight when they stirred in the breeze, shimmering like quaking aspens. Then the flowers appeared, goblets of delicate pink, each borne singly and twice the size of apple blossoms.

First there were eighteen small, round fruits, light brown, with a star-shaped marking on their blossom ends. Eleven fruits fell to the ground in early June, when quinces and some other fruits habitually thin their crop. The remaining seven quinces began to swell and change, ballooning out sharply at their blossom ends, much like Bartlett pears. Their color changed from tan to light green to deep and brilliant green; their skin turned downy, and then as fuzzy as a tennis ball. My seven fruits grew heavier and heavier, and by summer's end the branches that bore them bent under their weight. Now they have turned smooth and golden and ripe, beautiful things, even if there don't seem to be any recipes calling for a mere seven quinces.

It won't be long before the quince tree outside the kitchen window is bare of both fruit and leaves, but its silhouette in winter is attractive. In any season, quinces are quintessential.

The Sedum Family Reunion

The interests of gardeners and botanists do not always coincide. For one thing, they speak different languages. To a gardener a flower is a flower, even if it's more correctly a bract. A leaf is a leaf, even when it's a modified stem. Petals are petals, even if some petals are really sepals. Some gardeners have a precise hold on the distinctions among bulbs, corms, and tubers; others just stick their bulbs in the ground, hopeful that they will come up and not troubled that some of their bulbs, the gladiolus for example, are really corms. For another thing, gardeners who think it's a good idea (and it is) to learn the Latin binomials for the plants they grow and proudly talk of *Thalictrum anemonoides* instead of rue anemone are sometimes vexed to find that the old binomial has passed into oblivion by botanical decree. The rue anemone nowadays is *Anemonella thalictroides*.

It's not at all surprising, then, that few gardeners have had the slightest use for a scheme for organizing collections of plants which botanists came up with in the sixteenth century, when the first botanical gardens were established in Europe for the scientific study of plants collected all over the world by Western explorers. At Padua and elsewhere, plants were neatly arranged in separate beds according to their mutual kinship, so that all the Capparaceae would congregate here, all the Violaceae there, in a kind of reunion of the members of families previously separated by their geographical distribution. As sensible as this idea may be for scientists, it serves gardeners very poorly. To make a garden for our refreshment and delight, we must have variation and contrast. Rudbeckias and pyrethrums and Shasta daisies, as well as a great many other common garden perennials and annuals, may be cousins, as members of the Compositae family, but an entire bed given over to them is tedious, as anyone may witness who has been to Kew Gardens and strolled through a planting called the Herbaceous Ground, where no fewer than thirty beds are devoted to the many members of this family. Rudbeckias and the rest should be grown alongside plants that offer some contrast of form—tall delphiniums, huge misty mounds of gypsophila, loose spikes of artemisia—not next to one another. Combination of the dissimilar is the very nature of the gardener's art.

That said, I must go on to confess that on my own patch of earth nothing delights and pleases me more than a small bed—three feet by ten feet—in a mostly sunny spot alongside the pathway covered with fir bark that leads into my perennial garden. This bed is planted almost entirely with a single genus of flowering plants, a collection of some twenty-five species and named cultivars of sedum. In grouping together all my sedums— which accumulated gradually, from generous neighbors, from mail-order catalogs, and from roadside stands out in the country —I wasn't acting out of scientific principle, but simple practicality. Except for one shady corner, the bed where they grow is sun-drenched, sandy, and parched for most of the summer. As hardy succulents, sedums are well suited to such a location.

My passions are horticultural, not botanical, and I feel no hesitation in admitting that I don't know the names of many of my sedums. A neighbor donating a start of some fetching sedum or other over the fence seldom says, "Here's a nice clump of *Sedum spathulifolium* for you to try." Roadside stands are usually not especially precise about botanical nomenclature. (Sometimes they even badly miss the mark on common names, as when I recently saw lemon balm offered as "lemon bomb"— something to ponder.) I've never bothered to call in a sedum specialist to help sort out what I've got.

I do, however, know some names in the procession of sedums that come into bloom from midspring to late fall. The season begins with the flattened clusters of yellow blossoms of

S. kamtschaticum, a low creeper from eastern Asia. It reaches a climax in late August with *S. maximum atropurpureum,* a tall variety with fine dark purple leaves, and with several named cultivars of *S. spectabile,* which are impressive for their long-lasting flower heads in shades of soft pink, deep salmon, and creamy white. (These particular sedums grow in the slightly shaded part of the bed, as they appreciate some protection from the blaze of July and August.) The season ends most elegantly in October when *S. sieboldii* (described in the catalog of Lamb Nurseries in Spokane as "having thick blue-green leaves with rich pink edging resembling pieces of broken china") bursts into rosy bloom on stems that arch out from the center.

Even though everything that grows in this bed is a sedum, together they offer precisely that variation and contrast that gardeners crave. They have in common the thick and fleshy leaves that enable them to get by with infrequent watering, but the leaves vary from tiny, rounded ones to large, flat ones as thick as shoe leather. Some are evergreen, while others die back to the ground in the winter. Some hug the ground in thick mats, others stand bold and high, and others form graceful mounds of intermediate size.

In the case of sedums, planting many species of the same genus together turns out to be a splendid idea for gardeners as well as botanists. But I've excluded from my sedum bed one species: *S. acre,* the goldmoss stonecrop from Europe. A spring-blooming, relentless colonizer that quickly forms an evergreen mat and will grow from the slightest sprig dropped on the ground, it is a suitable ground cover for dry and otherwise barren soil. But if I gave it room among its kin in that small bed by the garden path, its insinuating and pushy ways would soon result in a stand of only one species of sedum, instead of a family reunion of great and ever-changing interest throughout the growing season.

Sempervivums

Aaron's rod, bullock's eye, healing blade, hen-and-chickens, houseleeks, Jove's beard, Jupiter's eye, live-forever, thunder plant—the diverse and resonant set of common names that have attached themselves to the plant known botanically as *Sempervivum* suggests that it's a prodigy and a wonder.

According to herbal lore, this genus of succulent perennials native to Europe and North Africa is almost a pharmacy in itself. Its crushed leaves, like those of the aloe vera, are said to soothe minor burns—and also to reduce fever, if applied to the forehead. Its juice is proclaimed to be an infallible remedy for corns, freckles, warts, and mosquito bites. Some people insist that a nasty-tasting tea brewed from its leaves cures the jitters and the blues.

What's more, apart from all these alleged medical uses, not one of which I have the faintest intention of exploring, the sempervivum has been believed to be a darling of the gods, especially the ones who play with lightning and take glee in claps of thunder. Neither Jove nor Thor would ever strike it with his wrath. Such belief persisted well into the Christian era: Charlemagne ordered his subjects to plant one species, *S. tectorum*, on their rooftops as protection against lightning, from which practice derives the common name houseleek.

It strikes me that much of the legend surrounding sempervivums is pure twaddle, idle superstition. Nevertheless, they're so carefree and easy to grow and so much fun to have around that I'd say any gardeners who don't try them are needlessly impoverishing their lives.

All sempervivums are built to the same design. Their thick and fleshy leaves grow in rosettes, each rosette soon becoming the mother plant for a brood of spreading offsets flocked so closely together that another common name, hen-and-chickens, rings of inevitability. And all sempervivums produce bloom stalks, usually late in the growing season, bearing extremely peculiar, rather shaggy and starlike flowers which look as if they might have evolved on some other planet.

But there's so much variation among sempervivums that it's possible to imagine a garden of nothing else, with maybe a few sedums thrown in. The forty species that make up the genus interbreed so lasciviously that some botanists throw up their hands at trying to tidy it up in a neat scheme of classification.

Some sempervivums make large, open rosettes as much as eight inches across. Others form tight balls the size of walnuts. The foliage varies widely across the spectrum. Grayish-green, deep green, red, wine purple, purple-black—all of these are possible, and there are some cultivars which alter with the season, starting out, for example, as wine purple in the spring but then changing to bright green in the summer. The flower stalks range in height from four to twelve inches, according to kind, and the blossoms may be white, greenish-yellow, pink, deep rose, or purple.

Sempervivums are undemanding in their needs. Given the sunny location and lean and gritty soil they prefer, they will thrive and spread, forming a thick mat that weeds can't easily penetrate. Neither the heat and drought of summer nor the icy winds of winter will faze them. They are amiable and jolly when stuck in odd corners, in crevices in walls, and in containers, especially terra-cotta strawberry jars. (Anyone who ever sees several different kinds of sempervivums planted in such a jar will never so much as flirt with the ridiculous notion of putting strawberries in them.)

I can think of only one negative thing to say about sempervivums, hen-and-chickens, houseleeks, thunder plants, or what you will: the nurseries who specialize in rock-garden plants and who are the best sources for this genus list such a dazzling variety that it's hard to know which ones to pick. As I write, there are two catalogs in front of me. Rocknoll Nursery in Hillsboro, Ohio, offers at very reasonable prices forty-five different sempervivums. Lamb Nurseries in Spokane, Washington, offers another twenty-five, but indicates that it sells others it doesn't list. As far as I can see, there is no overlap: what Rocknoll lists, Lamb doesn't, and vice versa.

So I shall proceed according to the rational gardener's best rule. Pick a catalog by flipping a coin. Decide how many sempervivums will be added to the flock this year. Close my eyes. Stab at the list the proper number of times with a pen. Order accordingly.

I can't really lose.

Cleome

For the last several years something bad has been going on in the seed racks of American hardware stores and discount garden centers, at least for the tribe of procrastinating gardeners like me, people who sometimes forget to mail off their orders for seeds to Burpee and Harris and Gurney until it's too late and they're forced to buy locally. On our local seed racks, the number of annuals has suffered a precipitous decline. These days, if your heart is set on four-o'clocks or moonflower vines or tithonia and you neglected to order them by mail, you are pretty much out of luck. Even nasturtiums are hard to come by.

It takes no Sherlock Holmes to find the causes of this minor catastrophe. First, more and more of us are growing vegetables, so the packets of celeriac and string beans encroach on territory that once belonged to the four-o'clocks. Second, those of us who grow annuals have also grown a bit lazy: we buy them already blooming in plastic or fiber six-packs, and in such great numbers that petunias and impatiens have become the emblematic flowers of the suburban landscape. And third, there's that new trend in American horticulture I've already mentioned and will probably mention again, since I think it's important—a swelling interest in perennials, in aconites and astilbes, heuchera and hemerocallis, liatris and lythrum, and many other plants that come back faithfully every year, increasing in size and vigor until they finally must be divided and shared with friends.

My heart has long belonged to perennials, but not because

they're all easy and carefree. Some of them aren't. Few really thrive on neglect: there's a substantial difference between a well-grown phlox and one poorly tended year after year. Sometimes a perennial that's always been reliable fails to come back; in 1985 I lost my purple coneflowers, every last one, for unknown reasons. Perennials also can take two or three years to look like much. Furthermore, as more and more gardeners leap on the perennial bandwagon, it's a good idea to remember that annuals have their place in the garden too. There's no point in despising impatiens or petunias just because everyone grows them. And there's every reason to study the seed catalogs and remember to buy seeds for some of the old-fashioned favorites no longer available on the seed racks. One excellent case in point is cleome.

Cleome has its detractors, and they have their reasons. Some people who detest it call it stink plant, and indeed, the foliage goes to the yonder side of "aromatic." It is also unpleasantly sticky, even clammy, to the touch, and before the flowers start appearing in midsummer, the plants bear sufficient resemblance to marijuana to cause a police car to slow down to take a closer look, if they're grown close to the street. And as a cut flower, cleome is perfectly useless, unless it's plunged into a deep bucket of lukewarm water the instant it's cut.

Nevertheless, just as we sometimes overlook flaws in our friends because of their virtues, I'm willing to grant their every point to the detractors of cleome and yet go on to say I like it a lot. The dozen or so plants I grow massed together in a far corner of the garden fill an empty spot with commanding dark green foliage and bright pink blossoms unfolding in unbroken succession at the top of the stalks.

To add to the interest, the seed pods that form in a loose spiral down the stalks from the flower cluster strike me as jolly and humorous somehow, giving each plant a shaggy and bewhiskered air. On dry days, there's a modicum of amusement in touching a mature seedpod and listening to the small explosive sound it makes as it scatters its crop to the earth.

Best of all, like a perennial, this annual from the American tropics will return, with no necessity whatsoever of my remembering to buy seeds again next year. A dozen cleome plants produce, by conservative estimate, a hundred thousand seeds. Almost every one will germinate next spring within a few days of one another, but the excess is a cinch to get rid off. A few swipes of the hoe, and there's only a dozen left, to brighten up the garden from summer into autumn.

Summer Bulbs

It was really too late in the spring when I did so, but I ordered summer-blooming bulbs this year anyway from Anthony J. Skittone, a bulb specialist on the West Coast whose catalog is crammed with bulbs I've never heard of—some very uncommon things from South Africa and Australia—as well as the usual staples. The order was shipped with dispatch, but it was May 31 before I got the bulbs in the ground, so it's not Mr. Skittone's fault that the tuberoses, montbretias, and chlidanthuses (reportedly terrific for their primrose yellow, intensely fragrant flowers) failed to bloom. I'll dig them up in the fall for storage and try again next year, this time getting them in the ground right after the usual date for the final frost of the season.

I did learn some things, which I will report here for the benefit of anyone else who may be thinking of planting summer bulbs, as well as the more usual spring ones. First, the tigridia or Mexican shellflower is enormously photogenic. I've never seen a picture of tigridias in a garden catalog that didn't make them seem wonderfully cheerful to have around, with their spotted blossoms in Technicolor hues of crimson and scarlet and orange and buff. In the garden, however, they are downright lurid, all tarted-up in garish colors that have a lacquer sheen. Tigridias went off my list of plants I like to live with as soon as the first ones opened. The blossoms last but a day. I'd prefer an hour. I won't dig them up this fall, so that the cold will get them.

I had higher hopes for the two dozen galtonia bulbs I planted. They burst through the ground almost immediately, pushing up very attractive wide rosettes of strap-shaped leaves followed by rapidly growing flower stalks, which started to bloom in late June. The blossoms were rather sparsely set in a pyramid of bloom, each greenish-white, bell-shaped blossom hanging gracefully downward. Two feet high, the galtonias were lovely for a week, somewhat reminiscent of some yuccas nearby, whose blooming season had just ceased. Unfortunately, the flowers open from the bottom of the stalk, and within ten days, when the blossoming is midway through, the stalks are an unsightly mess. I'm puzzled about whether or not to keep a plant which should clearly be allowed to get halfway through its blooming season and then be cut back to the ground.

It is my understanding that *Crocosmia masoniorum* is winter-hardy at my latitude (south of Philadelphia) and that it blossoms more and more heavily with every passing year. I very much hope so, for it's a marvelous garden plant, with sturdy, swordlike foliage, delicate, oddly twisted stems bearing small flowers of a deep burnt orange suffused with scarlet. A winner, Mr. Skittone!

But my pick of the crop would have to be the dozen acidantheras I planted in a thick clump. Again, the foliage is sturdy and swordlike, but the flowers are large, deeply fragrant, and a lovely soft shade of white, accented by a blotch of purple at the center. The blossoms open only one or two at a time, at the top of their constantly elongating stem, but the season of bloom is long—and just one blossom, with a sprig of fern, makes a superb small bouquet inside the house.

Next year I hope to find out about the chlidanthus and all the rest.

Santolina

One of the gardens in my neighborhood belongs to a horticultural minimalist, someone who has planted as sparingly as possible for the maximum effect. A curving flagstone walk leads from the street to the front door. On one side of the sidewalk, three large catalpa trees make a patch of shade, underplanted in English ivy. On the other side, he has put down a mulch of pea gravel (presumably with black plastic film below it to prevent weeds). There are no flower beds, merely groups of plants growing here and there in the gravel. This gardener's taste runs to rounded forms—to mounds of lavender and of both green and gray santolina. The result is tailored and austere, but still attractive.

I'm not a minimalist by any means, but this restrained planting convinces me that there's a great deal of merit in santolina, an evergreen shrubby perennial with two species sold commercially, whose foliage is neatly complementary. *S. virens* is a bright and sparkling green; *S. chamaecyparissus* a more somber bluish-gray. Both are covered in midsummer with long-lasting double flowers, like tiny gold buttons, and both have somewhat bristly thyme-scented leaves that can be used in herbal wreaths at Christmas and placed in dresser drawers to impart a spicy fragrance to clothing and to repel moths. Santolina, whose common name is lavender cotton, for reasons difficult to understand, is a plant that deserves more attention than it now receives. I mean to get some soon.

A Craze for Hostas

Today, among perennial nurserymen and a rapidly growing number of American gardeners, hostas are hot. People who didn't grow hostas ten years ago are growing them now. A lot of people who don't grow them now will probably be growing them two years hence.

There's a hosta craze abroad in the land, and it's easy to see why (though the question why it took so long to spring up is a bit complicated, involving sociological issues such as a hard core of hosta lovers whose hosta love runs from enthusiasm to fanaticism, and technological issues such as the advent of tissue-culture laboratories). Hostas' virtues are many and substantial, their faults few. They're bone-hardy. They grow well almost everywhere in the country. So long as they're adequately watered, torrid summer weather doesn't hurt them. Some grow perfectly well in full sunshine, except in the South. Filtered shade with a couple of hours of sunshine pleases them best, but they will grow in deeper shade, except that if it's downright gloomy and Stygian they may not bloom and the coloration of their foliage will not be typical.

Above all, hostas offer gardeners such a diversity of traits from one cultivar to another that it's possible—and some people do it—to make a garden in which they are the only herbaceous perennials. They range in size from wee things you almost have to squint to see to bold clumps higher and several times wider than a bushel basket. Leaf colors include a gamut of greens, blues (really a hazy blue cast, technically called pruinosity, which resembles the bloom on the skins of grapes and which generally wears off as summer progresses), chartreuses, and golds. Variegation—white or gold edges, splotches, streaks, splashes, mottlings, sometimes involving several colors—is increasingly found, especially in the newer cultivars. Leaf shapes also vary—rounded ones, lance-shaped ones, heart-shaped ones, and several others all occur. Some are cupped, in such a way that they will hold glistening drops of water after a shower or a heavy morning dew. The textures of the leaves also show considerable variation—pleating, ruffling, dimpling, and seersuckering all are possible.

Hostas flower freely, on spikes of bloom anywhere from a few inches tall to well over six feet, as in the case of a cultivar called, not very surprisingly, Tall Boy. The tubular blossoms, which open from the bottom of their stalks, are generally shades of lavender or lilac blue, occasionally white. They stay in bloom for two weeks or more, and since different hostas come into bloom at different times the flowering season is a long one, stretching from mid-June well into September. Some hosta lovers, it must be said, treasure them for their foliage alone and rush out into their garden, pocket pruners in hand, whenever a flower spike appears. The spikes somehow offend them, because they tend to lean toward the light. Furthermore, a hosta spike past its peak, when only a few buds and flowers are clustered at the top and spent blossoms and seed pods hang lower on the gangly stem, is no gem of beauty. Other hosta lovers put up with the somewhat graceless flowering habit for the sake of the bees and hummingbirds which are attracted by the abundant nectar. No one, however, faults the old favorite commonly known as the August lily, *H. plantaginea*, for its large, waxy, intensely fragrant white blossoms, which appear in the doldrums of late summer, when gardens look tired and bedraggled and flagging human spirits need a lift.

Compared with some other perennials, hostas come off very well. Unlike such things as delphiniums and scarlet lobelia, they are extremely long-lived. Unlike bearded iris and some perennial asters, they do not need to be divided, since they do not die out at the centers but just get more and more majestic with each new growing season.

According to the received wisdom, commonly passed on in general books on gardening, hostas are best used planted in masses, as ground covers. There's nothing wrong with such advice, except that it shows a lack of imagination and a failure to appreciate the further contribution of hostas to the garden landscape, beyond taking up space and keeping down weeds. Two or three plants of the larger hostas, such as *H. sieboldiana* Elegans, make wonderfully bold accents. Hostas with strongly variegated leaves pump color into shady nooks, lending further interest by changing with the changes in light and shade.

Hostas combine wonderfully well with one another, but they also are attractive companions for other perennials. They are splendid planted alongside astilbes, whose lacy foliage and feathery plumes of blossoms contrast pleasantly with their own more restrained and mounded form. Ferns are also suitable mates, and like hostas they come in such variety that a shady garden might feature only the two, without being at all monotonous. Ligularias and hostas are entirely handsome together. In my own garden, I am especially pleased by a serendipitous combination of hostas intermingled with three Oriental hybrid lilies, volunteer seedlings that just sprang up one year and that evidently find the cool shade beneath the hosta leaves much to their liking. I've also been eyeing some yucca that grows in a different spot in my garden, thinking that putting it with some hostas might be kind of dramatic, even pyrotechnic.

Hostas can also be combined very effectively with water. Little hostas, such as *H. venusta*, make charming specimens when planted along the edges of a small pool. One of the finest gardens I've visited in years, that of Dick Meyer of Columbus, Ohio, features near its entrance a large pond filling a former ravine. At one end, a huge planting of *H.* Royal Standard (a venerable and widely available cultivar descended from *H. plantaginea* and similarly fragrant) makes a splendid and stunning sight in early August, when its soft green foliage and its spikes of crisp white flowers are mirrored in the water, with goldfish swimming through their reflections.

❄

Hostas are generally so sturdy and unpersnickety that they are often certified to be problem-free. Not so. There are problems *of* hostas—and there is also a problem *with* hostas, which I will tackle a bit further on, since it has long been a source of embarrassment to hosta lovers.

The major problem *of* hostas is that a variety of creatures like to chomp on them, which is only to be expected, considering that in Japan people sometimes eat them as a vegetable. Cutworms, inchworms, and, in some parts of the country, earwigs add them to their diets. A deer will head as quickly to a hosta plant as a raccoon to a ripe ear of corn. The worst offenders, however, are slugs and taxus weevils, aka black vine weevils. Slugs eat holes through the emerging shoots in early spring in such a way that when a leaf unfolds after attack it will display a neat row of holes. Later in the season, slugs browse at random across the leaves in such a way that in an especially bad year a prized hosta may by summer's end look like gnawed lace. Taxus weevils deal a double whammy to hostas, and are unusually nasty for their capacity to reproduce themselves at some points in their life cycle by parthenogenesis. Their tiny larvae munch on the roots of hostas, and the adults eat notches out of the leaf margins. Slugs can be controlled by early and frequent application of commercial baits containing methaldehyde or mesurol, although organic gardeners may prefer leaving around the garden saucers of stale beer in which the slimy beasts may drown their woes. Taxus weevils, which also attack azaleas and rhododendrons, can be dealt with by keeping mulch well away from hostas and by spraying early and regularly with Orthene or similar pesticides.

The major problem *with* hostas has nothing to do with them at all, but a great deal to do with human beings. There has been, to put it very mildly, a great deal of confusion about what to call them, so much so that hostas are an easy mark for garden writers seeking a little fun at their expense. Henry Mitchell, for example, observed in *The Essential Earthman* that "the genus Hosta has always reminded me of the novelist Kafka and of various disorders of international politics." In the delightfully chatty catalog he writes for Holbrook Farm and Nursery, its owner, Allen Bush, complains that it would be an enormous chore "getting two people to call a group of ten hostas by the same name."

To explain all this confusion, some history is in order here as regards the involvement of European plant explorers, botanists, and nurserymen with hostas, almost all of which are native to Japan. A German physician with the Dutch East India Company in Japan from 1690 to 1692, Ethelbert Kaempfer, was the first European to pay heed to hostas, making a drawing of a plant he called, among other things, *Gibboosi altera*, following a Japanese word which today is generally romanized as "giboshi." In the 1780s, one of Linnaeus's disciples, Carl Peter Thunberg, classified one hosta as *Aletris japonica* and another as *Hemerocallis japonica*. For a time, hostas continued to be lumped with hemerocallis: the French naturalist J. B. Lamarck introduced to European gardens in 1798 from China the species he called *Hemerocallis plantaginea*. Still grown now as *Hosta plantaginea*, it accumulated an alarming number of additional names as it was distributed—*Hemerocallis alba* and *Funkia subcordata*, among others. By the 1830s, when Philipp Franz von Siebold, a plant lover who like Ethelbert Kaempfer before him had served as a physician for the Dutch East India Company in Japan, began introducing a large number of collected hostas, all under the name *Funkia*, the confusion would seem to have been almost complete. Not quite. Other genus names were proposed, including *Saussurea* and *Libertia*, before botanists were able to get their act together and settle on the name *Hosta* (but one also occasionally finds *Hostia*) early in the twentieth century, in honor of an Austrian physician who died in 1834, Nicolaus Thomas Host.

To make matters worse, nineteenth-century nurserymen began adding varietal names in Latin, such as aureo-marginata, after the genus and species names of particular hostas, creating a terrific muddle. The problem here is that hostas hybridize very easily among themselves, without human assistance and record-keeping. They also have unusually strong tendencies to mutate. The Latin names falsely suggested that what were really horticultural cultivars were botanical varieties instead. The names sounded precise and scientific, but they weren't.

One botanist, considering the genus *Hosta* in 1951, pronounced it "a taxonomic nightmare." Meanwhile, anyone buying hostas from nurseries found it not uncommon to get the same hosta three times, under three different names—or to get three different hostas under the same name. It was very untidy—another good example of the fact that the interests of botanists, nurserymen, and dedicated gardeners do not always coincide. It was also very troubling to some Americans who loved hostas so much that in 1968 they founded the American Hosta Society, one of whose purposes was to help clear up all the confusion. Maybe. Eventually.

I got started with hostas, after a lifetime of indifference toward them, about five years ago, on the day my neighbor Jean Plantan decided that she was sick of them. She ripped up from her back yard a vast colony of *Hosta undulata* Albo-marginata, a variegated green-and-white species which is commonly planted in our neighborhood. Jean carted three wheelbarrow loads out to the curb. I rescued them all, putting them in a shady new bed I had just dug on the north side of the house. They filled half of the bed quite nicely, but when I mentioned to Lola Branham, a friend in Richmond with whom I occasionally exchange daylilies, that I had planted some hostas, she asked what kind. Not knowing their name at the time, I said green-and-white ones. Lola, it turned out, was a lover of hostas as well as daylilies. She was also a generous soul, and she probably suspected that I was about to embark on yet another of those sudden and incurable passions for particular kinds of plants that have marked my life. A few days after we talked, a package arrived from Virginia containing ten hostas, each one labeled—Frances Williams, Krossa Regal, and so on. I planted them, far too closely together, I soon discovered, when they began elbowing each other for position. But they were wonderful. It wasn't long before I was strolling out to the garden early every morning, to see how Frances Williams was doing.

Last summer, I decided that I wanted not just to grow a few hostas but to know more about hostas—and to talk hostas with people whose passion for hostas was much more advanced than my own. I visited Alex J. Summers, the founding president of the American Hosta Society, at his home near Bridgeville,

Delaware, who loaded up my car with hostas he thought I'd like. I then drove up to Wilmington to spend time with Dr. Warren Pollock, who edits the annual bulletin of the AHS and who chairs the society's Committee on Nomenclature. I admired some very handsome hostas in Pollock's small suburban garden, and I came home loaded down with hosta literature. Later, I spent five days in Columbus, Ohio, at the annual symposium of the Perennial Plant Association, an organization of professional nurserymen and horticulturists. In the halls, the people came and went, talking about Frances Williams. I'm not a card-carrying hosta specialist, just a devout fellow-traveler, but I know a bandwagon when I see one, and hostas are it. And after immersing myself in the publications put out by the American Hosta Society since its founding in 1968, I find two things to be very clear.

First, Americans have dominated overwhelmingly in promoting the good name of hostas both in this country and abroad and in developing the new cultivars which are now appearing in commercial trade. The latest catalog of Alan Bloom's Bressingham Nursery, England's leading grower of high-quality perennials, lists over forty hostas. Except for species from the wilds of Japan, most are cultivars originating in the United States. (An exception to this American preeminence must be made for Eric Smith, a British plantsman who took advantage of the fact that in England the early-blooming species *H. plantaginea* sometimes reblooms, simultaneous with the late species *H. tardiflora*. He crossed the two to produce a splendid series of hybrids, known collectively as the *H.* X *tardiana*, which are much valued for their persistently blue foliage and for their hyacinth-like flower spikes.)

Second, the history of hostas in America falls fairly neatly into four major periods, each more promising than the one previous, and each contributing to a time not too far distant when any gardener who doesn't have at least five different hostas within ten yards of his back door will feel sorely underprivileged.

The first period covers the years prior to the late 1920s. Hostas, imported from England in the nineteenth century, were the old-fashioned plants of Victorian times, useful in their limited way to line pathways or to be stuck in odd and shady corners of the garden, where little else would grow. This attitude toward hostas—mild appreciation blended with faint disdain—is still expressed in some fairly recent books on gardening. A handsome book I much admire, Ippolito Pizzetti and Henry Cocker's *Flowers: A Guide for Your Garden*, after likening hostas to "the maiden aunt of herbaceous perennials," hands out this halfhearted and grudging bit of praise: "In spite of their relative monotony and general similarity, hostas are not to be despised."

The second period started around 1935 in Winchester, Massachusetts, when a remarkable woman named Frances Williams began to take interest in hostas and to raise them in her small, shady garden. Sending off for plants and seeds, corresponding with others who shared her interest, and visiting nurseries whenever possible, she hit what turned out to be the first real hosta jackpot very early, in 1936, when she spotted an unusual and striking seedling of *H. sieboldiana* Elegans at a commercial nursery in Connecticut. The parent plant, still highly regarded today, is described as follows in the most recent catalog of Wayside Gardens: "An unusually fine variety with large, blue-green leaves that make a lively contrast with lighter foliage. Superb in shady places, it forms a stately and magnificent clump." Wayside's description of its offspring says: "This rare plant will appeal to even the most discriminating gardener. It forms 3 x 4 foot clumps with very large puckered blue-green leaves with broad golden-yellow margins that deepen in color as the season progresses . . . A standout in the shady border. A future classic." Mrs. Williams introduced this future classic through Fairmount Gardens, a small retail nursery that specialized in iris and day-lilies, and later, to an increasing extent, in hostas. Somewhat predictably, since it was a hosta, as it began to spread into more and more gardens, both here and in England, it accumulated several names—*H. sieboldiana* aureo-marginata, Gold Edge, and Golden Circles.

Today this hosta, only one of several that Frances Williams introduced, is most commonly known as Frances Williams, but not out of any immodesty or self-advertisement on her part: in 1963, a few years before Mrs. Williams died, G. W. Robinson of the Oxford Botanic Garden registered the plant in her honor.

A Craze for Hostas

It is still an eye-catcher, a plant which, once seen, is sufficient to convert the indifferent and convince them that hostas, far from being dull and dowdy old maiden aunts among perennials, have more panache than Auntie Mame. In 1985, Frances Williams stood in first place on the American Hosta Society's popularity poll. It wasn't the first time and it probably won't be the last.

The third period, one in which a diffuse interest in hostas on the part of a small group of people took on a sharp focus, began in 1968 when thirteen of the plant's aficionados took time out from a lily show in Philadelphia to meet in Swarthmore at the home of Dr. and Mrs. John Wister to form the American Hosta Society, a group whose membership fairly quickly expanded to four hundred persons under the leadership of Alex J. Summers, the organization's president for its first ten years of existence. It was a crucial, if transitional, period in the history of hostas in America, and the AHS deserves much credit for both its goals and its achievements. The society, as one of its early bulletins put it, was "dedicated to the advancement of knowledge about Hostas, their introduction into cultivation, and the development of new and improved varieties." It meant to achieve these goals by diverse means: meetings, newsletters, exchanges of seeds and plants, auctions, exhortation of the faithful and preaching the good news to the uninitiated, and an annual bulletin which like the publications of many other plant societies presented a mixture of technical scientific information, historical commentary, cultural tips, and enthusiastic remarks about hostas in general and about especially promising or worthy cultivars.

History is the simplification of complexity, for the sake of understanding. One historical period does not march off into oblivion, merely because another one has dawned. The third period in the hosta's history thus continues, even though some brand-new things, on a much larger scale, are stirring in the wings. The American Hosta Society still thrives, now numbering about seven hundred fifty members, all of whom love hostas, some no doubt to the point of obsession. (I hear tell that one member grows over seven hundred different ones.) The society's annual bulletin has grown fatter and slicker, and it now sports

[105]

color photographs which help hosta lovers show less enamored gardeners what the fuss is all about. Over the years, the society's Committee on Nomenclature has done much to straighten out the pesky and embarrassing problems with names, insisting that new cultivars arising through hybridization or mutation be given so-called fancy names (Antioch, Pearl Lake, and the like) instead of Latin ones. The society has also cooperated with commercial nurserymen—and prodded them at times—to try to assure that the right name accompanies the right hosta when it is offered to customers.

But the fourth period in the history of hostas has already dawned, thanks to two converging forces. First, American gardens are getting shadier. The trees planted in suburban yards during the baby boom following World War II are now well on their way to maturity: that pitiful and unpromising maple sapling planted in a lot carved out of a potato field on Long Island in 1949 now towers high and spreads wide, casting a great deal of shade in whose fringes shade-tolerant plants like hostas will grow well, provided that they are amply fertilized to offset the competition for nutrients from the greedy tree roots. Furthermore, in recent years there has been a new trend in suburban development of wooded areas, an effort to leave as many trees as possible, so that new houses often now spring up not on naked, bulldozed earth but in the midst of ready-made shade, with all the special opportunities and problems it offers.

Second, American gardeners are getting more sophisticated. We're less and less inclined to call it quits with a few petunias and geraniums from the local garden center. As I've already mentioned several times, the interest in hardy perennials is everywhere on the rise, and hostas are one of the most sought-after items, thanks to their undeniable intrinsic merit and to the evangelism of members of the AHS, who have touted them highly.

But the love of hostas alone is insufficient to spread them far and wide across the land. A high demand for hostas is useless unless there is a good supply, and herein lies a problem. Mark Zilis of T & Z Nurseries, which he founded in 1981 with David Tyznik, has pointed out that hostas increase by natural division at something less than breakneck speed. A choice new plant, whether a seedling or a mutation, will produce, on average, two hundred fifty plants after ten years—a dishearteningly small yield.

The solution, as Messrs. Zilis and Tyznik and a great many other commercial nurserymen have discovered, lies in the technique of micropropagation or tissue culture. The technique is complicated, and sometimes troubled by problems involving contamination or the reluctance of some plants to perform as well as hoped, but its essence lies in the repeated dissection of bud or flower-spike tissue, under sterile conditions in a laboratory, to induce, with the chemical assistance of several hormones, tiny plants which eventually root and grow large enough that they can leave the laboratory for the greenhouse. The important point is that tissue culture leaps the hurdle of a hosta's slow rate of increase. A choice new plant by means of this new technology will produce, on average, twenty-five thousand plants in as little as two years. (A subsidiary advantage of tissue culture is that it seems to increase the number of desirable mutations in foliage color, probably because of the enormous numbers of plants being propagated.)

Tissue-cultured hostas are not a future promise but a present reality. Several laboratories are already in operation, and their business is brisk and humming. And because of tissue culture, hostas are rapidly moving from laboratory to greenhouse to wholesale nurseries to retail nurseries and eventually into more and more American—and British—gardens.

Mary Walters of Walters Gardens in Zeeland, Michigan, a wholesale nursery founded in 1946 by her father and now one of the very largest suppliers of perennials to retail mail-order nurseries, garden centers, and professional landscapers, testifies to the magnitude of the craze for hostas that is sweeping the land. Her company's catalog for the fall of 1985 offered some forty-six hostas, seven more than the preceding year, an increase of fifteen percent. Over half the cultivars listed, the newer and choicer sorts, were produced by tissue culture. "Orders have been almost embarrassingly strong," she told me in August, a month before the 1985 shipping season began. "We sold some kinds out completely within two weeks of mailing our catalogs— had to put people on waiting lists for 1986, and in some cases trade around with other wholesalers to fill orders sooner. At this moment, we've already sold three-fourths of the hostas we produced."

The plant Walters sells in greatest quantity—in the millions—is *Artemesia* Silver Mound, which costs seventy cents apiece for an order of twenty-five to forty-nine. But hostas, which can cost as much as ten dollars each wholesale, are the second most-frequently ordered plant. "Almost everyone who places an order with us will order at least a few hostas," Mary Walters told me, "and the higher price we have to charge for the ones our lab produces by tissue culture doesn't seem to be any obstacle. Hostas are here to stay."

For people who haven't tried hostas yet, or who have merely sampled one or two, there's a difficulty, however. The number of hosta species and registered cultivars available commercially has increased enormously over the past fifteen years. It in no way approaches the bewildering number of named daylilies, which are now reckoned in the tens of thousands, but it's large enough to give pause to anyone who picks up the latest mail-order catalog of Busse Gardens in Minnesota—an excellent source—and discovers 158 kinds for sale and another 119 listed as either being on display or withdrawn for increase. What follows is a list of worthy and recommended hostas, based on conversations with members of the AHS and with both wholesale and retail nurserymen. It consists of those hostas which are most consistently mentioned as outstanding, which are readily available by mail-order, which have been propagated in sufficient numbers that they are reasonably priced, in the three- to ten-dollar range in some catalogs, higher in others, and which have been tested and proven in gardens all over the country. It is not a list for people who are already hosta hobbyists and don't bat an eye at paying twenty-five dollars or more for the latest novelty.

Antioch. Lightly mottled, cream-edged leaves, lavender flowers, holds edge in sun. An older cultivar, recent recipient of the AHS Alex J. Summers Award.

August Moon. Large yellow leaves which hold color well; white flowers tinged with lavender.

Francee. Good green heart-shaped leaves with distinct narrow white margins that hold up well; lavender flowers.

Frances Williams (also sold as *H. sieboldiana* Frances Williams and *H. sieboldiana* Aureo-marginata). Bold and probably indispensable.

Ginko Craig. Good small edging plant, narrow white-edged leaves, abundant blue flowers, a rapid increaser.

Gold Crown (also sold as *Hosta fortunei* Aureo-marginata). Gold-edged green leaves.

Gold Drop. Small plant, gold leaves, white flowers.

Gold Standard. Light green leaves in spring, turning gold with thin green margin as growing season progresses; lavender flowers.

Golden Tiara. Heart-shaped green leaves with golden margin; lavender flowers.

Honeybells. An older cultivar, with large, light green leaves, good in sun, very fragrant white flowers tinged with violet.

H. decorata. Dark green leaves with white margins, purple flowers.

H. lancifolia. Narrow green leaves, lilac flowers, a rapid increaser.

H. plantaginea (August lily). Large light green leaves, fragrant, trumpet-shaped white blossoms, a slow increaser.

H. sieboldiana Elegans. Bold, textured, blue-gray leaves, white flowers.

H. undulata Albo-marginata. White-edged green leaves, very commonly grown, lavender flowers.

H. ventricosa. Large, glossy green leaves, blue-violet flowers.

H. venusta. Pleasing dwarf plant, green leaves, graceful lilac flowers.

Kabitan. Strap-like ruffled leaves, gold chartreuse edged light green.

Krossa Regal. Frost-blue leaves in spring, vase-shaped habit, lavender flowers on scapes five feet high or higher.

Pearl Lake. Blue-green, heart-shaped leaves, medium-sized clump, a winner of the Alex J. Summers Award.

Piedmont Gold. Creased and puckered yellow leaves whose

color persists through the season, white flowers, an immense clump, a rapid increaser.

Royal Standard. Large, with glossy green leaves, fragrant white flowers late in season, tolerates sun.

NOTE: Perhaps because hostas have presented both botanists and gardeners with such nomenclatural nightmare, the hosta lovers of today include in their number some of the pickiest people I've ever met—hosta names must run correctly, according to their particular standards. Latin should be used only for bona-fide species found in the wild. Any other hosta should have a so-called fancy name (some say Christian name), and the convention calls for it to be enclosed in single quotation marks, sometimes with the abbreviation *cv.* (for cultivar) preceding it: thus, either *Hosta sieboldiana* cv. 'Elegans' or *H. sieboldiana* 'Elegans.' I herewith apologize to any hosta fancier for choosing not to put the cultivar name in single quotation marks, but I have my reasons. First, this device of punctuation may be useful in avoiding confusion between Frances Williams the person and Frances Williams the plant, but the context usually makes clear what the reference is, as when someone announces that his Frances Williams is infested with slugs. Second, single quotation marks, in a book about gardening, strew up the page like so many fly specks. Third, the use of single quotation marks originates in England. Conventions about this mark of punctuation differ on one side of the Atlantic Ocean and the other: British books often use single quotation marks to indicate direct quotation, but in the United States the rule calls for double quotation marks. The important thing is not the rule itself but editorial consistency (book titles, I was taught, must be underlined or italicized, but *The New York Times* and some other weighty periodicals put them in double quotation marks), and I have chosen to forgo enclosing cultivar names in single quotation marks throughout this book.

One more matter concerns the word "cultivar" itself. I use it, but I think it's ugly and somewhat reminiscent of the bureaucratic degradation of language that both George Orwell and Anthony Burgess so despised. I was delighted to read in Alvide Lees-Milne and Rosemary Verey's *The Englishman's Garden* not long ago an essay by Lord De Ramsey in which he recounted how the late Sir Frederick Bawden "invented that ghastly word 'cultivar' and, not liking it himself, tried to recapture it, but it was too late." Botanists may need some way of distinguishing naturally occurring varieties of particular species of plants from varieties developed in cultivation. Gardeners, I think, do not.

III. INTO OTHER GARDENS

Mr. Shaw's Garden

The cabdriver parked in front of the Forest Park Hotel in St. Louis that dreary Sunday afternoon in January smiled when I told him where I wanted to go. "The Missouri Botanical Garden? Hereabouts we call it Shaw's Garden. I love it. Just last month it got me out of big trouble with my wife. The cold weather got to her, and she started bugging me to take her to Jamaica. Finally, I said I'd take her someplace tropical, but not Jamaica. I filled a Thermos bottle with rum and orange juice and took her to Shaw's, to a big ugly greenhouse with banana trees and stuff, a regular jungle. Now she says that if I take her there once a week till winter's over she'll shut up about Jamaica."

Shaw's Garden. I already knew a little about Henry Shaw. My interest in coming to St. Louis has been sparked by reading the remarkable last will and testament he had drawn up in 1885, four years before he died at the age of eighty-nine. Having seen the will and a brief biography about him, both published by the Missouri Botanical Garden—aka Shaw's—I now wanted to see something of his actual legacy.

Mr. Shaw's will showed him to have been unusually thoughtful of his friends, solicitous of his kin, and appreciative of his servants. To his architect and friend, George Barnett, he bequeathed an oil painting of the Falls of Terni in Italy and "two dozen bottles of my best sherry wine from the cellar in my city house." He left David Kaime, another friend, a carriage and two dozen bottles of port. To D. H. MacAdam went a gold

[115]

watch, a folio edition of Shakespeare, and two bottles of either claret or port, whichever he preferred. His sister Carolina may have been a teetotaler; he left her $4,000, a hardware store, and a hotel, but nothing alcoholic. His housekeeper, Mrs. Rebecca Edom, inherited $5,000, much of his furniture and silverware, a horse and carriage, the use of a house during her lifetime with all taxes and insurance paid, and four dozen bottles of assorted imported wines.

Shaw's will also showed him to be a philanthropic man and remarkably ecumenical in his benevolences. The Methodist Orphans Home, the Episcopal Orphans Home, the Protestant Orphan Asylum, the German Protestant Orphans Home, the Little Sisters of the Poor—each came away with $1,000 from his estate. To the Bishop of the local Episcopal Diocese went $200 annually, provided that he arrange each year for a sermon to be preached "on the wisdom and goodness of God as shown in the growth of flowers, fruits, and other products of the vegetable kingdom."

But his grandest legacy went to the citizens of St. Louis, the city he adopted as his home in 1819 when he sailed up the Mississippi River from New Orleans on the steamboat *Maid of Orleans*. A boy of eighteen, he brought with him a shipment of cutlery from his native Sheffield, England, and $3,000 in capital borrowed from an uncle to set himself up in the hardware business—a business which quickly prospered and thrived. Shaw left the people of his adopted city, in trust, one of the great botanical gardens of the world, the Missouri Botanical Garden, located on seventy-nine acres of former prairie land once on the city's outskirts but now well within its boundaries. His will provided that this garden, just below Tower Grove House, the country villa he built in 1849, should be open to the public for its pleasure and education.

The cabdriver dropped me off in front of the Ridgway Center, a new building dedicated in the summer of 1982, which serves as the main entrance to Shaw's Garden, as well as housing some shops, a restaurant, an auditorium, and several classrooms. Despite the howling blast of harsh January wind that would make an Eskimo keep to his igloo, I paused a moment to admire the building's architecture, which was handsome indeed. Two wings, each two stories high and as featureless and blank as a grain elevator, flanked a much taller barrel-vault, faced entirely in glass, so that my eye was drawn upward to some enormous cloth banners suspended from the ceiling high above the second floor. They glowed in pastel colors in shapes that were somehow reminiscent of Claude Monet's paintings of water lilies.

The evocation of water lilies was intentional, I discovered when I went inside and read a series of wall placards describing the building's design. But the water lilies concerned weren't those in Monet's garden in Giverny. Instead, they were *Victoria amazonica*, a native of tropical South America discovered early in the nineteenth century and remarkable for their rapid growth toward an immense size. The intricate system of branched veins on the underside of their huge leaves had given the British architect Joseph Paxton the inspiration for the design of that powerful symbol of the nineteenth century's unbounded optimism, the Crystal Palace—a design alluded to by the architects of the Ridgway Center.

Being an inveterate reader of whatever I find in front of me, including breakfast-cereal boxes and the lists of ingredients on bottles of steak sauce, I moved on from the placard about that water lily and Joseph Paxton to another placard, this one intended to give people some idea how fine a fellow Henry Shaw had been, before they visited his garden. I was not, at the moment, much inclined toward venturing outdoors. It was sleeting furiously, and the wind was whipping the stuff around in a very nasty way.

Mr. Shaw, I learned, was an ardent capitalist and a highly successful one. He had opened his hardware store at just the right time, in just the right place. Pioneers heading West needed his hatchets and knives. Indians and fur traders bought his traps. Shaw diversified his interests to trade in such commodities as tallow and hides and to invest in real estate—a great deal of real estate. An excellent businessman, he got very rich very young. But he seems to have lacked the greed that turned some other nineteenth-century go-getters into robber barons, and he knew when to stop pursuing the dollar and tend to higher pursuits. Discovering in 1839 that his annual profits had exceeded $25,000 ("more money than any man in my circumstances ought to make in a single year," he wrote), he decided to give up his business and devote himself to travel and the advancement of science.

Snow was now falling along with the sleet, so I kept reading, following the further adventures of Henry Shaw, ex-merchant of hardware. He traveled ten years in the United States, Great Britain, and Europe, returning to St. Louis at intervals to check on the progress of the country house his architect-friend George Barnett (who eventually got all that sherry) was building for him outside the city. When Shaw moved into the house in 1849, his thoughts turned to the great public parks he had seen in Europe, and he decided to develop part of his country estate as a botanical park for his own delight and instruction, and for the pleasure and edification of the public. But another distinguished immigrant to St. Louis, the physician and botanist George Engelmann, persuaded Shaw to enlarge his original vision, to go beyond a mere park by including green-houses, a botanical library, a herbarium, and a museum in his plans. Taken with the idea, Shaw commissioned Engelmann to go abroad to purchase herbarium specimens. Thus was born the Missouri Botanical Garden, the oldest such institution in the United States.

History fails to record what Shaw's friends thought of the wine he left them, but the people of St. Louis flocked to his grounds and conservatories from their first opening in 1859. They came to admire the formal rose gardens and to exclaim over the palms and other exotica grown under glass. They came to stroll the pathways alongside the young plantings of trees, the hack-berries and ginkgos and elms and bald cypresses that would, in time, bring new coolness and shade in the summer to a former prairie. They came to Shaw's Garden to have their pictures taken in their Easter finery, and during the summer they came in their Sunday best, the men in bowlers and the women carry-ing frilly parasols, to enjoy the fussy circular beds of annuals and cannas scattered haphazardly about the well-tended lawns. They still come—over half a million visitors a year.

They do not come, however, on snowy Sundays in January.

Mr. Shaw's Garden

Having read every placard in sight, I looked round the Ridgway Center and discovered that I was the only visitor, except for a young couple who were hovering near the entrance into the garden's grounds. Dressed in imitation-leather trousers and cute sweatshirts (hers said "Master"; his, "Slave") and each wearing a single diamond earring, they hovered a bit more and then pushed their way outside. I decided to follow their example. The Climatron was only a hundred yards or so away. I could go there and think some jungle thoughts, pretending I was in Jamaica. But I changed my mind when I got outside and saw a fully enclosed nine-passenger electric tram next to a sign reading "Garden Tours by Heated Tram—75¢." I paid the driver and climbed aboard, delighted to discover that it was toasty warm inside. Master and Slave were already there. Master was explaining to Slave her theory that a person could have several meaningful relationships at one time so long as she was open and truly sincere and the other parties involved didn't play mind games and screw things up. Slave was carrying on a parallel monologue about the stubborn refusal of his roommate, Tim, to face the fact that, no matter how much he might want the job, no airline was going to hire him as a flight attendant because of, "well, you know, the obviousness of Tim's situation."

I didn't learn more about Tim, although my curiosity was piqued, because the tram's electric engine began to whine and my companions' conversation ceased. As we started moving up the sidewalk, a tape-recorded message came on, welcoming us to the Missouri Botanical Garden and explaining a bit of its history. We were invited to cast our thoughts back to 1859, the year of the garden's founding. James Buchanan occupied the White House. Readers on both sides of the Atlantic were eagerly reading each new installment of Charles Dickens's *A Tale of Two Cities* as it appeared in magazine serialization. People were humming the tunes of Stephen Foster. Down South, slaves chopped cotton and worked on indigo plantations. Closer at hand, the city of St. Louis, the gateway to the West, had experienced several decades of explosive growth and was finally becoming civilized. A former hardware merchant named Henry Shaw conceived an idea that some people may have thought preposterous. On a fair-sized tract of tall-grass prairie, he wanted to start a botanical garden that would eventually rival the greatest of them all, the Royal Botanic Garden at Kew, which Shaw had seen in his travels.

Ahead of us lay a small greenhouse. Just beyond, on a slight rise of earth, loomed the Climatron, a geodesic-dome greenhouse much resembling a gigantic puffball of plastic and metal. The tram, swaying on its rubber wheels, came to a stop in front of the small greenhouse and the tape recorder announced that it was the Mediterranean House, devoted entirely to vegetation that thrives in the long, parched summers and the short, cool winters of the world's Mediterranean regions—in California, coastal Chile, southern Africa, and Australia, as well as in the lands of the Mediterranean Basin proper. Here, if we visited later, after the tour was over, we would find figs and grapes and pomegranates growing. Here we would see yellow acacias in full bloom and sniff in the air the wonderful and spicy fragrances of rose and lemon geraniums, of lavender and rosemary, and of *Laurus nobilis* or sweet bay.

On the way to the Climatron, a structure inspired by the ideas of Buckminster Fuller, although the actual architect was a firm in St. Louis, our ghostly electronic Virgil (who sounds a lot like Garrison Keillor) told us that its half acre encloses some two thousand species of plants, most of them native to the world's tropical rain forests, and that the tram would stop there on the return trip. Next, the tram looped back to the lower part of the garden, stopping in front of a long, low building of red brick, its façade pierced by symmetrically placed arched windows, its roof made of glass. Slave had resumed his disquisition about Tim's unrealistic expectations, Master her own about simultaneous relationships. Neither had the slightest interest in learning that what we were seeing was the Linnaean House, built in 1882, named for the great Swedish taxonomist Carolus Linnaeus, originally used as an orangery, and now home to about fifty camellia bushes just coming into peak bloom. Nor were my companions much interested in our next stop, the Gladney Rose Garden, nor the one after that, the scented garden for the blind, where all the plants either have interesting textures or heavy fragrance and where everything is labeled in Braille.

Mr. Shaw's Garden

Just above the Climatron, Master and Slave got off when we stopped at another small greenhouse, the Desert House ("a fine collection of cacti, agaves, and succulents"). The tram continued up the hill, stopping for a moment at a small building of white limestone, with windows on all sides and a cupola. Inside, there was a nifty statue. The tape explained that the structure was originally intended to be a mausoleum for the mortal remains of Henry Shaw. But when Mr. Shaw learned that the stone used in its construction would weather and deteriorate badly after several centuries of exposure to the elements, he used it instead to display a piece of sculpture celebrating one of his pet themes—"The Victory of Science over Ignorance"—and built another mausoleum, this one of sturdy granite, in a clump of trees just below Tower Grove House. His body now rests there, beneath a marble effigy that depicts him sleeping, his face turned toward his country house, a rose in one hand.

At Tower Grove House, the driver of the tram cut off the tape recording for a moment. He said he was a volunteer, one of many who work at the garden. And he told me what I was already beginning to suspect: January is not the ideal month to visit Shaw's Garden. "You should see this place in the spring, when everything's blooming. And for Tower Grove House, of course, the very best time to come is Christmas."

"Why's that?" I asked.

"They put up a real German Christmas tree, with hundreds of real, lighted candles on it. Thousands of people come here to see it."

"Sounds wonderful," I said. "It must bring smiles to children and nightmares to fire marshals."

The tram's next-to-last stop was at Seiwa-En, an extraordinarily impressive Japanese garden that owes its existence to a master plan Dr. Peter Raven had drawn up for the orderly development of the Missouri Botanical Garden in 1971, when he became its director. Raven had in mind putting in a fairly modest Japanese garden, as a result of a suggestion and a small grant from the Japanese-American Citizens League of St. Louis, but a consulting firm encouraged him to think on a much larger scale. Plans were already afoot to dredge a lake in the undeveloped southwestern corner of the grounds, and Raven's consultants suggested combining the lake with a garden in the Japanese style and recommended Koichi Kawana, a Japanese landscape architect, as designer.

Seiwa-En, whose name means, in English, Garden of Pure Clear Harmony and Peace, opened in 1977. Covering fourteen acres, with a four-acre lake at its center, it now surpasses even the Climatron as an attraction for visitors. It is a virtual encyclopedia—a living one—of Japanese gardening. There are several islands in the lake, including one with a ceremonial teahouse. A drum bridge arches a stream with notable elegance, and a zigzag bridge hugs the lakeshore near a huge stand of Japanese irises. A waterfall and a cascade tumble along next to a planting of black pines and azaleas, and a multitude of stone lanterns sit next to courses of raked stone. According to the tape-recorded guide, Seiwa-En had been designed to be beautiful in any season, including winter. I didn't doubt it for a moment. A stone lantern stood just outside the tram's window, covered with an inch of snow. A male cardinal perched there, its bright red feathers vivid and resplendent against the white snow and the deep black-green of an adjacent Japanese pine.

At the Climatron, I thanked the driver for the tour and pushed my way inside. Even without the rum and orange juice and a Jamaican pretense, I felt that I'd left St. Louis behind. In the warm, moist air of the Climatron, bananas and bamboos and palms soared upward toward the dome. A constant, random drip of condensation fell from the greenhouse plastic. The air smelled dank and fertile. Orchids bloomed on trees festooned with Spanish moss. In a lily pond fringed with papyrus, red and golden carp moved lazily through the algal water. Scarlet and apricot hibiscus bloomed brightly, joined by allamandas, anthuriums, ginger, lobster-claw heliconias, and lavender brunfelsia. Luxuriant vines of bougainvillea and of *Quisqualis indica*, the Rangoon creeper, embraced the Doric columns of a portico left standing from an old palm house torn down in 1959 to make room for the Climatron—a sight that somehow called to mind pictures of temples in Kampuchea or Yucatan being swallowed up by the encroaching forest.

The Climatron was a pleasant place, no doubt about it,

and on that snowy January afternoon I had it all to myself—my own private jungle for an hour, but a jungle tidied up for human comfort—no scorpions or malaria-carrying mosquitoes.

At the Ridgway Center, when I telephoned for a cab, the dispatcher said there would be a half-hour wait. I wandered about the building and noticed that its rooms and even some of its furniture were named in honor of various donors and benefactors. The garden shop was named for Henry L. Freund. A gallery displaying porcelain birds honored the memories of Blanche and Taylor Spink. The wing of the building housing the extensive educational programs offered to both children and adults was named for Mary and Ellie Johnson. Only the restrooms went unchristened. I parked my posterior on a bench named for the real estate developer Trammell Crow, waited for my cab, and thought how pleased Henry Shaw would be if he could know what good care the people of St. Louis have taken of the garden he gave them over a century ago.

Talipot Palm:
Bloom and Doom

Miami, Florida
In 1896, when he spent some eight months in the Dutch settle-
ment of Buitenzorg on the island of Sumatra, almost everything
that young David Fairchild encountered left an indelible impression on his memory. Many years later, in his delightful autobiog-
raphy, *The World Was My Garden*, he still recalled the graceful
young men carrying parasols and wearing indigo and brown
sarongs, the twin volcanoes gently smoking in the distance, the
bands of parrots chattering among themselves in the jungle, and
the colonial officials dressed in white, sitting in little two-wheeled
carts pulled by ponies.

But it was the flora of Sumatra that most captured his attention—understandably so, since Fairchild, who spent most of his
life working for the USDA, was arguably the greatest plant
explorer the United States has ever produced. If Fairchild hadn't
traveled the globe many times over, seeking out exotic plants,
American horticulture and agriculture today would be greatly
impoverished. He was responsible for importing the Japanese
flowering cherry trees that grace the tidal basin in the District
of Columbia, for popularizing zucchini and chayote and other
vegetables, for introducing many sorghums and other grains, and
for establishing groves of Chinese tung oil trees in Florida for use
in making fine varnish. He's unfortunately also the man to blame
for bringing us that highly pestiferous plant, the kudzu vine,

which since the late 1930s has had a stranglehold on most of Dixie.

In his memoir, which was first published in 1938 and reissued in 1982, Fairchild wrote vividly and lovingly about the aroids, bamboos, and orchids he saw in Buitenzorg. But what most impressed him, forty-two years later, was a specimen of the talipot palm (*Corypha umbraculifera*) which he witnessed in full bloom and called "one of the wonders of the tropics."

"In the early sunlight," he wrote, "I stood one morning watching clouds of the small white flowers drifting down from the enormous flower cluster in the crown of the immense palm. The ground was white with blossoms, and myriads of bees were busily gathering honey." David Fairchild's words bore special significance in 1984, when the chief attraction at Miami's Fairchild Tropical Garden, which was founded in 1936 and named in his honor by Robert H. Montgomery, was a talipot palm. Planted during the garden's second year of existence from a seed gathered in Jamaica, it burst in April into the glorious bloom that Fairchild had experienced in Sumatra earlier in the century.

Throughout its long lifetime, everything about the talipot palm (only one of four hundred species of palms grown at this stunningly beautiful botanical garden) gives credence to David Fairchild's assertion that it's a tropical natural wonder. Its leaves, which reach twenty-five feet across, are the largest of any plant and have considerable economic importance in its native Sri Lanka, India, and Indonesia. They are used for thatching, for woven mats, and for baskets. Buddhist monks dry them, cut them into long strips, and inscribe sacred texts on them. In a pinch during a sudden torrential rainstorm, a single leaf makes a passable umbrella to shelter up to a dozen people at one time.

At up to one hundred feet in height, the talipot is one of the most majestic of palms. But it's at its most prodigious and awesome when it flowers, just at the end of its life. (Botanists classify it as monocarpic, meaning that it blossoms only once and then perishes.)

The doom of this particular specimen at Fairchild, which rises some fifty feet above a pathway and the shore of a lake said to be inhabited by an alligator of enormous size but more retiring habits than the Loch Ness monster, was sealed in early January when workers observed that its newest leaves were much smaller than usual, a signal that it was abandoning vegetative growth and beginning the reproductive frenzy that characterizes the species. Soon a flower stalk appeared, rapidly elongating and branching out, until by early April, when I paid it a visit, it was twenty feet high—the largest inflorescence of any plant. Its individual blossoms were insignificant, but there were sixty million of them, a figure to reckon with.

Something over a year later, the fruits of the palm weighed a ton. I wasn't there to see it, but I'm told that this wonder of the tropics, its life cycle completed, shuddered slightly and then, in a sudden and mighty crash, crumpled and collapsed under the burden of its own offspring, perishing that some of them might live and renew the species.

Fruit and Spice Park

Homestead, Florida

The racks of brochures in the lobbies of Dade County's huge crop of motels offer many a wonder to entice tourists and part us from our cash. Parrot Jungle invites us to drop in and gawk at macaws riding bicycles and performing headstands. In four languages, Coral Castle compares itself to Stonehenge and the Egyptian pyramids, despite having been built by only one man, "alone, with nothing but primitive hand tools." Orchid Jungle promises that it's a place "where every lady gets an orchid," an offer that to my mind is blatantly discriminatory on the basis of gender.

For some reason, there aren't any brochures for a remarkable attraction that I'll call simply Fruit Park, since it's burdened down with a cumbersome name that must cause waves of despair in any employee when the phone rings and he's got to answer by saying "The Preston B. Bird and Mary Heinlein Fruit and Spice Park." Run by the Metro-Dade County Park and Recreation Department, this unusual twenty-acre park a few miles north of Homestead doesn't cost one cent to visit. Devoted entirely to tropical and subtropical fruits, spices, and vegetables, it will gladden the heart of any horticulturally minded visitor.

Despite the absence of brochures and other promotional hoopla, visitors do find their way to Fruit Park, which came into existence in the 1940s and which is now being expanded, especially in its collection of citruses, now numbering some seventy species and cultivars.

The staff at Fruit Park are friendly, the atmosphere relaxed and low key. Visitors are invited to sample any fruit that has fallen to the ground, with the notable exception of the castor beans, coral plants, machineels, and other highly poisonous plants grown in a fenced-off compound. From November through May, there are guided tours on Wednesday mornings at 10:30 and on Sunday afternoons at 1:00 and 3:30, but visitors who come at other times can explore on their own, with the help of a booklet that identifies the names and economic uses of over five hundred species of plants.

Some people come to Fruit Park, often from great distances, to do some serious bird-watching, with high hopes of catching a glimpse of the smooth-billed ani, the white-winged dove, or the black-whiskered vireo and adding it to their life lists. I came, however, to do some serious fruit-watching.

Chris B. Rollins, a very personable young man who has been the director of Fruit Park for four years, showed me round. Considering that I had come all the way from New Jersey to see some tropical fruit, he bent the rules a bit. We stopped off first at a fine large loquat tree (*Eriobotrya japonica*), a member of the rose family and, despite its botanical name, a native of China. Its golden fruits were so delicious that I got greedy and ate three, right off the tree. I wasn't so taken with the small, wine-purple Surinam cherry (*Eugenia uniflora*). It tasted like turpentine— just one was plenty. The eggfruit tree or canistel (*Pouteria campechiana*) was accommodating enough to drop a fruit as I approached, so rule-bending wasn't necessary. "Here, try this," Mr. Rollins said. "People add milk to it and make milk shakes that taste like eggnog. Right off the tree, it tastes like an odd combination of cooked egg yolk and baked pumpkin." I tried it. It tasted like an odd combination of egg yolk and pumpkin.

Although it really wasn't his fault, Rollins kept apologizing profusely for the fact that the best fruits in the park weren't ripe yet. No kiwis. No mangoes. No jaboticabas (an odd Brazilian tree which bears fruits the size and color of Concord grapes directly on its trunk and branches). It was unfortunate, he said, that I couldn't sample the luscious fruits of the only edible philodendron, *Monstera deliciosa*, which he described as tasting like "bananas and pineapples in a rich creamy pudding."

Worst of all, I was several months too early to experience the gustatory delights of the mamey sapote (*Pouteria sapota*), a Mexican native whose roasted seeds are added to cacao to make chocolate and whose two-pound fruits go for as much as seven dollars a pound in south Florida during their season, a price that makes sapote-rustling something of a local cottage industry.

Chris Rollins gave me the bad news about missing out on the mamey sapote as we walked past the tempting-looking fruit of *Dillenia indica*, the elephant apple. I reached out to pluck one, but he stayed my hand with the intelligence that the elephant apple was much like the durian except for one thing. The durian smells atrocious but tastes wonderful. The elephant apple smells awful and tastes even worse.

At last, we arrived at a row of papayas. They weren't ripe, of course. But Rollins offered me a green one anyway. Chopped fine, it makes a wonderful substitute for cole slaw, with one proviso: use salad dressing, not mayonnaise, since papain, the enzyme that makes this fruit so good a digestive and is extracted to make meat tenderizer, turns the egg in mayonnaise to a disgusting-looking glop.

I can't report about green papaya slaw. When I got home, the one in my suitcase was more than fully ripe, filling one corner of the suitcase with a disgusting-looking glop.

Ethnic Farming

Dade County, Florida
In its southern part, Florida's Dade County changes character. Somewhere well below Coral Gables, the condominiums thin out and then cease. The flow of tourists continues down U.S. 1 and the Florida Turnpike, but they're all on their way to Key West or to the Everglades National Park, and don't plan to linger in places like Homestead and Florida City.

Here, agriculture still rules the roost. Peaceful groves of handsome avocado and mango trees nestle against one another, as well as occasional citrus orchards and banana plantations. But the dominant crop here, as anyone who visits during the winter growing season will notice, is the tomato. Hundreds and hundreds of acres are devoted to its culture, on limestone covered with perhaps an inch of topsoil and vast stretches of black plastic mulch on which sprawl vines treated with so much chemical fertilizer that they could almost be said to be grown hydroponically.

All during the winter, huge open trucks piled high with fruit speed along the flat and narrow roads, spilling out scores of tomatoes as green as kelp and as hard as a bill collector's heart. The trucks roar past wholesale nurseries specializing in crotons and other foliage plants in a great rush to get to the packing sheds, so that people further north may be kept supplied with shippable inedibles to grace our salads.

There's little doubt but that all these tomatoes make some

people very happy. They provide jobs for farm workers and truckers and graders. They're a source of profit to the growers and middlemen and retailers along the way, not forgetting the fertilizer manufacturers, of course. Perhaps they even are a source of pride to the plant breeders who took summer's most glorious vegetable and turned it into a wan and faint imitation of itself.

I confess it. I'm a tomato snob. I don't eat the things during the winter. It wouldn't bother me a whit if everyone in Florida forgot to order seeds next year. These tomato farms are utter bores. Nevertheless, winter or summer, southern Dade County is a most interesting place for vegetable lovers to visit, because of just one thing: its ethnic farms, little patches of earth where people of Asian or Latin American heritage grow some very unusual vegetables, partly for their own families' use, partly for sale to ethnic restaurants in the major cities of the Eastern seaboard.

There are several Thai farms, where the specialties are tiny scarlet peppers of a remarkable ferocity, lemon grass for seasoning and for herbal teas, and eggplants—not the usual large, elongated purple ones that Americans grow, but round-fruited eggplants which are a glossy golden-yellow when ripe and which are about the size of a ping-pong ball. The plants on which they grow (perennials at this latitude) spread wide and handsome, making them perfect subjects for what Rosalind Creasy has called "edible landscaping," the practice of making food plants with attractive habits do double duty as ornamentals.

Although I didn't manage to find it, I'm told there's a Filipino farm somewhere in this vicinity that grows a vegetable that's a particularly hot item these days among people who are studying ways of improving the diets of the rapidly growing populations of the world's tropical and subtropical regions. This vegetable wonder is the perennial winged bean, a legume which not only contains more protein than the soybean but also is edible in its entirety—green beans, dried seeds, leaves, roots, and even flowers.

One particularly fine and accessible ethnic farm lies right on U.S. 1 in Florida City, just behind the Sea Glades Motel, whose owner, Mr. D. A. Patel, is of Indian extraction. The soft marl of his patch of earth is home to a small truck garden devoted to Asian vegetables, all of them unfamiliar to those of us who raise vegetables at home for our own tables.

One of his specialties is the ivy gourd, a member of the cucurbid family propagated by cuttings and grown on high trellises. Ivy gourd is eaten green, since it becomes unpalatable when it ripens and turns fire-engine red. Mr. Patel grows purple lab lab beans and something called the horseradish tree, a legume whose many uses rival the winged bean in culinary and nutritional versatility. Its young roots can be peeled and cooked. Its feathery, light green leaves make a fine pot herb. Both its flowers and its seed pods are edible.

Just past Mr. Patel's small garden, a large field planted in what seem at first glance to be elephant ears makes an important point: small ethnic farming of unusual vegetables can sometimes grow into big business. These handsomely striking aroids, which aren't elephant ears at all though they're close kin, are *Xanthosoma sagittifolium*. First planted on a small scale by refugee farmers from Cuba and known in Spanish as *malangas*, they are now a multimillion-dollar crop in south Florida, thanks to the large Cuban population, for whom they are as important a root vegetable as the Irish potato is to other groups.

I know it's not very likely to happen, but it would be pleasant if some of those tomato farmers of southern Dade would see the light, let tomato growing be a summer activity by truck farmers whose fields lie close to those of us who eat tomatoes, and explore the uses of their land for raising unusual vegetables that will lend variety to our winter larders.

Lob's Wood

Cincinnati

Shortly before he and his wife Mary died within a few months of one another in 1964, Cincinnati businessman Carl Krippendorf told his daughter Rosan Adams, "I don't know what you're going to do with it when we're gone. I think we're leaving you somewhat of a white elephant." Mr. Krippendorf's white elephant was Lob's Wood, 175 acres of forested hillside east of Cincinnati in Clermont County. He had spent his summers there as a boy, staying with a country doctor's family to improve his delicate health. In 1900, the year he married, he bought the place to keep the land from being cleared and planted in tobacco, and he and his wife built the huge two-story shingled lodge where they lived from early March to late November every year.

Lob's Wood in time became one of the most remarkable gardens in America, and well known to many people who never visited it, thanks to Elizabeth Lawrence's description of it in *The Little Bulbs: A Tale of Two Gardens*, which was originally published in 1957 and which Duke University Press has just reprinted. Miss Lawrence's own garden in Raleigh, North Carolina, which was modest in dimension but distinguished in its range of plants, was one of the two gardens in her book's subtitle; the other was Lob's Wood, which she came to know intimately during a decade of regular correspondence with its owner.

By any reckoning, Carl Krippendorf was a man obsessed, a man who gardened on a scale much grander than Elizabeth

Lawrence. While he had a considerable appreciation for native wildflowers such as columbines and trilliums, his special passion was for bulbs, which he planted by the millions during his long career as a gardener.

The season of bloom in Lob's Wood got under way every January with the first snowdrops and with the pale yellow winter aconites, each blossom standing out against a frilly collar of dark green foliage. It ended in fall, with the final flourish of deep pink colchicums and hardy cyclamens. In between there were anemones, grape hyacinths, trout lilies, scillas, chionodoxas, and daffodils in awesome number.

Carl Krippendorf's infatuation with daffodils I suspect to be without parallel in the history of gardening. He planted them in vast colonies, thinking nothing of ordering twenty thousand bulbs at a time from just one dealer and similar quantities from other suppliers. And this unmistakable narcissomaniac must have known, when he told his daughter he was leaving her a white elephant, that a garden such as his, built up over many years on a grand scale in the service of a deep personal obsession, would after his death be vulnerable to bulldozers: developers would see 175 acres of woodland underplanted in bulbs and wildflowers as the raw material of a new subdivision.

But Lob's Wood has survived its former owner for twenty-one years now, its future assured for generations to come. The lodge still stands. Aconites, great sheets of them, still carpet the woods each winter, followed by the scillas and grape hyacinths and other spring bulbs that have self-sown everywhere beneath the beeches and the oaks. Daffodils, whole battalions of them, enough daffodils to keep a gaggle of English romantic poets busy for decades, still march up and down the hills, filling the woods with explosions of yellow and gold from early March to late April. Then come the wildflowers of summer—dame's rocket and butterfly weed and evening primrose and bouncing bet.

The people of Cincinnati and its surrounding counties may thank Carl Krippendorf for the fetching beauties of Lob's Wood, but they must thank others for its preservation. Shortly after Krippendorf died, Karl Maslowski and Stanley M. Rowe, two public-spirited citizens with a passionate interest in conservation, decided that it would be a crime for his property to be split up.

They also thought that it would be perfect as a nature center which would educate both children and adults about ecology and environmental issues. Mr. Rowe and Mr. Maslowski acted swiftly. With the help of the National Audubon Society, they set up a nonprofit corporation establishing the Cincinnati Nature Center, which immediately attracted three hundred enthusiastic founding members.

Lob's Wood survived, and the Cincinnati Nature Center thrived, acquiring additional property until it now takes in some 755 acres traversed by thirteen miles of well-tended trails, plus Long Branch Farm, a 535-acre working farm near Goshen, Ohio, a bequest from Neil McElroy, Secretary of Defense under President Eisenhower. It now has over five thousand members, who have the place to themselves and their guests on weekends and holidays. (Other days, it is open to the general public, who are requested to make a donation, to keep to the trails, and to refrain from picnicking and picking wildflowers.)

It was a raw, sunny day in late March when I visited Lob's Wood. I paid my respects to the hordes of daffodils, a truly spectacular sight. I walked a bit of one of the trails, which led past one slope densely covered with trout lilies in full and graceful bloom and several slopes covered with a golden species of ranunculus with flowers like buttercups. I eavesdropped as a volunteer guide explained to a small group of third-graders the geology of a stream cutting its way through blue-gray shale and limestone.

Then, shivering with cold, I made my way to the Rowe Interpretive Building, which houses the center's extensive educational program. A cheering fire roared in the huge stone fireplace next to the bookstore. I sat down on a wooden bench just inside the plate-glass wall overlooking a pond and a great many bird feeders. More goldfinches than I had ever seen in one spot flew from one feeder to another, as bright and winsome as the daffodils in Lob's Wood. I had a plane to catch, but I was filled with a momentary sense of absolute well-being, tinged with envy for the people of Cincinnati, who can regularly enjoy Carl Krippendorf's legacy—no white elephant at all, but a genuine local treasure.

Ted Childs's Hillside Marvel

Serious garden lovers are a notoriously gossipy and gallivanting tribe. Among true aficionados, word gets around so quickly about any truly extraordinary garden that its owner is soon besieged by requests from people who wish to visit. The word has gotten out about Edward Childs's garden at his Connecticut home in the Litchfield Hills, just outside the charming village of Norfolk, and late every spring, when his garden is at its peak season of bloom, he increasingly plays host to visitors on tours pre-arranged by the botanical gardens and horticultural societies of the Northeast. Generally, he meets his guests in the driveway and then conducts them down a short flight of steps through a small Japanese garden to another, much larger garden so spectacular in its beauty that it is unarguably one of the finest in the Western world.

On first sight, the big garden seems to have been wisely and deliberately designed to overwhelm the viewer with its grand vistas and its bold use of masses of glowing color. From a wide graveled ledge just below the Japanese garden, one looks down a steep hillside covered with huge granite boulders and criss-crossed by a network of pathways and stairsteps. Forty feet below, rhododendrons and conifers are clustered on the valley floor, and in the distance, beyond a country lane, a hillock rises, planted with apple trees.

There's also a great deal of bold color. Dense mats of crimson, magenta, and white creeping phlox don't creep but fairly spill over rocks like brooks in torrent. Gentians in electric shades of blue assert themselves against the softer blue haze of forget-me-nots. Everywhere, something catches and holds the eye—columbines, for instance: soft purple ones like amethysts in the lee of an enormous boulder halfway down the hillside, dark red ones like rubies growing atop a limestone outcropping at the bottom of the garden.

But first impressions deceive. As it turns out, this garden wasn't thought out in advance. The vistas and the bold colors are undeniable, but they are incidental and serendipitous. The total effect may be grand and overwhelming, but unintentionally so. The true purpose here is to make each member of a collection of individual plants with very special needs happy enough that it will survive in a setting far from its native home. The pleasure that its owner hopes visitors will find in it lies not in attending to the overall whole but in paying close attention to small, even tiny things. For Ted Childs, it's the details that count.

When Edward Childs first started gardening in 1969, his ambitions were modest, as compared with his achievement many years later. His dominant interest lay in trees, not flowering plants. He studied forestry at Yale in the early 1930s, worked out West in the mining industry after graduation, and spent the war years with Claude Hope in Costa Rica developing a cinchona plantation to replace the sources of quinine lost when the Philippines fell. At his home in Norfolk, long before he took up gardening, he was an avid forester, tending the trees on his 6,400-acre private preserve on Great Mountain, on whose lower slope his house stands.

Childs's first venture into gardening was the Japanese garden just below his driveway. In the 1960s there was keen interest in the principles and practices of the Japanese school of gardening, which impressed Childs for its emphasis on simplicity and formal restraint. On the eve of a trip to the Orient with his wife, he asked a friend from nearby Falls Village, H. Lincoln Foster, to design and build a garden in the Japanese manner within an enclosure formed by the granite foundations of a barn that had been destroyed by fire some years previous.

Childs made an excellent choice in turning to Foster. He was

America's leading authority on rock gardening, a style of horticulture developed in Britain in the late nineteenth century, when
English hikers began cultivating plants brought back from the
Swiss Alps. Foster's own garden, just outside Falls Village, is a
Connecticut landmark. Called Millstream, it stands on a precipitous hillside dominated by a dramatic stream plunging down
a course of enormous granite boulders—a point of pilgrimage for
horticulturists since the 1930s. Foster quickly set about designing
and planning the modest Japanese garden Childs wanted, and it
was finished when the Childses returned. The result was superb,
a classic of its kind. Childs now possessed a complete and self-
contained garden, based on Buddhist ideals and meant to inspire
quiet meditation about humanity's place within the natural order.
Although small and intimate, it symbolically embraced the entire
universe, its raked gravel standing for water, its partly submerged
boulders representing earth.

Something happened to Childs after this small garden was
built. He fell in love with alpine plants. Although he still retains
a passionate interest in forestry, for the past twenty-six years he
has devoted more and more time and attention to ferreting out
alpine plants in every corner of the globe and adding them to his
collection.

"Alpine," it should be noted, is a generic term. It denotes
plants that grow at the timberline or above or plants native to
arctic and sub-arctic regions where climatic conditions are similarly harsh. What all alpines have in common is a tendency
toward shortness of stature and the absolute need to complete
their annual cycle of growth in sixty days or fewer, from initia-
tion of new leaves to ripening of seed. One finds alpines in the
Alps, yes, but also in the Pyrenees, the Urals, the Himalaya, the
higher mountains of northern New England, and the Rockies
and other Western ranges, as well as at lower elevations in the
Far North.

Ted Childs is a gracious and charming man—if it irritates
him to have strangers on the premises inspecting his Alpine
garden, it doesn't show. But he gets a bit impatient with certain
kinds of comments or questions.

If someone tells him he has a beautiful garden—and he *does*, by any measure—he replies by pointing out, "Well, it's really very much an experimental garden. That's the way it started out, and that's the way it still is. It's a place to try things out, to see what it takes to make some plant happy. And plants do let you know very quickly when something displeases them." Walking over to a tiny green plant growing in a crevice between two rocks, he points to it as example. "Here's just what I mean, this little arenaria from Spain. I thought it looked as if it would like a limy situation. I kept it in one until there wasn't much left but two green leaves, so I snatched it up and put it in where the soil is more nearly neutral and it just said thank you and came right back. As you can see, it has reseeded itself quite splendidly."

Childs also is spectacularly uninterested in quantitative questions. How many acres does his garden cover? He doesn't know. (But three seems a reasonable guess.) How many individual plants are in his care? No idea. Does he keep track of the number of species, perhaps on a computer?

"Heavens, no," he answers. "It would be foolish even to try because plants come and go. It keeps changing so. You even come to welcome losses, first because there's no sense coddling things beyond a reasonable degree, second because it opens up room to try new things. There may be gardeners who strive just to get everything right once and for all. Not me. I'm always trying to spread my horizons, with plants that may or may not do well. If they die, they die, but there's always something new—like some seeds my son just collected in Bhutan that I've high hopes for."

What seems to interest Childs the most in a visitor is curiosity about the individual plants that grow in his garden, each one neatly labeled by genus, species, and place of origin. Scrambling over the rocks with remarkable spryness—a gardening friend who lives nearby says that Ted Childs is "seventy-eight going on fifty"—to reach some rare botanical treasure, he talks animatedly about it, then goes on to something new. This wee little mat of dark green leaves and clusters of cobalt flowers is *Ajuga pyramidalis metallica crispa,* and it's one alpine that's actually from the Alps, as is the nearby clump of *Gentiana acaulis,* which is purely astonishing for the depth of color of its host of large, cup-shaped flowers. A few feet farther on there's a low-growing yellow lady's slipper. "That's *Cypripedium calceolus,* from Eurasia—an unusual orchid in that it likes a slightly limy soil."

In Ted Childs's alpine garden there are so many plants to see and his enthusiasm for each—he shows no favoritism whatsoever—is so high that hours in his company seem like minutes and one soon forgets to look at the vistas and the masses of bold colors, to see what Childs must see, such as a fine assortment of lewisias, which are extraordinarily toothsome American alpines, or a prostrate mat of a very northern species of gaultheria, collected on Mt. Katahdin, pleasant for its tiny flowers, somewhat resembling blueberry blossoms, but truly notable for the fruit that follows. ("The berries are quite large and white and delicious," Childs says, his face lighting up at the memory of obvious firsthand experience. "They've got a delicious slight wintergreen flavor. You can take handfuls and quench both thirst and appetite in a very wonderful and refreshing way.")

Even if Childs can't list the plants he grows, the list is obviously a long one: for starters, there are many different species of sedums, violets, penstemons, poppies, tiarellas, saxifrages, geums, phlox, geraniums, campanulas, lobelias, and their names march on and on, including scaled-down species within genera whose more familiar species are much, much larger, such as an arctic willow barely two inches high.

Ted Childs's collection of alpines is one of the wonders of American horticulture today. But he's a modest man. Mention to him the legendary collection of alpine plants at Great Britain's Royal Botanic Gardens at Kew, and he will tell you that, yes, it's very fine indeed. But not being interested in mere numbers, he won't make the justifiable claim that his alpine collection stands up well in comparison with Kew's. And he's too gentlemanly to mention one salient fact. Ted Childs grows his plants out in the open in a region where winter is long and ferocious.

The royal gardeners at Kew play it a little safer, giving many of their alpines the protection of a special greenhouse.

Viette's Place

In 1976, when Andre Viette sold the well-known nursery and garden center near Muttontown, Long Island, that his father, Martin Viette, had founded almost fifty years earlier, he knew what he was escaping. Profits were up, but so were taxes, labor costs, and his blood pressure. Pleasure in his work had ebbed. He didn't have enough time to pursue his program of hybridizing daylilies as much as he would have liked. He couldn't devote himself to the perennials that were his first love. He still raised them and sold them, but the bulk of his business lay in ho-hum junipers and pyracanthas shipped in by the truckload from California, market packs of unremarkable petunias and salvias, imported Dutch tulips and daffodils, and sacks of lawn fertilizer. He loved plants, but he was coming not to like selling them to the suburban retail trade. He felt especially harried at Christmastime, when his business in cut firs and spruces was brisk and lively.

That year, when he moved with his wife, Claire, their sons, Scott and Mark, and their twin daughters, Heather and Holly, to the hillside farm he had bought in Fishersville, Virginia, not far from Waynesboro in the Shenandoah Valley, Mr. Viette thought he knew almost precisely what the future would bring. He had considered the move carefully, scouting other locations in Virginia and also North Carolina before settling on Fishersville. There, on more than two hundred acres of rolling fields, pasture, and woodlands, he would lay the foundations of a small perennial nursery, a retail business whose clientele would drive over from Charlottesville, Richmond, or Washington to buy the very select plants he would grow—hostas, iris, peonies, phlox, Oriental poppies, but, above all, daylilies, his favorite.

Things did not go according to plan, not at first at least. The fate of a small perennial nursery wouldn't seem to have much to do with world affairs on a massive scale, but it did. Andre Viette's Farm and Nursery and OPEC collided head-on. Gasoline prices rose dramatically, and people weren't driving over to Fishersville from Charlottesville, Richmond, and Washington to buy perennials. Viette quickly decided that if people weren't coming to his plants he'd take his plants to people. To move them into the market, he followed a two-fold plan.

First, he began to develop a wholesale trade. Leaving his elder son, Mark, in charge of the farm, he and Claire traveled up and down the state of Virginia, visiting the better garden centers from Norfolk to the suburbs of Washington, with samples and colored photographs of his perennials. They also called on landscape architects and municipal-park authorities, touting the great merits of the daylily as a free-blooming, virtually carefree perennial. Viette's enthusiasm for his plans was so infectious that he became a highly successful salesman. It didn't hurt that an interest in perennials was beginning to surface throughout the country. Orders began pouring in. And besides garden centers and landscape architects, Viette soon found himself with another kind of wholesale customer altogether—some of the large and very well known mail-order nurseries serving the mass market. I hope I shatter no one's illusions here by stating one of the plainer facts about American horticulture today: a handsome color catalog with dazzling photographs of tempting floral goodies is no guarantee that a nursery actually raises all, or even *any*, of the plants it sells. Some nurseries that used to raise their own stock now find it simpler to buy from wholesale growers, keeping the plants in cold-storage warehouses until they're ready for shipment to customers. Sometimes the plants even come from England, shipped here with all the soil washed off their roots to satisfy the strict regulations of the USDA, and they may linger in cold storage for many months, a fact which explains their sometimes puny condition when gardeners finally receive them in the mail. Mr. Viette's wholesale business with mail-order nurseries is now of sufficient order that many people grow his perennials without knowing it.

The second step Andre Viette took to develop his nursery was to move, very cautiously, into mail-order retail trade on his own, with a modest, twenty-six-page, no-frills catalog listing almost two hundred kinds of flowering perennials, herbs, and ferns, although only a fraction of the plants he grows on the farm. The catalog is admirably understated, remarkably free of the glowing prose that some nurseries use to sell their wares. It offers no wonder plants, no amazing bargains, no dollar daylilies. And as things have turned out, the catalog, combined with word-of-mouth among the horticultural cognoscenti, has brought the in-person customers Viette had hoped for back in 1976. There's a small notice in the catalog inviting visitors to drop by, and about six thousand people per year now do so, from early spring, when the anemones and epimediums are blooming, to mid-autumn, when the oaks and maple trees reach their peak of color on the lower slopes of the nearby Blue Ridge Mountains and Viette's closes to the public. During the long growing season, there's always something in bloom, even if some times are more spectacular than others: those who come in mid-May, when whole fields of Oriental poppies, peonies, and more than six hundred named varieties of iris are in full and radiant bloom, covering the entire spectrum of color, say that not even the tulip fields of Holland can match the spectacle, except for their greater extent.

I would respect Andre Viette, even if I had never met him. The prices in his catalog aren't cheap, though I've seen some that are more expensive. But the plants he mails out are well grown and big enough to establish themselves quickly. As should be clear by now, I'm a regular customer of quite a few mail-order nurseries with which I've had good experiences. From time to time, I write out an order and mail it to the Viette Farm and Nursery. But usually I just get in the car and zip on down from southern New Jersey to Fishersville, which is only a day's drive, with some spectacular scenery along the way. I've been making this particular excursion about twice a year since 1983, when a regional daylily meeting was held at the Viette place. I was hooked by the Viettes' hospitality, by the beauty of the farm's setting in the Blue Ridge foothills, and by the obvious fact that the entire Viette family are something more than nursery people who earn their living by raising plants in the fields and numerous plastic greenhouses on their premises. They're also *gardeners*, and good ones. Visitors, once they've parked their cars by the barn up the hill from the Viettes' attractive brick house, are free to roam wherever they please, and there's an inspiring horticultural idea almost everywhere they look. When I first visited Fishersville, the first thing that caught my eye was a two-hundred-foot-long perennial border tucked into the hillside behind a low retaining wall of stone, artfully designed to give a long succession of bloom and also to display appealing combinations of plant textures and forms. The area devoted to perennial beds keeps expanding, especially as regards berms (raised, mounded beds, good for displaying plants and also good in providing drainage for the heavy clay soil Viette has got).

A visit to the Viette Farm is much better than leafing through even the most lavishly illustrated nursery catalog, because you can see for yourself mature specimens of the plants for sale. It's also slightly dangerous for gardeners like me, who always go overboard at the slightest opportunity. Almost everything that Andre Viette grows in his garden is available in the large sales area below his barn, and it's all growing in containers, so there's no shock to the plants when they're transported and transplanted. (Nor is there any rush about planting them once back home; they can sit in their containers for months, if need be.) The last trip I made, I drove to Fishersville with the car empty except for a small overnight bag. I came back with the car so loaded down with astilbes, daylilies, hostas, and other wonders that the toll-booth collector at the Delaware Memorial Bridge shot me a suspicious glance, as if all those plants were meant to divert attention from some more illicit cargo.

At least half the plants growing in my garden now came

from Viette's. If I keep making those trips to Fishersville, the time can't be very far away when I'll have to buy some acreage out in the country—and start a rival nursery. Until then, praise be to Andre Viette, who hasn't had to sell a Christmas tree in years.

Sissinghurst

It's no secret that, of all nations, Great Britain is home to the greatest number of people who are passionate about gardening almost to the point of dottiness. Horticulture pervades British culture to a greater extent than the bullfight pervades that of Spain. More acreage is devoted to the raising of daffodil bulbs there than in Holland. (In fact, the Dutch import large numbers of bulbs from Britain.) While the United States has at best—and I'm stretching a point here—five decent magazines for gardeners, the London news kiosks sell well over a dozen, several of them weeklies. Gardening gets better coverage on television in Great Britain than cooking does in the U.S.

It's obvious, therefore, that if garden-loving Americans can visit just one other country, Great Britain should be their choice. And if there's time to visit only one garden, it's my firmest conviction that they should make a beeline for the garden that the late Vita Sackville-West and her husband, Harold Nicolson, designed and planted at Sissinghurst, about an hour's journey south of London. This garden is not ancient by any means. It dates back only to 1930, when Nicolson and Sackville-West, a strangely mated but nonetheless affectionate pair, bought Sissinghurst Castle, an odd assortment of sixteenth-century brick-and-stone buildings in a sorry state of dilapidation and disrepair.

When they moved in, there was no garden at all. The buildings were surrounded by what Sackville-West later described as an "appalling mess of rubbish," including "old bedsteads, old plough-shares, old cabbage stalks, old broken-down earth closets, old matted wire, and mountains of sardine tins, all muddled up in a tangle of bindweeds, nettles, and ground elder." After the rubbish was hauled away, Nicolson began to design the garden, laying out its walks and hedges and walls, while his wife started to select the plants that would grow there.

A longtime admirer of the brief but lapidary garden columns that V. Sackville-West wrote for the London *Observer*, twice published in collections in the United States, I have always wanted to go on pilgrimage to Sissinghurst, something I finally accomplished a few Septembers ago. But I almost didn't make it, thanks to a hotel clerk who assured me that the train from London to Hastings stopped right at the entrance to the garden. No such thing. The closest it gets is Tunbridge Wells. From Tunbridge Wells there's bus service, but it takes four hours, three transfers, and a three-mile walk at the end. My problem was solved in the person of Mr. Peter Plume, who was willing to take me there and back for a hefty £35, plus an hourly charge for waiting. Our journey took us through woodlands and fields of hops ready for the harvest, a sight that inspired Mr. Plume to launch into a lengthy diatribe against brewers and people who quaff what they brew.

Just before we arrived at Sissinghurst, I was suddenly gripped by misgivings. Garden writers sometimes exaggerate just a bit when they're writing about their own real estate. Perhaps V. Sackville-West gardened with pen and paper better than she did with shovel and hoe. Or perhaps her garden had fallen into neglect after her death, despite now being part of Britain's National Trust. Perhaps there would be weeds in the herbaceous border, litter on the pathways, a forlorn look to the shrubbery. Furthermore, I was visiting in the autumn. Perhaps nothing would be in bloom.

All my misgivings were groundless. As soon as I entered the archway through the long, fairly low rectangular building that Harold Nicolson had used as a library and saw in front of me the tall, vine-clad tower where V. Sackville-West had her quiet retreat, I knew that the picture I had of Sissinghurst from her writing was right on the mark: it was, and it remains, one of the world's most beautiful gardens.

Nine Million Flowers
under One Roof

Aalsmeer, the Netherlands
Niek Hoffman, the staff writer for the Flower Council of Holland
who volunteered to take me through the celebrated cut-flower
auction at Aalsmeer, was a most amiable and considerate young
man. Knowing that I couldn't get any coffee at my hotel in The
Hague at 5:00 a.m., he brought some in a thermos bottle so I
could jolt myself awake with a strong dose of caffeine before we
hit the busy highway and headed toward Aalsmeer, which is just
a few kilometers from the Amsterdam airport.

The trip took only half an hour. Along the way, as the sky
changed from black to leaden gray, Hoffman enlightened me
with some statistics about the Dutch flower trade. There are
twelve cut-flower auctions in Holland, each conducted every
weekday from well before dawn until shortly before noon, and
Aalsmeer is the largest. Some four thousand growers belong to
the cooperative which runs it. An equal number of registered
buyers use its services, although it isn't very likely that all of
them will show up on any given day. At 300,000 square meters,
the warehouse it has occupied since 1972 is reputedly the largest
commercial building under one roof in the world.

By the time we reached the parking lot at Aalsmeer, already
thick with trucks and vans belonging to growers and registered
buyers, the caffeine was wearing off and my mind was awash
with numbers. If it was a typical day, some nine million flowers

and 700,000 potted plants would change hands by noon, in 60,000 individual transactions ranging in magnitude from a single bunch of twenty roses to several truckloads of them. Although the bulk of the flowers and plants I would see were raised in Holland, there would also be dendrobium orchids from Thailand, spray carnations and anemones from Israel, and even a few plants, mostly leatherleaf ferns, from the U.S.A. The Dutch, it seems, are in the business of selling flowers, and they are remarkably unchauvinistic about where they come from.

The Aalsmeer auction draws over 200,000 visitors each year, mostly foreign tourists, including an estimated 40,000 Americans, who are generally delighted to find out that even if they've missed out on tulip time and the lavish display of the bulb gardens at Keukenhof they can still come to Aalsmeer any weekday morning and boggle their eyes at the sight of nine million flowers assembled briefly in one spot before they are dispatched by truck to every country in Northern Europe and by jet transport to several cities in the United States and Canada. (The small admission fee of 2.50 guilders amounts to less than US $1.)

Although it wasn't even six yet and the auction doesn't open to visitors until the slightly more civilized hour of 7:30, Hoffman led me in through the tourists' entrance and up a flight of stairs to a suspended sidewalk on the second story, where he promised I would find a good overview of what goes on at a flower auction.

Numbers—300,000 square meters, nine million flowers—don't call up any pictures in my head, but their meaning became clear as soon as we pushed open the door from the staircase and saw the vast and extremely busy warehouse below us—so vast and so dimly lit by cool fluorescent lights hanging from the ceiling that I couldn't see the other end of the building, whose area, Hoffman told me, amounts to something like sixty football fields.

Several hundred yards ahead of us lay the first of the five auction rooms that are arranged at regular intervals along the central walkway of the warehouse—an auction room, I was told, where only roses were sold. Below us was an immense staging area filled with hundreds of large metal trolleys, each loaded with 2,880 roses packed in twelve plastic containers and each worth up to $4,000 retail, for top-grade long-stemmed tea roses.

From time to time, workers would connect five or six trolleys into a train which was placed on a track to be pulled into the auction rooms where buyers waited.

The rose auction clipped along at such a swift pace that without Niek Hoffman's explanation I would hardly have understood what was going on. The buyers sit at desks arranged in broad, steeply raked tiers, like medical students observing an anatomy lesson. Below them the flower trolleys arrive in procession, each one pausing briefly as it is auctioned to the highest bidder.

High on the wall above the flowers, a pair of very large clocks permit two separate auctions to take place simultaneously, each with a single hand pointing to midnight, representing a preset maximum price. When the auction for a particular lot begins, the pointer rapidly descends toward the minimal price for whatever merchandise is being sold, which will be thrown away if no one bids in time. By pushing one button, buyers can switch from one auction to the other. By pushing another, they make a bid, which is recorded by the computer, which then sends the trolley to the shipping area, where the buyer's representative takes delivery within fifteen minutes of purchase.

The tension in the auction room is palpable. If a buyer pushes a button a second too soon, he will have bought too dearly. If he's a second too late, he has lost to another bidder some flowers he wanted to buy.

While Hoffman was explaining to me the reasons for the expressions of nervousness and worry on the faces of most of the buyers, the auction's smooth efficiency was interrupted by a mechanical failure. A trolley of pink cluster roses, just bought by a successful bidder, got stuck on the track, refusing to budge at the computer's command. Four workmen removed it by much pushing and nudging, and the roomful of buyers erupted in disorder, like a study hall of ninth-graders when their teacher has left the room. There was much hooting addressed to the balky trolley and claps and cheers for the men wrestling it off its track. One buyer wadded up a paper napkin and threw it at another who was sitting at a desk three tiers up. It seemed a good moment to leave to explore the warehouse's deeper reaches, after first stopping off for coffee and the Dutch equivalent of a prune

Danish at one of the several small cafés in the building. (There's also a bank, a post office, and a barbershop.)

I hope I offend no one by saying that long-stemmed cut tea roses bore me just a trifle, though seen 2,880 at a time they do make a certain impression. But beyond the auction room for roses there were staging areas for other trolleys loaded with other flowers in enormous variety—alstroemerias, lilies, liatris, anemones, gerberas, heather, freesias, many of which would fly to Atlanta and New York and Los Angeles on the 2:00 flight from Schiphol Airport. It was possible that some of the alstroemerias I saw on the trolleys would be sold for export to the U.S. within the hour. They might even end up tomorrow at the florist we patronize back home.

Count Bernadotte's
Floral Disneyland

Konstanz, West Germany
I went to Mainau, a small, turtle-shaped island near the eastern
shore of Lake Constance—Bodensee to German-speakers—with
many mental reservations and none at a hotel, since I was making
a quick day trip of it from Zurich. My mood was that of someone
who lets a tent barker at a county fair persuade him to come
inside and behold a genuine, living and breathing three-headed
calf. I had learned about Mainau from a brochure put out by an
American travel agency specializing in arranging overseas tours
for travelers with particular interests, in this case for horticultural-
minded Americans bent on cramming as many European gardens
as possible, from Wisley in England to the Boboli Gardens in
Florence, into a hectic two weeks of bus travel, with scarcely a
spare moment to recover from jet lag or cope with gastrointesti-
nal protest.

According to the brochure for the tour, the allotted time for
visiting the gardens on the isle of Mainau would be brief, only
an hour or two, but the pleasures would be immense—and also
quite astonishing. The island, it was claimed, was noted for its
lush tropical flora. Bougainvillea clambered up palm trees, and
bright hibiscus and gaudy birds-of-paradise bloomed alongside
banana plants. It all sounded pretty improbable. Palm trees
growing on an island in a lake between Switzerland and West
Germany seemed about as likely as finding decent food in London by reading the menus in restaurant windows. Or that living

three-headed calf. There had to be a trick. When I arrived I would probably find all those palm trees growing inside a conservatory. Nevertheless, I filed Count Bernadotte's garden away in my mind, doubts and all, and when I found myself in the vicinity one late summer day I decided to visit the place.

Doubt changed to dismay when I pulled into the parking lot, enormous but still so crammed with BMWs and Opels, plus the occasional Mercedes-Benz, that it was no small matter finding a parking spot. A second lot was filled to overflowing with tourist buses from Bremen and Cologne and Düsseldorf. Very depressing: it's always a downer to discover that tens of thousands of other people have a destination in common with you.

The causeway leading over to Mainau and its gardens was so clotted with visitors that a pedestrian traffic jam seemed imminent, as throngs of tourists strode briskly along a footway lined with larches to join the throngs who had already arrived. Some of my fellow pilgrims complicated the flow of traffic further by bringing dogs. One woman had two boxers on a tandem leash, each straining in a different direction.

Once over the causeway, I set out to find those highly touted tropical plants. There were some—not only palms and hibiscus but also daturas, heliconias, and orchids. My suspicions were fully grounded, nevertheless. If Mainau is tropical, then so is Brooklyn. Most of the island's more exotic flora grew in pots or large containers easily transported to greenhouses before the first good frost. As for the palm trees, undeniably an astonishing sight with the cool blue waters of Lake Constance in the distance, a guard told me that they were covered over with glass for winter protection. He also told me that the island gets over two million visitors each year.

I thought he may have underestimated the number. On this particular Saturday afternoon in early fall, there seemed to be about 400,000 people on hand, most of them trying with little success to take pictures of flower beds without another human in sight to mar the view.

In coming to an opinion about any garden open to the general public, it's crucial to know the exact intentions of those who created it. Was its original purpose to display the power of an absolute monarchy, as at Versailles? Or did it come into being because some wealthy citizen had both a horticultural passion and a desire to share it with his fellows, as was the case with Henry Shaw and the Missouri Botanical Garden he founded in the nineteenth century or with Pierre Du Pont and Longwood Gardens, closer to our own day?

Having known little about Mainau except that I would find tropical plants growing there, I decided to remedy my ignorance by buying a book about the place, written by the island's owner, Count Lennart Bernadotte. Planting myself beneath a palm to peruse his brief text in three languages, I discovered that the story was fairly simple. The count's great-grandfather, Grand Duke Frederick I of Baden, who was the Kaiser's son-in-law and an ardent dendrologist, bought Mainau in 1853 and started an arboretum, including a grove of sequoias from California which have now reached immense size and are in their own way just as remarkable as the well-advertised palms and bananas. When Count Bernadotte inherited the island in 1930, it was wild and overgrown and he was financially strapped. After a brief and unsuccessful try at farming, he decided to turn it into a lavish garden that would attract paying tourists. In his own words, he speaks of "creating this green refuge from the rush and roar of everyday life for nearly two million visitors each year."

The count's intentions are something of a contradiction, of course. Two million visitors a year to a tiny island nowhere near the size of Central Park bring a good bit of rush and roar with them, as well as the occasional pair of boxers. Nevertheless, it's perfectly apparent what Bernadotte had in mind: he wanted Mainau to be a crowd-pleaser. And he has certainly succeeded. There's nothing subtle about the place, and the plantings of flowers are something of an indiscriminate mishmash, an explosion of brightly colored annuals everywhere, with a strong emphasis on gaudy cannas and sumptuous dahlias glowing in their radiant fall colors from a hundred yards away. Much use is made of the outmoded Victorian style of carpet bedding, with circles of assorted bedding plants plopped here and there in the lawn without much rhyme or reason. One bed on a hillside is a floral map of Lake Constance, done entirely in red begonias, with a dwarf banana tree marking the island's location.

But there's no sense in being peckish, judging the gardens at

Mainau as other than they are. Mainau is no cloister, nor is it a Japanese garden meant to inspire meditation about the human condition and our transactions with the natural order. It's a horticultural Disneyland, an amusement park where flower beds take the place of roller coasters. And seen in this light, it's really lots of fun, especially for the children's zoo near the exit, whose animals—a spreading peacock, a mother duck and three ducklings, an owl, a bunny rabbit, and three whales ("Moby Dick and His Friends," the sign says)—are all twelve feet tall and made of wax begonias, ageratum, dusty miller, and other flowers growing in peat moss inside a wire-mesh framework.

The children loved it. So did I. And after admiring that owl, whose beak was made of houseleeks, for almost half an hour, I bought some cotton candy, the first I'd had in years.

Corn among the Edelweiss

Zurich, Switzerland
At first glance, they seemed to be shantytowns, something I hardly expected to find in Switzerland. High fences of wire mesh surround these large colonies of small shacks scattered through the outskirts of Zurich, as if to keep them segregated from the general prosperity of this pleasant city. Here, my first thought was, live the poor of Zurich. My second thought was that the poor of Zurich live far better lives than those who inhabit the other shantytowns of the world. Their houses may be tiny, dollhouses almost, but they are all neatly painted. Almost every shack flies the Swiss flag from its rooftop or from a pole out front. Each house sits in an immaculately tended garden. During the season, tidy rows of Brussels sprouts, perfect heads of lettuce, and very fetching-looking Swiss chard with leaves of emerald green and stems that glow an incandescent ruby red grow in well-cultivated beds without a weed in sight. Late raspberries and blackberries, their canes heavy with ripe fruit, serve as hedgerows separating one garden from the next. Geraniums and petunias spill from window boxes, and immense clumps of dahlias, each so exactingly staked and tied as to exemplify the phrase "Swiss precision," delight the eye in half the gardens at least.

These tidy plots are not, however, the gardens of the poor, and no one lives in the huts. They are *Schrebergärten*, named after Daniel Schreber (1808–61), an orthopedist from Leipzig who worried that the rapid growth of industrialization and urbanization that took place throughout the nineteenth century was inimical to both physical and mental health. In addition to promoting gymnastics in the schools and the establishment of public playgrounds for children, he urged that the municipal authorities in cities and large towns should make garden plots available to their inhabitants, giving them the chance to escape the stress of modern civilization. Dr. Schreber's ideas caught on. Today the gardens named after him abound in Austria, Germany, and Switzerland.

A *Schrebergarten* is a small piece of land, averaging seven hundred square feet, that an apartment dweller may lease from his municipality for a long enough period, typically twenty years, to make it worthwhile not only to put in a garden but also to build a small hut, a place to store tools and supplies, and a place to sit, enjoying coffee and cake or quietly reading or playing a game of cards with friends. These gardens and their huts are grouped together in large complexes covering many acres. Wide asphalt alleys penetrate each complex in parallel rows. Locked gates at the end of the alleys and a high fence around the perimeter prevent strangers from slipping in to snitch the zucchini or pick a free bouquet of dahlias.

It is great fun to wander around a *Schrebergarten* complex, peering through the fence to see who is growing what and learning again the old lesson that gardeners, no matter where they may live or what language they may speak, are such thoroughgoing individualists that no two gardens are ever exactly alike, although they can be roughly classified. Some of Zurich's gardeners specialize entirely in vegetables, raising tomatoes trained on hoops (their fruit shrouded in clear plastic to keep out insects and to hasten ripening in the cool climate), beds of asparagus and rhubarb, row upon row of common things like carrots and turnips and the ubiquitous beet, and of less common things like celeriac and sweet corn (which Europeans have only lately learned not to despise). Other gardeners, content to get their vegetables from the grocery store or to absorb their neighbors' excess, devote their plots to flowers. Morning glories scramble up strings to the tops of their huts, covering the roofs with a

thick sheet of bright cerulean blue against a background of soft
green. Every square inch of earth is taken up with an appealing
jumble of roses, delphiniums, tall pink and white Japanese anemones, and ornamental annuals, which perform better in the
clear cool air of Zurich than in any other place I've seen. Some
gardeners specialize in one particular flower to the exclusion of
all others: I saw one plot entirely covered with wooden frames
protected by lathing, each frame planted with nothing but tall
chrysanthemums, the big, shaggy "football mum" sort, pruned
to one stem per plant, each stem disbudded to one flower, carefully staked to support the weight of the pampered blossom. But
most of the *Schrebergärten* are mixed plantings: flowers, vegetables, berries, and small fruit trees—especially the purple prune
plum, which makes an unusually fine cake called *Zwetschen-
kuchen.*

In addition to flying the Swiss flag, all these gardens have
two things in common. Each has several compost heaps, in various stages of decomposition. And virtually all, even those devoted
to vegetables, have copious numbers of sunflowers, of several
kinds. The Russian mammoth sunflower, whose sturdy stalk can
exceed fifteen feet and which produces a single composite flower
as much as two feet across, rises in solitary glory from many a
garden plot. Other sunflowers, the bushy multiflora sort, grow in
hedges along the fencerows, their colors a revelation to those
who think all sunflowers are golden yellow—the sunflowers of
Kansas and of Vincent van Gogh. There aren't any blue sunflowers or true reds, but there are mahogany ones and burnt
siennas and rosy purples and lemony yellows and creams so pale
that from a distance they seem to be white. Although these
annuals are native to North America, they grow much more
magnificently on Swiss soil than on our own and in such numbers that they would seem to have nudged aside edelweiss in
the affections of the Swiss people.

Schrebergärten, it must be noted, have their equivalents in
places where German isn't spoken. Since 1906, Norwegians have
been planting small plots, also with huts and flagpoles, which
they call *kolonihager.* The Dutch have their *volkstuinen*, the
British their small "allotment gardens," devoted mostly to potatoes, mammoth cabbages, vegetable marrows, and other practical

plants. In Boston, New York, the District of Columbia, and other American cities today, a number of groups actively promote the notion of urban gardening. But thanks to Dr. Daniel Schreber, German-speaking Europeans got there first, and if Zurich is typical, they've done the most to show us all just how wonderful a tiny garden can be.

The Gardens of Montjuich

Of all the earth's gardens that I've ever seen, surely one of the strangest in its beauty is the one known in the Catalan language as the Jardí Mossen Costa i Llobera—the Garden of Father Costa i Llobera, a nineteenth-century Roman Catholic theologian who wrote lyric poetry about nature in his native Mallorcan dialect. The garden named in his honor sits precariously on the steep eastern slope of Montjuich, a mountain overlooking Barcelona and its busy harbor.

For the busloads of Danish and German and French tourists who are deposited there briefly, Montjuich is pretty much synonymous with El Pueblo Español, a complex of monumental buildings put up for the ill-fated Barcelona International Exposition of 1929. The basic premise of El Pueblo Español was that the architectural styles of every region of Spain should be reproduced on one site, so that visitors could have the feeling of being in Old Castile one moment and Asturias the next. Although the place can claim some historical significance as a forerunner of Disneyland and the other theme parks that have sprouted like mung beans in the past few decades, it's a gigantic bore, perfectly dead except for the tourists who rush from one small shop to another before it's time to crawl back on the bus, clutching their purchases of such authentic Iberian handicrafts as Samurai swords and straw baskets made in the People's Republic of China.

The natives of Barcelona shun this hokey imitation of a Spanish town, but not Montjuich itself, a mountain quite close to the center of the city which offers many wooing attractions, including a fortified castle at the top (best reached by cable car), an amusement park with an outside concert hall where Julio Iglesias packs in the crowds whenever he plays town, an inexplicable Indonesian restaurant, museums devoted to the religious art of medieval Catalonia and to the works of the twentieth-century artist Joan Miró, and several notable gardens.

In a way, all of Montjuich is a garden. Oleanders, hibiscus, and bright beds of annuals line the broad and winding roads that climb its slopes, and handsome plane and eucalyptus trees shade the many park benches where people can read or admire the stunning view of the city or stretch out for a siesta. But Montjuich also contains several individual gardens with their own identities. Besides a somewhat forlorn and tatty botanical garden and the Maragall Garden (named for the poet Joan Maragall), whose chief distinction lies in the officious, finger-waggling guard stationed outside its high wrought-iron gate to turn people aside, except during the brief visiting hours on Sundays (a restriction I didn't at all understand at the time), there's the splendid Jardí Mossen Cinto—Father Jacinto's Garden, which is much loved and much visited by Barcelonans, with excellent reason.

The sloping emerald lawns of Father Jacinto's Garden are perfectly manicured. The enormous, irregularly shaped beds of bronze- or green-leaved cannas in full bloom in the light shade of cork oaks and olive trees take on an awesome radiance in the slanting golden light of late afternoon. Near the garden's entrance the huge, creamy blossoms of a row of *Magnolia grandiflora* pervade the air with their delicious lemony fragrance. And the sight and sound of water rushing down one side of the steeply terraced terrain from an informal pond at the top, down through a series of formal rectangular pools to a fountain at the bottom, are enough to give anyone an overpowering sense of well-being and the urge to linger for many an hour.

People throng Father Jacinto's Garden from earliest morning to late at night. Children run and laugh and play catch. Pairs of nuns stroll the walkways, talking softly. Young mothers push their infants in strollers. Lovers walk slowly, holding hands, pausing occasionally to enjoy the fragrance of jasmines or to admire the handsome plantings of calla lilies, gardenias, bird-of-paradise, and blue-lilies-of-the-Nile. And an almost unending procession of newlyweds come by car, right from the Nuptial Mass and still in their wedding clothes, to have their pictures taken next to the weeping willows near the fountain or in front of the glowing beds of cannas.

I had no idea who Father Jacinto was, but the garden named in his honor was clearly a very popular place, even though the tourist buses didn't stop there. But almost nobody came to Father Costa i Llobera's Garden, less than half a mile away. I couldn't explain this fact. By any reckoning it would be a prime contender for a spot on any list of the world's ten best gardens, but during two weeks in Barcelona I visited it seven or eight times and there were never more than two or three other visitors. Twice I had the place entirely to myself, except for a strolling guard, whose job must make him one of the loneliest men in Spain.

I stumbled on Father Costa's Garden completely by accident, which is the only way anyone is likely to find it. It went unmentioned in all the tourist guides. The kiosks on the Ramblas, the crowded boulevard leading from the elegant Plaza de Catalunya down to the city's seedier districts by the waterfront, didn't sell postcards showing it off, nor were there photographs of its attractions in the glossy picture book hawked at every newsstand in four languages—*Todo Barcelona, Tout Barcelona, Ganz Barcelona,* and *All Barcelona.* I had to tell cabdrivers how to get there, and the desk clerk at my hotel, a lifelong resident of the city and otherwise a treasure trove of information about where to go and what to see, knew nothing about the good father's garden.

I found it after taking a cable car from the harbor to the landing station halfway up Montjuich. My plan had been to turn right, toward the Miró museum, but a powerful thirst drove me left instead for a cold bottle of mineral water at a sidewalk café a few hundred feet away. Just beyond the café I found a faded sign announcing that I was at the entrance of a public garden devoted primarily to a collection of plants from regions of the world where winters are warm and annual rainfall scanty. Here one would find gazanias blooming from March through June, mesembryanthemums in April and May, yuccas and cacti from midsummer to early fall, and aloes from December until May. The sign didn't enlighten me about the garden's history or explain why it was named for the poetry-writing clergyman, but it did explain that bloom is continuous throughout the year, except for November, when all the plants go into a brief period of dormancy.

One look down the steep wooden staircase into the garden and I was thunderstruck by its drama and beauty. Below me, on some fifteen acres of tricky terrain, the garden dropped down toward the sea, a series of long, very broad gravel paths lined with date palms and palmettos—their course occasionally cut by stone stairsteps to serve as shortcuts from one level to another— crisscrossing the precipitous mountainside.

Since I garden on a patch of land as flat as a tortilla, I'm always depressed when I read that any garden worth the name must have a vista and several changes of elevation. But Father Costa's Garden convinced me that these claims are absolutely correct. Here was vista with a vengeance and change of elevation in spades.

Sharp, almost vertical cliffs smothered in crimson and dark purple bougainvillea loomed high above to the west. Several hundred feet below, the garden ended at a highway separating it from the blue waters of the Mediterranean and from Barcelona's harbor, dominated by tall grain elevators and long warehouses and bustling with merchant ships and huge cranes for loading and unloading containerized freight. From my mountainside vantage point I could hear all the sounds of the harbor, the bells of a tugboat, the long, low whistle of a passenger ship preparing to embark, and the clatter of the cranes as they moved ponderously along their steel tracks to deposit cargo in the holds of the waiting merchant vessels. This busy maritime setting at one of the commercial crossroads of the world seemed perfect for a garden of this sort—a cosmopolitan collection of hundreds of species of plants gathered from all the dry regions of the earth, from Mexico and the American Southwest, from Central and South America, from southern Africa, Australia, and the Canaries.

The view was breathtaking, but as I walked down the staircase I forgot all about it, for the plant life in the garden captured my entire attention. Little signs here and there admonished people to "Respect the Plants." A better admonition would be to marvel at them, to stand astonished before a plain fact: in several unrelated families of plants growing at different spots around the world where survival requires that moisture be stored during a brief rainy period and then conserved over many months of parching drought, there has been an evolutionary impetus toward forms and shapes that have a fantastical air about them.

Everything in this garden caught my eye, and I was delighted to find that neat labels identified every plant by scientific name and place of origin. I was fascinated by a dense planting of an odd native of the Canary Islands, *Aeonium arboreum* Schwarzkopf, the tips of whose thick and fleshy stems bore flattened rosettes of leaves so dour a purple that they looked black. I gawked when a side path led me past a thicket of candelabrum-branched *Euphorbia lactea* into a forest of the Mexican cactus *Cephalocereus polylophus*, each plant a single green column twenty-five feet tall and prolific with neon-red buds and waxy flowers much visited by ants. I was amused by a specimen of *Harrisia tortuosus*, a sprawling and languid native of Argentina which somewhat resembled a green octopus with stickers and plum-red fruit. I was not so amused by the cactus that attacked me when I pushed it aside with my foot to read the label identifying it as *Cylindropuntia rosea*. It is now classified as *Opuntia rosea*, and commonly and very appropriately known in English as the jumping cholla. Its three-inch, glistening and silvery spines were very beautiful, but they also penetrated shoe leather with no trouble at all, to my sharp and sudden discomfort.

Atop one of several overlooks with a view of the harbor and the sea, surrounded by a planting of lavender in full bloom, there was a statue of a young woman weaving on a simple handloom. But it seemed superfluous, for almost everything that grows in Father Costa's Garden had a bold and dramatic sculptural quality—the groves of saguaros, the creamy spikes of yucca blossoms on well-branched trees thirty feet high, the succulent hedges of jade plants in full bloom, the high flower stalks of century plants rising like marks of punctuation along the tiers of pathways.

But for sheer fantasy I took my hat off to something I encountered for the first time in this garden on a mountainside, a plant called *Furcraea bedinghausii*, a native of Mexico which looked as if it might have evolved in another galaxy or have been dreamed up by Hieronymus Bosch for his *Garden of Earthly Delights*. An absolutely singular plant, it stood thirty-five feet tall, with a palm-like lower trunk, a band of dead leaves girdling its middle like a hula skirt, and a lime-green inflorescence topping it off, a most peculiar thing somewhat resembling the framework of a half-opened umbrella. It was quite striking even here, among many other striking plants in this most striking of gardens. I had a hunch that if someone were to set a couple of these strange vegetative marvels at a street intersection in midtown Manhattan, so many drivers would slow down to stare at them that it would bring on gridlock.

I returned many times to Father Costa's Garden, observing the wonderful changes in the light as the sun made its way across the sky until it disappeared behind the tall cliffs above. I went once at night, when it took on an entirely different, almost unearthly aspect under the floodlights illuminating it. I seldom saw another human soul, although higher on Montjuich the Garden of Father Jacinto was crowded with nighttime visitors and the distant sounds from the amusement park's calliope filled the air.

After my return from Spain, the beauty of the gardens of Montjuich—especially the strange beauty of Father Costa's Garden—haunted me, so much so that I made repeated efforts, at first unsuccessful, to learn something of their origin and history. None of the experts on the history of public gardens whom I checked with knew anything about Montjuich, nor did those who specialize in cacti and similar plants (all of whom, however, commended a like garden in Monaco). Months and months after I mailed it, I despaired of ever receiving an answer to a letter of inquiry to the Spanish Embassy in Washington, and I wondered why the Spanish tourist authorities kept urging us all to come see the gardens of the Alhambra in Granada but ignored those on Montjuich. Meanwhile, I published in the October 1984 issue of *American Horticulturist* an article, fully illustrated with some color photographs I had taken of the saguaro groves and that amazing *Furcraea bedinghausii*, describing these wonderful gardens and expressing dismay that they were so unknown and unpublicized outside of Spain.

What happened next—until events took an unexpected tragic

turn—was fun, and also satisfying, since like most writers I often entertain the dark suspicion that I have no readers, except a few editors and proofreaders. In early December of 1984, a letter arrived from José Carrillo, Director of Parks and Gardens for the City of Barcelona. Señor Carrillo had seen a copy of my article, and he thanked me for my interest and promised that additional information would soon be coming my way. His letter was followed by one from Joaquín M.ª Casamor de Espona, who turned out to be the landscape architect who had designed not only Father Costa's Garden but also Father Jacinto's and the Maragall Garden I never got to see because of that finger-waggling guard. Señor Espona surprised me by saying that the three gardens on Montjuich—"monographic" gardens, he termed them, meaning that each was devoted to a particular kind of plant or to a thematic style—had been opened to the public only in 1970. (I had supposed them to be much, much older.) With his letter he sent the text of a lecture he had recently given in a course on landscape architecture at Barcelona's Higher Technical School of Architecture.

The lecture, which explained the history of these gardens and the principles of design on which they were based, was highly informative. It seems that the single most important event leading to their existence took place on May 8, 1960, when the Spanish government ceded to the municipal authorities of Barcelona the fortress high atop Montjuich, setting in motion a process of planning the redevelopment of the whole mountain for public use and recreation. New highways and parking lots were built first, and in 1966 planning got under way for the gardens. There were some notable obstacles. Where the Garden of Father Jacinto now stands, with its procession of bloom from bulbous or rhizomatous plants (hyacinths and daffodils in March, tulips and ranunculus in April, iris in May, followed in summer and fall by lilies, amaryllis, agapanthus, dahlias, cannas, and daylilies), there was a large shantytown whose occupants had to be relocated to public housing elsewhere in the city, for example.

I learned something about the Maragall Garden, including the reason it was usually closed to the public. This garden surrounds the Palacete Albéniz—originally a small pavilion with a modest formal garden, built for the 1929 Exposition in Barcelona as a place where King Alfonso XIII and Queen Victoria Eugenia could receive official guests and dignitaries. After the monarchy fell, the pavilion became a music museum, named for the composer Isaac Albéniz. In the late 1960s the authorities in Barcelona decided to enlarge the pavilion and its garden and to offer it to the Prince of Spain—now King Juan Carlos I—as his official residence in the city. Today it is used by visiting heads of state and other guests of honor and also serves to house important meetings and conferences.

I took particular interest in Señor Casamor de Espona's description of Father Costa's Garden, whose cacti and other succulents had come from nurseries in many places, but most notably Bordighera, Italy, where the Pallanca Collection, especially fine for the maturity of its plants, was acquired. The site for this garden, once occupied by cannonworks guarding the harbor and ceded to the city at the same time as Montjuich's fortress, seemed ideal for cacti, given its particular microclimate. "The terrain was climatically superior, on account of protection from the north wind. And its orientation and exposure to the sun made it warmer (by one or two degrees) than anywhere else in our city, staying ordinarily above 0°C. on the coldest days. And the humidity was low, on account of the good circulation of air. These factors, combined with its privileged position by the sea . . . made it particularly well-suited for a garden of tropical exotic plants, under conditions which would be difficult to find elsewhere on our Mediterranean coast."

José Carrillo wrote again on January 16, sending the additional information he had promised, including some photocopies of biographical articles on Fathers Costa and Jacinto and clippings of some recent newspaper articles he thought might be of interest. Miguel Costa i Llobera (1854–1922), I learned, was the firstborn son of a well-to-do Mallorcan family, who began a legal career in Barcelona when he was eighteen and was ordained a priest at thirty-four. He was a prolific poet, writing in Catalan, whose style combined romantic and classical elements. Father Jacinto, Jacint Verdaguer (1845–1902), was the son of a poor farm worker, and he himself worked in the fields even after he entered seminary. For a time in the 1870s he served as chaplain of a ship trading between Barcelona and Havana, this period

being his most prolific as a poet. Good as it was to learn these
things and more about these two poet-priests, I was much more
fascinated by the newspaper clippings, both editorials dealing
with my article about Montjuich. One, from the December 4 issue
of *La Vanguardia*, was in Castilian. It described me as a doggedly
tenacious American professor of philosophy who had discovered
a fabulous but almost unsung cactus garden, it quoted the article,
and it vowed that the whole world should now hear of this
garden. The other, from the January 4 issue of *Divendres*, in
Catalan, called me a "desconcertat profesor de Nova Jersey,"
urged that Barcelonans pay more heed to Father Costa's Garden,
and translated large chunks of the article, affording me a rare
chance to see how I would write if I were writing in Catalan.
("No puc explicar-me per què no el visita gairebe ningu. Des de
qualsevol punt de vista, seria un candidat privilegiat per a ocupar
un lloc en la llista dels deu millors jardins del món.") These two
editorials were peculiarly delightful. My article had not meant
to criticize people for not massing to Father Costa's Garden,
merely to say how wonderful I thought it was when I stumbled
on it. For me, the garden was the hero of the story—and a hero
about which I wanted to know more. In the editorials, I was a
minor hero for having found a "secret" garden. Odd, since I was
hardly some horticultural Christopher Columbus, and the garden
was there in plain view for anyone to see. One thing in Carrillo's
kind and helpful letter disturbed me—its worried tone, a slight
overtone of apprehension. For several nights, there had been
severe frosts in Barcelona. He feared that there might be some
significant loss of plants in that garden overlooking the harbor
and the sea, if the cold weather continued.

He wrote again on February 1, again enclosing newspaper
clippings, news stories this time, and bad ones. The big chill
began in mid-January, continuing for thirteen days, with
temperatures as low as $-7°C$. The loss of plants all over Barcelona was enormous, a loss estimated at 80,000,000 pesetas. Over
half of the monetary loss took place in Father Costa's Garden,
where 79,018 individual plants representing 186 species either
died from the prolonged cold or were severely damaged. The
newspaper photographs showed workers shoveling huge piles of
dead plants into trucks. The mayor of Barcelona was quoted as

saying that the garden would be replanted with cactus and other succulents from the city's nurseries and from nurseries in the Canary Islands, but it would be impossible to replace some of the larger specimens with their like. Not everything in Father Costa's Garden perished, but the list of those that did was appallingly long. Señor Carrillo enclosed with his letter and the clippings a seven-page inventory of the damage, arranged by family, genus, and species. I immediately checked up on those *Furcraea bedinghausii*. All, 130 at various stages of maturity, had been killed by the freakish winter freeze.

"We intend to restore the garden with all the vegetal species it had," José Carrillo concluded, "but it will take time to find all the plants and grow them."

I wish him well. I wonder if there's any lesson in this story. Some, the safety-minded souls of this earth, might conclude that Father Costa's Garden should never have been planted, since it's obviously possible for Barcelona to suffer almost two consecutive weeks of sub-freezing weather. But 1985 was a bad year in the United States, too, especially in the South. Florida's citrus groves sustained tremendous damage. Much of the boxwood in middle Tennessee, including some plants over a hundred years old, either died entirely or were killed back to the ground. Many of the crape myrtles that line the streets of Norfolk, Virginia, and make the city so beautiful in August were badly damaged. There is no such thing as risk-free gardening, and thus I admire the city authorities of Barcelona for trying to save what they've got, for picking up the pieces, and for starting over once again.

The lesson, I think, may be this. The loss of plants is always saddening, whether it's one little jasmine on the windowsill that inexplicably sickens and dies, 79,018 specimens in a public garden in Catalonia, or vast numbers of whole species, some of which haven't even been named scientifically, in the Equatorial rain forests. "Respect the plants," say those signs in Father Costa's Garden.

IV. GARDEN
READING

Thomas Jefferson,
Garden Writer

Such places are generally crowded with paying customers, so I
suppose that many people don't share my disdain for those gift
shops associated with our national shrines, where you can buy
ashtrays bearing the likeness of Andrew Jackson or place mats
depicting the portico of Mount Vernon. But last summer when I
spent a day inspecting the progress made since 1977 in the ambitious program to restore the gardens, orchard, and vineyards
of Thomas Jefferson's home at Monticello, a sudden and violent
thunderstorm drove me to take refuge in the hillside gift shop
overlooking the spot where our third President grew his peas
and pumpkins. After the storm subsided, I came away prepared
to make an exception to my general rule about gift shops for the
one at Monticello, which sells no ashtrays, vinyl place mats, or
bumper stickers saying "Honk If You Love Tom Jefferson." It
does sell potpourri and flower seeds harvested on the ground,
linen place mats woven in designs common in late-eighteenth-
century America, and a great many fine books, including one that
now has a prominent place in my horticultural library—*Thomas
Jefferson's Garden Book*.

The title is somewhat misleading. Mr. Jefferson didn't exactly write a garden book in the same sense that Eleanor Perényi
wrote *Green Thoughts*. He did, in a rather casual way, keep a
garden journal, starting in 1766 and continuing until 1824, two
years before his death. Had the publisher of *Thomas Jefferson's
Garden Book*, the American Philosophical Society (of which

Jefferson was president for many years), restricted itself to publishing his garden journals, the result would have been of quite limited appeal. He sometimes neglected them for years at a time, when he was occupied with matters of state, and when he did write in them, his entries were so terse and laconic that admirers of his considerable gift at turning a phrase may suffer disappointment; on May 14, 1774, for example, he wrote, "Cherries ripe." But the journals take up less than ten percent of the volume. The remainder, arranged in chronological order by the editor, the late Edwin Morris Betts, who taught biology at the University of Virginia, consists of extensive notes, together with excerpts from the correspondence between Jefferson and other people who shared his horticultural passion, including George Washington, William Bartram, André Michaux, and the Marquis de Lafayette.

Any gardener who loves to read about gardening will treasure the Jefferson book for its revealing portrait of one of the finest gardeners America has ever produced, the man who wrote these words in a letter to a friend in 1811:

I have often thought that if heaven had given me choice of my position and calling, it should have been on a rich spot of earth, well watered, and near a good market for the productions of the garden. No occupation is so delightful to me as the culture of the earth, and no culture comparable to that of the garden. Such a variety of subjects, some one always coming to perfection, the failure of one thing repaired by the success of another, and instead of one harvest a continued one through the year . . . Though an old man, I am but a young gardener.

Jefferson's horticultural concerns were often familiar and parochial. He lavished much attention on the improvement of the grounds at Monticello, ordering apples and pears for his orchard, tuberoses and tulips for his flower borders, and writing a friend in Ohio to inquire if he could possibly obtain a few seeds of a cucumber there that was rumored to produce fruits five feet long. But his concerns clearly transcended his own back yard. He was directly responsible for introducing many fine native American plants, such as *Magnolia grandiflora*, to Europe. And the

Spanish-broom plants that grow in large colonies to brighten a great many patches of sandy, infertile soil throughout the Middle Atlantic states may be descendants of broom he imported and planted almost a decade before he wrote the Declaration of Independence. Throughout his life, his letters show him cajoling friends in Europe and Great Britain to send him seeds, bulbs, and plants, with precise instructions on how to pack and ship them to give them the best chance to survive the trans-Atlantic crossing. And it was a two-way trade, since Jefferson in his turn sent them new things to try.

Jefferson's influence on American agriculture was of course profound. He invented a moldboard plow, which was much praised and of which he was very proud. He urged the practices of contour plowing and crop rotation. He tried, without much success, to get the farmers of Virginia to produce grapes and to make wine—advice now proved sound by the success of several fairly new wineries in the Shenandoah Valley. He was quick to see the value of trying out new crops, such as benne or sesame. Although his conviction that South Carolina was ideally suited for growing olive trees and cork oaks was wildly mistaken, his advice that the farmers of the South Carolina lowlands plant certain varieties of rice he had located in Italy had a much happier outcome. ("Located" isn't exactly the right word. The Italian authorities forbade the export of rice in the husk, which could be germinated and thus lead to possible foreign competition. In 1787, when he was the U.S. Minister to France, Jefferson visited the rice country of Italy and smuggled out seed in his pockets, also taking "measures with a muleteer to run a couple of sacks across the Apennines," as he put it. One could say that our third President was a smuggler. Or one could say that he was a man who lived by his oft-stated principle that nothing, neither national boundaries nor even warfare between states, should be permitted to interfere with the exchange among peoples of scientific information and useful or ornamental plants.)

Thomas Jefferson's Garden Book is hardly new. The American Philosophical Society in Philadelphia first published it in 1944 and has had the excellent good sense to keep it in print ever since. It makes wonderful reading. One just can't keep from liking a man who can write James Madison one day to promise that "your ploughs shall be duly tended to," and his own daughter the next day to say, "I sincerely congratulate you on the arrival of the mocking-bird. Learn all the children to venerate it as a superior being in the form of a bird, or as a being which will haunt them if any harm is done to itself or its eggs."

Bernard M'Mahon's
Declaration of Independence

No one knows exactly when the question occurred to Bernard M'Mahon after he immigrated to Philadelphia from Ireland in 1796, at the age of twenty-one. Why was it that the citizens of his new homeland—"an intelligent, happy, and independent people, possessed so universally of landed property, unoppressed by taxation or tithes, and blessed with consequent comfort and affluence"—had made such slow progress in horticulture? This matter struck M'Mahon as deadly serious. Horticulture, as he defined it, was no trivial pursuit, but the indispensable "art of improving every kind of soil; of producing a plentiful supply of wholesome vegetables and fruits, so necessary to health in all countries, especially in warm climates; of cultivating the various plants designed by INFINITE GOODNESS to minister to the comforts of animal life, by correcting the divers maladies to which it is subject by nature, and still more so, in the human race, by intemperance; and of raising many articles of luxury and commerce, as well as materials for ornamenting the whole face of the country."

The basic cause of America's horticultural backwardness at the turn of the last century, M'Mahon believed, was easily explained: we were reading the wrong books—books imported from abroad, and especially from England. Considering the "peculiarities of our climates, soils, and situations," information that was "excellent and useful" for English gardeners could only "mislead and disappoint the young *American* Horticulturist,

[179]

instead of affording him that correct, judicious, and suitable instruction, the happy result of which would give impulse to his perseverance." The remedy for this unfortunate state of affairs was obvious. America needed her own garden book, so M'Mahon set out to write it, the words quoted above coming from his preface.

The result, published in 1806, was *The American Gardener's Calendar*, which bore the whopping subtitle *Adapted to the Climates and Seasons of the United States, Containing a Complete Account of All the Work Necessary to Be Done in the Kitchen-Garden, Fruit-Garden, Orchard, Vineyard, Nursery, Pleasure-Ground, Flower-Garden, Green-House, Hot-House, and Forcing Frames, with Ample Practical Directions for Performing the Same.* The subtitle said it all. M'Mahon's *Calendar* was not only the first truly American garden book but also the progenitor of a horde of subsequent books, some very bossy, telling gardeners on a methodical, month-by-month basis what we ought to be doing to keep everything going in the garden as it should.

In 1776, in Philadelphia, Thomas Jefferson wrote the Declaration of Independence, announcing America's intent to put an end to British colonial rule. Thirty years later, in the same city, M'Mahon published what amounted to a horticultural declaration of independence from British books on gardening. And, by an odd coincidence, it was Jefferson who introduced me to M'Mahon and his *Calendar*. On page 313 of the copy of *Thomas Jefferson's Garden Book* which I had picked up at Monticello, the following letter to him from M'Mahon was reproduced:

> *Philadelphia, April 17, 1806*
> *I have much pleasure in requesting your acceptance of one of my publications on Horticulture which I forward you by this mail. Should my humble efforts meet with your approbation, and render any service to my adopted and much beloved country, I shall feel the happy consolation of having contributed my mite to the welfare of my fellow man. I am Sir,*
> *With sincere esteem and best wishes yours,*
> *Bernard M'Mahon*

I found M'Mahon's scheme of sending a copy of his *Calendar* to the President admirably bold and canny. Certainly Jefferson was receptive to the idea of a book on horticulture tailored to American conditions. Some years later, in a letter to one George Jeffreys, he commented that "there is probably no better husbandry known at present than that of England, but that is for the climate and productions of England. Their books lay for us a foundation of good general principles, but we ought, for their application, to look more than we have done into the practices of countries and climates more homogeneous with our own." At any rate, Jefferson answered M'Mahon immediately, calling his book a "useful aid to the friends of an art, too important to health and comfort & yet too much neglected in this country." He also complained that he had been having a devil of a time locating tarragon seeds and wondered if M'Mahon, who owned one of the first mail-order seed companies and nurseries in the U.S., might send him some. Thus began the correspondence between the Philadelphia plantsman and the Sage of Monticello, which continued at regular intervals until M'Mahon's death in 1816. Jefferson consigned to M'Mahon's care many of the first plants collected in the Lewis and Clark expeditions, ordered vegetable seeds and flower bulbs from him, and asked his assistance in sending native American shrubs and trees to botanically minded friends he had made in France.

My curiosity piqued by the Jefferson–M'Mahon correspondence, I decided to see if I could locate a copy of *The American Gardener's Calendar*, so I did what any reasonable person living in New Jersey and looking for an old book on gardening would do: I telephoned Hopewell to talk with Elizabeth Woodburn, a leading dealer in antiquarian books on the subject. She congratulated me on my interest in the *Calendar*, calling it not only the first real American gardening book but also one of the most consistently popular throughout the nineteenth century, going through some eleven editions under M'Mahon's name between 1806 and 1857. (There had even been one pirated edition, brought out in Baltimore in 1819, with the author given as "An Old Gardener.")

Mrs. Woodburn had on hand two copies of the eleventh

edition. One, in excellent condition, cost thirty dollars more than the other, some of whose pages were "slightly foxed." I allowed that for thirty dollars I could put up with a little foxing. A couple of days later, our postman presented me with my new acquisition, America's oldest garden book, to be read, savored, and then tucked on my library shelf.

In many respects, the gardening life as M'Mahon's *Calendar* describes it is still the same today. Garden chores must be done in their proper season, and procrastinating gardeners pay their price. Hyacinths are still lovely things, likewise carnations and primroses, plants for which M'Mahon obviously had special affection, considering the great number of pages he devoted to their culture. People who have their own kitchen gardens, where they may harvest peas and lettuce and beans at their freshest and bring them straight to their tables, delighting not only in their flavor but also in the knowledge that their own labor helped produce them, are still most fortunate souls.

The particular charm of old books, however, lies in the differences they reveal between our day and the time from which they come, and what makes M'Mahon's *Calendar* such fascinating reading 180 years after he published it is its testimony to change. Some things remain the same, yes, but many a thing in M'Mahon is so passing strange as to be quite remarkable.

For one thing, the distinction between organic gardening and any other sort was meaningless. Justus von Liebig (1803–73), the German professor of chemistry who revolutionized medicine by discovering chloroform, cookery by inventing baking powder, and agriculture by concocting chemical fertilizers, was barely out of diapers when M'Mahon's *Calendar* appeared. The so-called artificial manures whose use von Liebig advocated didn't exist, but there was plenty of the real stuff, piles and piles of it. Thus, M'Mahon provided his readers with detailed information on the proper uses of the various kinds of manures— information sufficient to provoke fits of envy in the suburban gardeners of today, who have to make do with fifty-pound bags of dried cow dung. Furthermore, the arsenal of chemical pesticides we find all too easily available at our local garden centers was something M'Mahon could not have foreseen. The best weapons against mealybugs he could come up with were decoctions of tobacco, wormwood, walnut leaves, henbane, snuff, and pepper, sometimes mixed with a little sulfur. To keep curculio beetles at bay in an orchard, he suggested letting hogs and chickens run loose among the trees.

For another thing, a good many of the fruits and vegetables whose culture he explained are either extremely exotic or else unfamiliar. He said very little about growing tomatoes, although he said enough for it to be clear he didn't look on them as poisonous. He wrote at length and lovingly about how to bring "pines" (pineapples) to luscious ripeness in the home hothouse and how to raise mushrooms from spawn. Apparently such horticultural triumphs were a matter of course—or at least not outlandish—in early-nineteenth-century America. Today, the gardeners who tend their own pineapple plants under glass could probably hold congress in a telephone booth. Ditto for those who raise their own mushrooms. (It is of incidental interest, by the way, that M'Mahon describes catsup as a sauce made from mushroom juice, salt, and spices.)

Then there are the skirrets, whose seed he recommended sowing in March, with the advice that "the fleshy tubers of these roots are considered very delicious." One hundred pages later, when he was giving his instructions for what had to be done in April, his enthusiasm for this plant waxed even higher. "The *Sium sisarum*, or skirret, is greatly esteemed as a garden vegetable; its root is composed of several fleshy tubers, as large as a man's finger, and joining together at the top. They are eaten boiled, and stewed with butter, pepper, and salt; or rolled in flour and fried; or else cold with oil and vinegar, being first boiled. They have much of the taste and flavor of a parsnep, but a great deal more palatable." You hear very little talk of skirrets nowadays; T. H. Everett's massive *Illustrated Encyclopedia of Horticulture* dismisses these Eastern European members of the carrot family as "of decidedly minor importance."

I've heard some talk of people who eat nasturtium blossoms as a lark, but M'Mahon took them very seriously indeed, stating that "the *Tropaeolum majus*, or large nasturtium, is very deserving of attention, as well on account of the beauty of its large and numerous orange-colored flowers, as their excellence in salads and their use in garnishing dishes." Their abundant green seeds "make one of the nicest pickles that can possibly be imagined." (Thomas Jefferson was also a nasturtium enthusiast. Nasturtiums almost always appear in his annual lists of the vegetables planted in his kitchen garden, and in May of 1824, some years after Bernard M'Mahon went to glory, he wrote a friend in Richmond, complaining of a seed-crop failure and asking for enough nasturtium seeds to fill a bed of 190 square yards!)

The American Gardener's Calendar not only discussed the proper culture of vegetables Americans were already growing but exhorted them to try new ones. Sea kale was a notable case in point. "The *Crambe maritima*, or Sea Kale," M'Mahon wrote, "is yet very little known in the United States, though a most excellent garden vegetable, and highly deserving of cultivation." After devoting several thousand words to its history and culture, he concluded that it was similar in flavor but superior to asparagus and a most promising perennial vegetable for farmers with ready access to city markets to raise as a profitable cash crop. (We may never get a chance to check up on M'Mahon's judgment of skirrets, but at least one of our mail-order seed catalogs, that of Thompson & Morgan, offers sea kale.)

One also finds two kinds of rhubarb in M'Mahon's book. He gave only faint praise for the rhubarb we all know, *Rheum rhabarbarum*: "Its roots afford a gentle purge . . . esteemed for pies and tarts . . . considered very wholesome for children." For another rhubarb, Chinese rhubarb or *Rheum palmatum*, he tried to start a virtual crusade, terming it "an article of considerable consumption, consequently of national importance, and highly deserving of attention in the United States . . . Shall we despair of bringing it to perfection where soil and climate are perfectly congenial, and nothing wanted but the enterprise of a few spirited individuals to make a commencement?" M'Mahon advised that Chinese rhubarb should not be harvested until the fourth year after planting it from seed, and that certain unspecified "medicinal virtues" appeared only in plants eight years old or older. It was not the stalks but the roots of this rhubarb that were eaten, after being peeled, sliced, and dried on threads in a heated room. M'Mahon went into curious detail in describing the exact merits of his beloved Chinese rhubarb.

"The marks of the goodness of rhubarb are, the liveliness of its color when cut; its being firm and solid, but not flinty or hard; its being easily pulverable, and appearing, when powdered, of a bright yellow color; on being chewed, its imparting to the spittle a deep saffron tinge, and not proving slimy or mucilaginous in the mouth."

M'Mahon had a like affection for "the *Glycyrrhiza glabra* or cultivated liquorice, a plant that brings enormous profit to the industrious cultivator." Because of its uses in medicine and brewing, he commended its planting to all "spirited persons, who may have the welfare of their country, as well as their own, at heart." And he became virtually ecstatic when he contemplated the possibility that some unusually spirited persons might contrive to grow both cultivated licorice and Chinese rhubarb: "The crops would more than adequately repay the cultivators; and although a partiality to articles of customary culture is in the way, it is to be hoped that new and necessary plants will, from time to time, be introduced with advantages to the individuals and the nation at large."

Some measure of the differences between M'Mahon's day and our own can again be found by checking the Everett encyclopedia. It discusses the ornamental merits of *Rheum palmatum*, but doesn't mention its edibility. The legume *Glycyrrhiza glabra* has some value in making candy, cigarettes, stout, and certain sorts of fire extinguishers, but there's "little to recommend it to gardeners."

I have emphasized here the things I find strange in this historic piece of American garden writing, but there's something sound and sensible on every page. And one thing stands out as especially right—his commendation, to American gardeners, of American native plants. I'll let M'Mahon speak for himself, from a passage quite early in his *Calendar*:

I cannot avoid remarking that many flower gardens, &c., are almost destitute of bloom during a great part of the season; which could be easily avoided, and a blaze of flowers kept up . . . from March to November, by introducing from our woods and fields the various beautiful ornaments with which nature has so profusely decorated them. Is it because they are indigenous that we reject them?

[185]

Ought we not rather to cultivate and improve them? What can be more beautiful than our Lobeilas, Orchises, Asclepiases, and Asters; Gerardias, Monardas, and Ipomoeas; Liliums, Podalyrias, Rhexias, Solidagos, and Hibiscuses; Phloxes, Gentianas, Spigelias, Chironias, and Sisyrinchiums; Cassias, Ophryses, Coreopsises, and Cypripediums; Fumarias, Violas, Rudbeckias, and Liatrises; with our charming Limodorum, fragrant Arethusa, and a thousand other lovely plants which, if introduced, would grace our plantations and delight our senses? In Europe, plants are not rejected because they are indigenous; on the contrary, they are cultivated with due care; and yet here we cultivate many foreign trifles, and neglect the profusion of beauties so bountifully bestowed upon us by the hand of nature.

These are not the words of a chauvinist, but of an immigrant-patriot, arrived in the United States only ten years before he wrote them. He had such prescient appreciation of native North American flora that I regret that he didn't live long enough to learn that, like Jefferson and Franklin, both born on this soil, where they lived much longer than he, he would have an American plant named for him—the mahonia or Oregon grape holly, like yucca much beloved by Gertrude Jekyll.

Old Gardening Books

With something of a sigh, Elizabeth Woodburn tells me that she must drive down to Delaware within a couple of weeks to appraise a large collection of books on gardening, bequeathed to a young man profoundly uninterested in gardening by an uncle who was both an avid gardener and a prodigious reader. The nephew, who wants to sell this legacy, is in for something of a disappointment, she fears. Given the fact that his uncle died at seventy, the books he left behind were most likely acquired in the 1930s and after, with perhaps some from the 1920s. They are thus secondhand books, not old enough or rare enough to command much of a price in the specialized market which Booknoll Farm serves. There's a strong chance that many of them turn up with fair regularity for twenty-five cents apiece in cardboard boxes at flea markets and lawn sales. Old and out-of-print don't necessarily mean rare and valuable.

No doubt Elizabeth Woodburn is correct. That said, I must go on to add that one of the greatest pleasures of being a gardener who likes to read is rummaging through those cardboard boxes and finding some dusty volume on gardening from another day, then browsing through it or dipping deeply to measure the things that have changed and the things that have remained the same in the gardener's world. I have, for example, a tattered copy of the 1936 edition of Wm. H. Wise & Company's *The Garden Encyclopedia*, and find it fascinating, both for what is missing and for what is present. Most of the insecticides and herbicides it advocates are no longer in use, which is not necessarily a good thing, considering the unforeseen side effects of some of the stronger chemicals marketed and highly touted since World War II. The short shrift Wise gives to both hostas and daylilies testifies to the progress amateur hybridizers in this country have made in turning these two perennials into the indispensable staples of the summer garden. And I am always amused when I browse through Wise and come to this entry, on p. 216, where it says of one plant: ". . . occasionally grown in gardens as ornamental screen or background plants. Requiring no special care or soil condition, beyond a good supply of humus and moisture, they are raised from seed sown in spring outdoors or, earlier, in flats." The plant in question is *Cannabis sativa*, whose common name is given as "mariajuana."

But it is not the books dispensing solemn and objective advice which I love most, rather those in which a personal voice still sounds through, decades after it was written and long after the writer no longer walks and tends the earth. There is, to start with one of my favorites, Charles Dudley Warner's *My Summer in a Garden*, originally published in 1870. (I have a much later edition, 1896, which cost $4.50 in a secondhand bookstore in Bell Buckle, Tennessee.) I know of no other gardening book which gets under way with such force and authority. Warner's opening paragraph is something like the first four notes of the Beethoven Fifth, so I shall quote most of it here, with a nudge to the reader to consider that the author was writing before Freud got going:

The love of dirt is among the earliest of passions, as it is the latest. Mud-pies gratify one of our first and best instincts. So long as we are dirty, we are pure. Fondness for the ground comes back to a man after he has run the round of pleasure and business, eaten dirt, and sown wild-oats, drifted about the world, and taken the wind in all its moods. The love of digging in the ground (or of looking on while he pays another to dig) is as sure to come back to him as he is sure, at last, to go under the ground, and stay there. To own a bit of ground, to scratch it with a hoe, to plant seeds, and watch their renewal of life—this is the commonest delight of the race, the most satisfactory thing a man can do.

Warner's book is chock-full of wonderful lore, for example some strange facts about ecclesiastical solutions to horticultural problems. *Item.* During the Middle Ages the monks under the rule of St. Bernard of Clairvaux excommunicated an unproductive vineyard. *Item.* St. Bernard also excommunicated the flies in another monastery. *Item.* In 1120 a bishop took the same measure against the caterpillars in Laon. The problem with *My Summer in a Garden* is that it is quotable without end, so I'll go on to the next old gardening book, Beverley Nichols's *Down the Garden Path*, with just one more tidbit from Warner's long and charming disquisition on salads: "You can put anything, and the more things the better, into salad, as into a conversation; but everything depends on the skill of mixing."

Early in the Great Depression, a sudden urge to own a house and a garden overtook the British novelist Beverley Nichols during a storm at sea as he was sailing toward England on the *Mauretania*. Reading an old newspaper in the vessel's library, he came across the obituary of an American, a slight acquaintance, whom he had once visited at his thatched cottage in the English countryside, with a garden that was "a blaze of roses" and deliciously fragrant with Madonna lilies. He immediately sent off a wire to the owner's sister in Timbuctoo, making an offer to buy the property. The offer was accepted. A week later Nichols took possession of the cottage. Ignorant of gardening, he promptly dismissed the gardener who had come with the place, a man who made Melville's Bartleby look like a chatty, cooperative fellow in comparison.

Down the Garden Path, which was published in 1932, is a delight, because Nichols writes as an unabashed amateur gardener who has committed his share of follies, who will doubtless commit more, who has learned some things from his experience but knows there is much yet to learn. He tells of the sudden passions that overtake him, for cyclamens for example, about which he grows lyrical: "A flight of butterflies, frozen for a single, exquisite moment in the white heart of Time." And he describes his initial frustration in trying to grow them, issuing this warning to "all who first grow cyclamen from seed. You will read on the packet that the seeds 'germinate' in from four to six weeks." He continues for several paragraphs, as for months and months ambiguous things sprout in his seed boxes, until the triumph comes one day when he inspects his crop: "Oh . . . these were cyclamen, without any doubt . . . they held themselves sturdily against the fawning weeds . . . there was a fine flourish about them which set them apart from the rank usurpers of their place. And as I bent over them they regarded me gravely, as though they were saying, 'Well? Weren't we worth waiting for?' "

Another old book on my shelf, published in 1933, is Richardson Wright's *Another Gardener's Bed-Book*, a sequel to his previous *A Gardener's Bed-Book* and subtitled *A Second Crop of Short and Long Pieces for Those Who Garden by Day and Read by Night*. The underlying idea is similar to that of certain books of religious devotion, providing for every night of the year a morsel for gardeners to read before snapping off the bedside lamp. Wright offers a pleasant hodgepodge of practical advice ("Grapes should be sprayed twice with Bordeaux mixture—just before and after blooming"); high praise for plants that especially please him (halesias, for one); and discussions of the history of gardening (Zen gardens, Versailles).

There's one more pleasure often found in these old, though not pricelessly rare, garden books picked up at lawn sales and in dusty old shops. As the advertisements from automobile dealers for used cars put it, they're previously owned, and sometimes one can find the traces of their previous owners in them. My copy of Wise's *Encyclopedia* is inscribed on the title page: "Happy Birthday to Bessie, From Dick, Mae, Betty, and Dick Junior—1940." I don't know who first owned *Another Gardener's Bed-Book*, but whoever it was was a busy underliner and writer of marginalia, sometimes applauding the author ("Terrific idea"), sometimes throwing brickbats ("Just plain stupid!"). Reading the text together with the commentary is like eavesdropping and carries the same guilty pleasure. There's no marginalia in my copy of Beverley Nichols, no name on the frontispiece, but tucked in its pages are two scraps of yellowed paper with messages in pencil, memoranda I think. One reads: "Snow Drop. Galanthus elwesii. Plant not less than six inches deep. Christmas Rose. Grow under glass bell in shade of evergreen." The other: "Delia, we are using 4666 lbs. of coal a month in range. Please see if we can reduce this by ¼." These scraps of paper, not meant for my eyes at all, don't tell me very much. Just that the person who wrote them was a gardener. And that there was a whole lot of cooking going on out in the kitchen.

Dahliagrams

His name is Harry, and when I briefly met him last spring a year ago, he was sitting at a small table outdoors at a horticultural fair in northern Virginia, selling dahlia tubers on behalf of the National Capital Dahlia Society.

My experience in raising dahlias has never been what anyone could call exciting. Some years I plant them, and some I don't. On the advice of a friend I consider knowledgeable in most horticultural matters, I no longer try to save the tubers from one year to the next, since, when I did, the outcome, alternating between desiccation and rot, was never happy. My friend informed me that the fat, waxed tubers from Holland which reliably appear in garden stores every spring were perfectly fine. They are inexpensive and they are easier on the nerves than tubers you have stored yourself, since, he explained, there's something far worse than desiccation and rot. "Suppose you plant ten dahlias in the spring," he said. "Each tuber will increase to six or seven at least, so if you get them safely through the winter storage period and each has multiplied sixfold, you'll have 60 next spring, then 360, then 2,160, and in four years' time 12,460. No one has any use for that many dahlias, not even people who belong to dahlia societies, who are the wildest-eyed of all flower freaks—worse even than the daylily people." Harry didn't look at all wild-eyed, even if he was a member of a dahlia society, so I asked him about those waxed clumps from Holland.

He told me first of all that there were far better cultivars available from American sources and second that planting a whole clump was pretty silly, since just one little tuber produces in a few months as much dahlia plant as you can say grace over. Most of the tubers on his table looked a little puny, in comparison with waxed clumps, but I asked him to pick out ten good ones for me, gave him fifteen dollars for his society's treasury, and started to leave. He detained me to offer advice about proper staking and above all about the proper planting time—in June, after the soil had really warmed up. Then he asked for my address, saying he would put me on the mailing list to get the NCDS's monthly newsletter.

I waited till the soil really warmed up. Alongside each tuber I put up a stake, a little less sturdy than the one Harry suggested, for despite his words, I really doubted that such scrawny tubers—further wizened and shriveled after so long a wait—could produce much in the way of plants. He was right and I was wrong. By mid-August most of my new dahlias were shoulder-high or higher and so loaded down with blossoms that I wished I'd used steel I-beams instead of the flimsy bamboo stakes that had seemed sufficient. One August morning, after a fierce thunderstorm the night before, I found the dahlias only knee-high, having toppled in the wind. They leaned at strange angles, but they still kept producing blossom after blossom in those clear and cheering colors that dahlias have—deep maroons and dark purples, lilacs and lavenders, bright yellows, and molten shades of red. I did have to lean over to pick them, but they kept us and some of our neighbors in cut flowers right up till the plants were blackened by the first frost.

Harry was right about something else. The display from his ten unpromising tubers was at least twenty times better than any dahlias I had ever grown from those waxed clumps.

I would like to say that I now love dahlias, but the harshest truth ever uttered by Professor Freud was that what we do is what we want to do, and the fact is that I neglected those dahlias. I didn't bother to record their names on the stakes, though I know that one, a flamboyant dark red with blooms larger than a Frisbee, was named Envy. When frost came, I cut the stalks back, but I didn't get round to lifting the tubers until it was too late. This spring I told myself that I must order new dahlias from a good mail-order company, but I never did.

There's a little more to tell. Harry was true to his word. Every month since we met, the NCDS newsletter *Dahliagram* arrives faithfully by mail, and it makes wonderful reading. I haven't met other members of the society, except in the eight or so mimeographed pages of their newsletter, but they are a caring lot, united in their devotion to this most magnificent flower of late summer, and mindful of one another. It's almost like a church. The faithful rejoice when someone new is converted and joins the fold, and they grieve when someone dies who loved dahlias. They pass information back and forth, providing tyros with the basic facts and allowing the experts to explain what they have learned, by very precise observation, about such matters as the changes that take place in a dahlia tuber from the time it is first harvested until it is ready to be planted. (These changes, it seems, are important: stored tubers, to avoid those twin dangers of desiccation and rot, should receive different treatment at different stages.)

The members of the society meet together regularly, they hold auctions, they put on flower shows, they volunteer to sell tubers in shopping malls and in grocery stores—and all of this good fellowship is reported in the monthly *Dahliagram*. I read it avidly and faithfully, for its testimony that gardening is no trivial pursuit, nor a solitary one, either. Affection for flowers binds people together, and that's no small thing.

V. TIDBITS AND OBSERVATIONS, DREAMS AND PRACTICALITIES

Cats and Plants

My wife and I have been houseplant people, to put it mildly, for twenty-six years now. We own several asparagus ferns that are older than our elder son. Over the years, through several moves from one state to another, we have been horticultural magpies, picking out a Christmas cactus here, an *Aeonium arboreum* there, to add to our household flora. Our old house is so richly blessed with windows perfectly placed to make houseplants thrive that I sometimes wake at dawn and think I'm in a greenhouse, if not a tropical rain forest.

I just counted, and discovered that I live with fifty-seven hanging baskets containing a considerable variety of vegetation, including one enormous Boston fern, several orchid cacti, the numerous progeny of a pot of Swedish ivy we bought at the grocery store a decade ago, and several different sorts of jasmines, for which I have a special and long-standing affection. Add to these the potted ficus trees and ancient philodendrons on the floor, and all the African violets and begonias and other plants on ledges and windowsills, and our houseplants exceed one hundred. There's an awful lot of photosynthesis going on around the place.

But we are also cat people, and here the problem lies. A year ago, our houseplants lived in peaceful coexistence with our cat, a nineteen-year-old calico whose destructive tendencies extended mostly to mice, although she took an occasional nibble at a potted papyrus in the living room. One Saturday last June, after a long and remarkably healthy life, Melissa abruptly stopped eating and sought out a hiding place at the back of a closet. We took her to the vet, and Tuesday morning she died.

There was an unspoken understanding among my wife, our one son still at home, and me. A cat was indispensable. Melissa could never be replaced, but there was no disrespect to her memory in bringing a kitten into our midst right away— or, more precisely, two kittens, so they could keep each other company while the humans were away. That same Tuesday afternoon, I visited the local animal shelter and picked out two stray kittens, sisters from the same litter, I was told. I named one, a fat yellow tabby with affectionate ways and no whiskers to speak of, Franny. The other, a severely undernourished tortoiseshell with a wild, somehow owlish expression and a disposition to hide under sofas and tables, was, of course, Zooey. Those names were vetoed instantly, as soon as my wife and son got home from work. Franny became Sheba, and Zooey was rechristened Samantha.

We quickly discovered that two kittens were much more fun than one. It was fascinating to observe the differences in their personalities. Sheba was somehow feminine, in all the old stereotyped ways—demure, cuddly, and warm. Samantha, once she stopped hiding under things, turned into a tomboy, racing around the house with enormous energy and little grace, and ambushing her sister at every opportunity. In early August, two things happened. First, I discovered that the animal shelter from which our kittens had come, the vet who had given them their shots, and I had all missed out on a notable difference between them: Samantha didn't have testicles. The erstwhile Franny or Sheba now became Thurber. Second, both the kittens discovered the houseplants.

The first casualty was the papyrus. Melissa had nibbled; Thurber and Samantha devoured it down to the roots. Next came a venerable asparagus fern, which they sat on and polished off in a single morning. They stripped a small gardenia of every bud. When I noticed that they were starting to chew the leaves of a favorite sambac jasmine, I sprayed it with an impromptu concoction of water mixed with garlic, dry mustard, and cayenne pepper, which only caused them to eat with more pronounced relish. (They have oddly sophisticated tastes anyway; Thurber loves cantaloupe and tomato, and his sister is the first cat of my acquaintance who licks her chops for Stilton cheese.)

They've left certain plants alone, including dieffenbachia, English ivy, and lantana, whose poisonous properties they seem instinctively to recognize. They also shun clivia, making me wonder if it might not be toxic also, and avoid the pot of rye grass I planted for them at the suggestion of a friend, convincing me that the most wonderful thing about cats is their way of ignoring our all-too-rational and simplistic strategies for dealing with them.

Their warfare against our houseplants extends far, far beyond eating them. The *Ficus benjamina* they've used as a jungle gym looks as if someone took a machete to it. Several philodendrons have bit the dust. In climbing a six-foot-high schefflera they knocked off all its leaves, reducing it to a gaunt stick. They scaled a huge hoya vine in our entranceway, to its permanent damage. The toll of African violets knocked down from windowsills is immense. The lower reaches of our houseplant collection so strongly resemble what Rommel left behind in Africa that I fear a telephone call from the Society for the Prevention of Cruelty to Plants.

But at least the hanging baskets have been safe—until four this morning, when Thurber somehow managed to climb up a curtain, stalk along a bookshelf, and pounce into a prized new winter-blooming jasmine, which fell to the floor with so mighty a crash that we thought the roof had caved in.

I love cats. I love plants. I stand in awe of the wonders of the reproductive process. But this awe is outweighed by the hope that surgical intervention on the part of our vet will calm the fierce hormonal storms of our feline teenagers, that they and we and our philodendrons may come to live together in harmony and peace.

Gardening's
Dirty Little Secret

As a member of the gardening tribe, I take considerable pride in all those catalogs that arrive early every summer from firms specializing in Dutch bulbs. "Send no money," they advise. We are invited to order our daffodils and fritillaries and tulips right away, according to our hearts' desire, and inspect the shipment when it arrives to make sure the bulbs are all plump and sound. Payment can wait until Jack Frost arrives.

This policy is extremely heartening. Not only does it help with cash flow; it also conveys a lesson about all us gardeners. These companies trust us. It follows inescapably that we are upright, unswervingly honest, and incapable of acquiring anything for our gardens that is not rightfully ours. When some plant or other that we lust for is for sale, we willingly pay fair-market value.

But what if the object of our affection is not for sale at any price? Once this question is posed, the darker parts of a gardener's soul are exposed to view. It's not a pretty sight, for the fact is that some, perhaps many, maybe even all, gardeners sometimes are tempted toward a little larceny. (Possibly the great majority haven't committed it—but without the impulse, they don't get credit for their restraint.)

Here's some anecdotal evidence. A good many years ago I stopped by the greenhouses of a nursery and seed company whose name would be instantly recognized by anyone who has ever planted so much as a single package of zinnias. It's one of several in this country with a catalog sporting photographs of the bearded patriarch who founded it in the nineteenth century and of successive generations of proprietors down to the present . . . or it was, until some art designer or other got hold of the management and persuaded them that old-fashioned charm was a marketing vice.

Halfway through my visit, I spotted the most remarkable specimens of impatiens I'd ever clapped eyes on, their flowers twice the usual size and their foliage wonderfully variegated in rainbow hues. (They were later introduced as the New Guinea strain.) I picked out two and carted them over to the clerk, who shook her head and informed me they weren't for sale. I asked if I might buy a cutting. "No," she said. "But I'll be away for the next half hour having coffee in the canteen."

I stood in puzzlement. She repeated her announcement of her impending coffee break. Finally, seeing that I didn't get the point, she blurted out a company secret. "The old man," she said (referring to the proprietor at the time, who was about to retire and let the next generation take over), "whenever he visits somebody else's greenhouse, he takes a hollow walking cane with a little water in it."

Her meaning was unmistakable. Her boss sometimes snitched cuttings of plants he wanted, evening things up with the competition, so if I really wanted a start of that impatiens, she would turn a blind eye to my malefaction. I resisted her implicit invitation, but there's no need here to say that I did, for it's the principle that interests me—and the principle seems to be that gardening and theft are not strangers one to the other.

History backs me up in exposing this dirty little secret of the horticultural life. Out of scores of possible examples, there's the tale of the plant the Aztecs knew as cocoxochitl, which was imported from Mexico to Spain, primarily because it was thought that its tubers might make agreeable eating. They didn't, but the flowers were so handsome that the royal gardeners at El Escorial, who renamed it "dahlia" for the Swedish botanist Andreas Dahl, guarded it covetously but not carefully enough to prevent a few seeds or tubers from being stolen by a visitor from France, who turned them over to the Empress Josephine for her garden at Malmaison.

Josephine was a greedy and possessive gardener. She refused to share her dahlias with anyone, but one of the ladies of her court persuaded her lover to steal some tubers. When she learned that she no longer had sole and exclusive possession of the dahlia in France, the Empress flew into an imperial snit. According to Tyler Whittle's instructive book *The Plant Hunters*, she instantly "had all her Dahlias chopped up and dug in, and never would hear the plant named in her presence."

More contemporary evidence comes frcm Christopher Lloyd, the eminent British garden writer, whose own garden at Great Dixter in East Sussex is open to the public seven months of the year. In his amusing and instructive *The Adventurous Gardener*, a wry chapter details the theft he has experienced and the countermeasures he has taken, such as neglecting to label real rarities or fixing them to the ground with long wire staples. "Finger Blight," Lloyd calls the larceny he decries, and he asserts that the worst thieves are to be found among the most enthusiastic of all gardeners, those who collect (by fair means or foul) alpine plants for their rockeries. I'm not a collector of alpine plants, but something tells me I'd better not throw the first stone at those who collect them in less than scrupulous ways.

Just a few weeks ago I dropped in on Hillside Nursery, just outside Norfolk, Connecticut. It doesn't sell by mail order, but it's sufficiently known as a source for perennials both uncommon and ordinary that a good many discriminating gardeners in the Northeast call ahead to place orders and then drive there to collect them.

The owners, Frederick and Mary Ann McGourty, gave me an impromptu tour of their perennial garden, which is notable enough to have been featured in several national magazines.

There's much to admire there—astilbes in grand abundance, cimicifugas, epimediums, and so on, through the horticultural alphabet. But the plant that started my pulse to race and my lust for acquisition to rise was a mutation of one of the more common perennials on earth, something I have held in some disdain for years. I won't mention it by name, lest I inspire someone to pile a shovel in the trunk of his car and make a midnight raid on Norfolk. Suffice it to say that its leaves are variegated in green and white, rather than the solid green of its common form, and that it's a real snazzy plant, something that stands out forty feet away.

It wasn't for sale as yet, but it was being propagated. I asked politely and was given a spot on the waiting list. I will acquire it one of these days, and honestly.

But I couldn't help noticing that there were several offshoots around the clump, small enough to fit in a pocket without a noticeable bulge. I resisted finger blight, but my fingers did itch just a bit. Had my visit been longer, I might not have come away with a clear conscience. After all, ever since Adam it's been clear—gardens are places of temptation and sometimes fall.

Horticultural
Hide-and-Seek

All gardeners who go on vacation from their own home turf to see what's going in gardens other than their own sooner or later get struck dumb when they wander across some new plant so purely wonderful that they have to have it, and right away. Often there's a disappointment in store, for the unfortunate fact is that the kind of person Christopher Lloyd singles out in the title of his book *The Adventurous Gardener* often finds himself playing a frustrating game of horticultural hide-and-seek. Far too frequently, the plants you fall in love with in someone else's garden turn out to be unavailable. You lust for *Urginea maritima*, the Mediterranean sea squill—an odd bulb that grows halfway out of the soil and produces a single long spike loaded with hundreds of small white flowers, before the leaves appear, but it's not in any of the mail-order catalogs you get, and the clerk at your local garden center just gives a shrug when you ask about it.

But there are three places that people on the prowl for special plants can turn to. First, the Mailorder Association of Nurserymen, a trade organization which says its primary objectives are consumer education and industry watchdogging, offers *The Complete Guide to Gardening by Mail* to anyone who sends a self-addressed, stamped envelope to its headquarters at 210 Cartwright Blvd., Massapequa Park, N.Y. 11762. This thirty-two page booklet is somewhat mistitled, because a considerable number of fine and reputable mail-order nurseries haven't bothered to join the association and are therefore not listed. Nevertheless, the guide does provide a handy starting point, listing over five hundred kinds of plants and keying each to those of its ninety-four nurseries which sell it.

Second, Longwood Gardens has recently put out a more ambitious booklet giving both retail and wholesale commercial sources for over 1,300 of the 14,000 kinds of plants grown on its grounds and in its conservatory. Covering herbs, annuals, perennials, vegetables, evergreens, and exotic tropical plants, this booklet, *Longwood Garden Plant and Seed Sources*, is available postpaid for $2.50 by writing Visitor Center, Longwood Gardens, Kennett Square, Pa. 19348.

Finally, the truly adventurous gardener will want to become a member of the American Horticultural Society, not only because it's a worthy organization but also because it maintains an extensive and up-to-date collection of nursery catalogs at its headquarters in Mount Vernon, Virginia, and gladly assists members in locating plants, something which happens about forty times a week. Sometimes the search fails, of course. None of the catalogs will turn out to carry *Distictis laxiflora*, the Mexican vanilla trumpet vine, or *Muscari botryoides* carneum, a rare pink grape hyacinth. The society will then publish the names and addresses of people who are looking for some rarity or other, in the hope that some other member might grow it and be willing to share. This measure of last resort often works: gardeners are a generous tribe.

Garden Volunteers

Just recently an acquaintance who doesn't garden pressed me to define gardening, somewhat in the way that Socrates used to press his young friends for definitions of such virtues as justice and piety. Never having thought very deeply about the matter, and fairly well convinced after forty years of digging in the earth that such a summation is inessential to the art, I offered nothing, but he filled in the gap. "Gardening," he said, "means, it seems to me, to put the plants you choose in the earth and make them grow according to your will. It means deciding what you will grow and what you won't—and then acting on that decision."

"Maybe so," I mumbled. Nevertheless it struck me that this definition was the horticultural equivalent of what theologians call the sin of pride. I also suspect that anyone who began to garden with the above as a guide would soon be humbled or at least deeply humiliated: every garden is a battlefield, and its owner only one contender among many.

Take aphids, for example. From the human point of view, aphids are enemies, wretched creatures who infest our plants and weaken them by drinking their sap. But for certain ants, aphids are their dairy cows, producing the honeydew on which they feed.

Or take weeds. The distinction between weeds and desirable plants is purely anthropomorphic, corresponding to nothing in nature itself. If one views the matter dispassionately—a hard trick to master if crabgrass is galloping all through the perennial beds and the vegetable garden—a weed is just a particularly successful plant that people don't like. One purslane plant, I am told, can produce almost 200,000 seeds in a single season, most of which will germinate at some point in the following five years. In addition to this frenzy of reproduction, purslane isn't especially bothered by being rooted up. A purslane plant left on the ground merely puts down new roots and gets on with its business of producing seeds. I call that a triumph of success; never mind that it's nothing a gardener can brag about.

To turn to a much more pleasant topic, there's another class of plants which, like weeds, simply appear in the garden without our invitation but which are so desirable that we allow them to stay. These are the garden volunteers, and they can be divided into two classes.

Some volunteers are as predictable as purslane, for they reproduce themselves with equal enthusiasm. Sweet alyssum is a reliable reseeder, as are Johnny-jump-ups, rudbeckias, foxgloves, and honesty or money plant. Tiger lilies are sterile, but one soon grows into many, thanks to the dozens of fat bulbils in the leaf axils which fall to the ground and start new plants, each a perfect clone of its parent. (Hardy phlox self-seeds prodigiously, but its progeny should be removed without hesitation, since their flowers are almost always an ugly magenta which clashes with everything else in the garden.)

Then there are the shy volunteers, especially delightful because they appear unexpectedly. In my garden right now there are several such plants: a couple of cotoneasters that must be accidental hybrids, because they don't match any of the several species I grow; a tiny clematis that just popped up this spring, conveniently next to a fence post. There are also quite a few self-sown lilies, which can be recognized by their narrow petals. Jan De Graaff, the great American lily hybridizer of the twentieth century, would have rooted them up and composted them immediately had they appeared in his seedling fields at Oregon Bulb Farms. He would have been perfectly correct, but I'm no Jan De Graaff, and my narrow-petaled lilies, which I'd call ugly ducklings except that there's not an iota of a chance that they'll ever become swans, can stay in my garden along with some other volunteers. I take no credit for any of these plants. Their presence here is not of my doing and not according to my will, but I wouldn't dream of uprooting and discarding them. They are gifts that came unasked.

The Grandeur
of Trees in Winter

It is in winter that trees reveal what they most truly are—alien
presences possessed of a stark and foreign beauty that owes
little to the human race. In this season, I come to understand
the reasons the Druids among my ancestors had for giving them
worship. In other seasons we may almost deceive ourselves into
believing that trees exist for our purposes, that they are exten-
sions of ourselves, meant to serve our wants and needs. In early
spring, when the willow twigs change from yellow-gold to pale
green, we find a metaphor of hope for a world made new. In
summer we find refreshment in their cool green shade. In
autumn they so dazzle the eye that we forget the approach of
winter's harshness. And in their deaths, trees serve us in myriad
useful ways, giving us fuel and shelter, pencils and paper, ax
handles and broomsticks.

Their leaves departed, trees in winter stand naked to our
gaze, their structure laid bare. We see the architecture of an
aged grove of honey locusts, their spreading crowns all angles
and arches, suggesting all the energy and dynamism of a Gothic
cathedral. We see the pendant branches of the weeping mulberry, falling in discrete stages like a frozen cascade of wood.
We see a farmhouse dwarfed by sugar maples planted a century
ago, their massive, dark, and solemn trunks tapering off into a
delicate tracery of gray.

In the winter we see the wounds that trees have suffered
in their lives, hollow places, and the decay. We see the other

things that trees are home to—the bird nests, the places where squirrels sleep, the mosses and algae and lichens that grow on trunks and branches.

As children, we "learn" that tree trunks are brown, when we are taught the colors of a box of crayons and told which to use when drawing a tree. But in the winter, if we only look, we learn a truer lesson. Tree trunks are sometimes black, sometimes whitish-gray, sometimes reddish-gray; more often than not, their colors are ones we have no name for. In what language is there sufficient precision to describe the bark of an ancient sycamore tree, and get it right?

In winter we see the fragility of trees, and their pliant strength as they bend before the howling wind; we see them gleaming silver in a coating of early-morning ice; we see them changing in the changing light of late afternoon, reflecting the golden light of the setting winter sun.

We may see ourselves in a different way if we truly look at our trees, for they are oblivious to our most feverish concerns. They are the largest living beings on this earth. The oldest of our planet's trees, a stand of bristlecone pines in California, was growing there before the Great Pyramids were built and was well advanced in age when the foundations of the Parthenon were laid.

Meadows
and Other Wild Thoughts

Steve Davis, the head horticulturist at River Farm, a plantation in Mount Vernon, Virginia, once owned by George Washington and now headquarters for the American Horticultural Society, had a bright idea a couple of years ago. He decided to plow up six acres of lawn at the farm and replace it with a flowering meadow. Now he's very happy with the result. But that first season he thought he had a catastrophe on his hands. The reasons for putting in the meadow were sound enough. Some twelve of River Farm's twenty-five acres of rolling hillside above the wide and placid Potomac were planted as a lawn. Gasoline and labor to mow it during the long growing season were increasingly expensive, as were the fertilizer and water to keep it lush and green. Meadows require much less maintenance than lawns, merely an annual, late-winter mowing to keep out the woody plants that eventually turn meadows to forests. Planting the meadow would cost almost nothing, since Spruce Brook Nurseries in Litchfield, Connecticut, was willing to donate fifty pounds of seed.

Mr. Davis lost no time accepting the offer. The land was plowed deeply and raked smooth, the seed scattered. All that winter he looked forward with eagerness to the glorious outcome, hundreds of thousands of wildflowers in bright bloom from early spring until Indian summer—and six fewer acres for his crew to mow. What he got instead was a great shock and six acres of *Phytolacca americana* or pokeweed, a tall, rapidly growing, poisonous herb that immediately muscled aside the evening primroses and black-eyed Susans he had dreamed of. By late May, to his puzzled consternation, the "meadow" on the broad slope between the river and the mansion that houses the society's headquarters was a solid stand of the lusty stuff. Visitors to the farm asked embarrassing questions. Why was the AHS taking such obsessive interest in a weed, growing so many poke plants that they dwarfed the formal rose gardens nearby? Or had an organization devoted to improving American horticulture become just a bit slipshod in tending its own grounds?

Steve Davis first suspected that the wildflower seed had been contaminated, but the quality-control department at Spruce Brook keeps samples of each batch and was able to establish that the mixture it sent had been okay. Davis was mystified. Mowing keeps out pokeweed. The former lawn where it had reigned had been regularly mowed for over fifty years. Birds do spread this plant by eating its purple-black berries and excreting the undigested seeds, but this fact was insufficient to account for more than a tiny few of the specimens of *Phytolacca americana* in Davis's meadow. A little detective work in the River Farm archives and in the scientific literature on *Phytolacca americana* solved the mystery. Before the lawn was a lawn, it was a neglected field, precisely the kind of territory pokeweed is apt to colonize. And this damnable plant's seeds have tremendous viability. A few inches underground, they can lie dormant for as long as two hundred years. When the lawn at River Farm was plowed, tens of thousands of seeds were brought to the surface. There, after waiting since Herbert Hoover's Administration, they found the right conditions for germination.

Furthermore, pokeweed has a great advantage over many other plants, in that it doesn't require the presence of certain associated soil fungi in order to thrive. It is even believed to produce chemicals through its root system that suppress or destroy these fungi, thus giving it a double advantage in competing for territory.

The mystery solved, the farm's crew sprayed the pokeweed and everything else with Roundup, a potent contact herbicide which acts quickly and leaves little in the way of troublesome residue. Meadow number 1, mostly *Phytolacca americana*, withered away, and meadow number 2 was sown with fresh seeds, this time without the deep plowing that would have brought up more poke seeds.

It worked. Mr. Davis's bright idea was realized. On a recent summer day, he took me on a tour around River Farm, showing me the new orchard along the winding drive from the entrance to the mansion, the display beds of daylilies and dahlias, and the wooded ravine that was being rescued from brambles and poison ivy to become a garden for shade-loving wildflowers. He saved the sunny meadow for last. There was still a little poke-weed, since some of the seeds unearthed by the original deep plowing had taken their time in germinating. But the meadow was a splendid sight no doubt, a tapestry of bright bronze-gold and dark rose. The dominant colors were those of golden black-eyed Susans and raspberry-maroon coneflowers, mingled with the off-white of Queen Anne's lace and the sky blue of chicory. Ablaze with radiant color, the meadow also teamed with life. Garden spiders large and small spread their webs from plant to plant. Bees hummed, and wasps quietly stalked up and down the plants, fanning their wings in a no-nonsense, down-to-business way as they foraged for prey. A great many birds flitted about the place, looking for insects or for the ripe seeds of the plants that had bloomed in early spring and finished their annual cycle. When I commended Steve Davis on the beauty of his accomplishment, once he'd solved the mystery and the problem of *Phytolacca americana*, he said I should remember that I was seeing the meadow at only one point in its annual cycle, that it was very much a seasonal thing, constantly changing in character and color from the first field daisies and violets of spring to the days in early winter when dawn would find the somber browns of the plants left standing all ashimmer with radiant hoarfrost. I thought that I'd really like a meadow—or would recommend one to anyone who had yard to spare and hated mowing it.

This thought was reinforced a couple of days later when I was driving north on Route 340 in Virginia from a trip through the Shenandoah Valley. Everywhere I had been struck by how lovely the roadside wildflowers were, despite a bad drought.

Low drifts of crown vetch, their blossoms an attractive haze of rosy pink, hugged the steep banks where the road had been cut through hills. Pink-and-white perennial sweet peas grew in huge colonies in the areas separating lanes of traffic. Golden coreopsis was cheerful and bright. As at River Farm, there were coneflowers and black-eyed Susans, clusters of Queen Anne's lace and the ragged blue blossoms of chicory. Here and there, yellow spikes of verbascums and purple loosestrifes stood out like exclamation points. Native wildflowers and European escapees from colonial gardens alike, both graced the roadway landscape. I thought I knew what I was seeing: nature at work, strewing the roadsides with some very nice wildflowers to cheer the eye and make automobile travel more pleasant. But I was wrong. I was seeing something like the lawn Steve Davis turned into a flowering meadow, but on a much grander scale.

I realized my mistake as soon as I crossed into West Virginia, but I turned around and drove a few miles back into Virginia to make certain I'd seen what I thought I'd seen. The character of the roadside vegetation changes at the state line and most abruptly so. The wildflowers disappear at the West Virginia border. Cross the line, and there's nothing but grass, closely mowed right up to the fencerows, where mulberry and ailanthus trees and brambles slug it out for dominance.

A state line is a political demarcation, not a botanical one. It was clear that Virginia's roadside wildflowers were not there just because nature had been at work. The Commonwealth of Virginia, obviously, was intentionally managing some of the rights-of-way in her highway system to encourage the growth of a wide variety of highly attractive flora. West Virginia—and many other states—had a roadside lawn not all that different from many of the lawns in my own neighborhood, a lot of grass to mow. Virginia had its lawn too, but less of it, set off by a considerable amount of flowering meadow. The people responsible for its highways, it seemed sure, were following the lead of Texas, whose Department of Highways and Public Transportation has planted so many wildflowers along its roadsides since the 1930s that they are now estimated to cover one million acres—easily the largest wildflower garden in the world.

When I got home from Virginia, I rang up Richmond to

find out what was going on and eventually found myself talking with Bob Huntley, an environmental engineer with the state highway department. He seemed happy that someone had noticed that the flowers begin and end at the Virginia border and was ready with an explanation. The wildflower policy was initiated in the middle 1970s in cooperation with the Virginia Federation of Garden Clubs, which has eleven thousand members in 144 separate groups. In a program called Operation Wildflower, club members undertook to plant seeds in half-acre plots along selected highways. For its part, the state followed up with a plan of maintenance designed to insure the spread of wildflowers from one place to another.

"Partly it's a mere matter of timing, of knowing when to leave things alone," he explained. The general policy is to cut the grass short only at the immediate edge of the pavement, in a mown strip four to six feet wide. Beyond that, the rest of the right-of-way receives as little attention as possible. The grass predominantly planted by the highway department, Kentucky 31, isn't mown until it's some twelve to eighteen inches high and has gone to seed, after which point it remains green but ceases active growth. Herbicides are used very sparingly, mostly against Canadian thistles, multiflora roses, Russian olives, and kudzu, all extraordinarily pestiferous plants. The entire right-of-way is cropped short in the autumn to keep out ailanthus and mulberries and other weedy trees.

The result of these enlightened policies in Virginia goes beyond providing human beings with beautiful plants to enjoy as they zip along the highways in disregard of the posted speed limit. Gasoline used for mowing is being conserved. A habitat has been created that offers shelter and food to birds and small mammals. There is even some anecdotal evidence that people don't throw as much litter out of their cars when there are wildflowers in view.

Now there's some chance that with federal assistance other states may do what Virginia has been doing for the last decade and Texas much longer than that. Senator Lloyd Bentsen, like Lady Bird Johnson a Texan who is accustomed to flowers on roadsides, introduced to Congress three years ago a bill to encourage the use of native wildflowers in highway landscaping by providing funds for that purpose. It has languished in committee ever since, partly because of the nervousness of some farmers who fear such pretty weeds as thistles (a fear unwarranted: no highway department would ever plant such known tyrants of fields and pastures). But a key member of the senator's staff believes that the bill may pass in 1986, turning more and more of our public roadside lawn into flowering meadows.

The idea of transforming a lawn into a meadow can be dangerous, however, for private citizens, as Steve Kinney started to learn right around the time when Steve Davis solved his problem with pokeweed. Kinney, a graduate student at the State University of New York at Buffalo, read an article in *Audubon* magazine about the need for people to plant wildflowers instead of lawns, partly to help out birds, but also to save on the energy resources consumed by the nation's lawns. Kinney decided to turn the tiny lawn at the house he rented in the village of Kenmore into a mini-meadow. He stopped mowing and planted a mixture of wildflower seeds, with much the same plants that Virginia sows along her highways or that Steve Davis sowed at River Farm. The result was a terrible ruckus. Some of the neighbors complained. It seemed, well, *un-American* somehow, not to have a neatly mowed and trimmed patch of rye and fescue, like everyone else. It was a betrayal of the suburban ideal. People expressed vague fears that Kinney's meadow, only fifteen by fifteen feet, would cause hay fever and attract varmints, maybe even rats. The insect population might explode. Kinney put up a small sign explaining what he had done and why he had done it, but it failed to allay neighborhood suspicion. He was hauled into court and ordered to mow his meadow, with a fine imposed for every day he delayed in doing so. Kinney, a student of Thoreau, sensed that there was a principle at stake, so he refused, appealing the verdict. At this writing, the ending of the story of Kinney and his little meadow is unknown. But whatever happens, he's learned some interesting lessons about the human race, both good and bad. His case was widely publicized at its outset on network television and in the nation's press. People all over the country wrote to support and encourage him. Some even offered to contribute money to help meet his legal expenses, which were considerable. But there were also anonymous telephone calls late at night, threatening him with violence. Someone drove a truck across his front yard and dumped out garbage and broken slabs of concrete. There were public mutterings that his Queen Anne's lace and black-eyed Susans had lowered property values. Meadows, the strange lesson seems to be, are not without their power to cause alarm, as well as bring delight in a touch of wilderness enshrined in an urban world.

Flamingos!

One of the most profoundly embarrassing experiences that anyone can have—especially someone like me, who's not very good
at concealing his thoughts with a polite fib or a discreet silence—
is to have someone else proudly show off something that's in
flamboyant bad taste. Something, for example, like pink flamingos
as garden ornaments.

It was a torrid and sultry July day in Raleigh, North Carolina. At the repeated urging of a good many horticulturally
minded friends from the area, I had finally worked in a visit
to the North Carolina State University Arboretum, where, I was
told, I would find an extremely fine herbaceous perennial border
designed by a young woman named Edith Eddleman, following
the principles laid down by Gertrude Jekyll. What's more, I
had Ms. Eddleman, who serves as curator of the border, as a
guide. She had graciously consented to drive over from her
home in Durham to meet me in the arboretum's parking lot.
We had exchanged pleasantries there, the usual bits of auto-
biography passing between us. Eddleman, I learned, had ma-
jored in Chinese history at the University of North Carolina at
Greensboro, then earned her Master's at Duke, in divinity.

Now, as we stood at one end of the border she had designed,
she explained how the color scheme began with pastel tones,
moved into warmer parts of the spectrum, and then, way in the
distance, shifted into pastel blues and lavenders. I hoped she

did not divine what I was thinking as I looked at the object immediately before my eyes—a pink wooden flamingo, high on a stake, as if frozen in its flight in front of a clump of tall ornamental grass. Perhaps, I thought, someone who didn't know any better had stuck it there—or someone with malicious intent. Eddleman hadn't seen it yet. When she did she would wade into the border with all the energy of Jesus going after the money changers, rip it to the ground, and throw it deep into the shrubbery until such time as it could be more properly disposed of—incinerated perhaps, as an effront to the dignity of a herbaceous border designed according to the principles of Gertrude Jekyll. Eddleman didn't see it. At least, she didn't wade in to remove it.

We began to walk down the slope alongside the perennial border. I forgot all about the flamingo, for the border was a wonder. I whipped out my notebook to record the things that pleased me, starting with several different kinds of hardy perennial verbenas, which I didn't even know existed. Sidalcea had never much attracted me in nursery catalogs, but it was a very winning plant, with blossoms a delicious shade of pink that combined especially well with the metallic-blue foliage of some elymus grass nearby. I was surprised to learn that joe-pye weed, the ordinary old joe-pye weed of our late-summer roadsides and waste places, makes a fine plant in the border, tall and commanding at its back. Eddleman obviously knew very well what she was doing, and she had a lot of taste, as well as a good eye.

We stopped for a moment, and there they were. Two flamingos. Plastic ones. "How do you like my flamingos?" she asked. *Her* flamingos: she admitted to it.

I mumbled something and bent down to inspect a label on a lovely goldenrod, lemon-yellow and only fifteen inches high. But my mind was on those flamingos. We walked farther down the border. I found some perennial salvia I'd never heard of, so lovely and bold that it argued right then and there for a place in my own garden and won. I also ran across a blue mirrored globe on top of a piece of clay pipe. By then I expected the plastic gnome, the jockey, the plaster Madonna of the Blue Bathtub, but none of these things appeared. There was a sign: "Beware—Nymph and Satyr Crossing." There was also a blush on my face, and a broad smile on Edith Eddleman's. As some contemporary British philosophers put it, when they want to speak of epiphanies in the midst of common life or other sudden understandings, "the penny dropped." I came to a sudden realization that it made a considerable difference to me that Edith's plastic flamingos in this public garden weren't there because she simply loved them in an unreflective and uncritical way. She had thought the matter through. She also had a lively sense of camp. And she had trapped me. *I was a garden snob.* The fact is that I hadn't given the plants in her garden a fraction of the attention they deserved, for brooding about those flamingos.

There is an art, taught me by one of my sons, of learning to appreciate the terrible. Since a VCR came into our house last year, there has also been a steady parade of films on video-cassette. Some have been good, some genuinely awful—inept, stupid, utter schlock. Many of the latter have been my son's selections. He knows how to appreciate cinematic failures, and he tells me it's an important point to learn. After all, he says, bad movies far outnumber good ones, and if someone has learned to sit through *The Attack of the Killer Tomatoes* he can sit through anything with no discomfort. He may be right. Søren Kierkegaard said something similar about bores. One never knows when one will meet one, so it's best to be prepared with a strategy. Perhaps as he talks, the bore will begin to sweat. Then he becomes interesting. One can then wager with oneself: Will that bead of sweat on the bridge of his nose turn left or will it turn right, or will he wipe it away before it does either? The fact is that I was being a terrible bore, as well as a snob, in that garden in Raleigh, with my knee-jerk reaction to fla-mingos of wood and certainly plastic. Edith Eddleman had some fun with me, and she set me thinking. The world is full of people who genuinely like such flamingos. Who knows but that on visiting that arboretum and finding them there they then will go on to discover that they also like a herbaceous border à la Jekyll?

We gardeners are serious people about what we do—sometimes too serious. Edith Eddleman has a refreshing sense of fun. She tells me that sometimes in midwinter when the border at the arboretum is dull and lifeless, she goes out and spray-paints some of the ornamental grasses, following Gertrude Jekyll's color scheme.

Moist Shade on Dry Soil

I suspect that most true gardeners are touched with irrationality in at least one respect, in wanting to grow certain plants ill-suited to their climate and soil. I know gardeners in the Deep South whose lips quiver when they think of the double peonies they can't raise. I also know people in Boston who feel that they labor under the curse of Cain because they can't have the hedges of gardenias or camellias their Southern counterparts take for granted.

I'm no exception to this rule. Among the plants I most admire are some tall and spiky perennials that look bold and wonderful at the rear of a border. Aruncus or goatsbeard, once established, grows so vigorously from the roots each spring that it seems almost a shrub by summer, when its foamy, cream-colored panicles catch the eye from halfway across the garden. The taller astilbes, which have similar leaves and flower spikes, but in pure white and clear pink and fiery red, depending on the kind, look even better. Cimicifuga or snakeroot lifts its flower spikes high, like ivory candles glowing in the shade. The list goes on and on. Meadow rue and meadowsweet are handsome things, as are such foliage plants as gunnera, rodgersia, and petasites, which have huge, rounded, leathery leaves that look like they evolved in some swamp back when coal was being formed. I almost forgot to mention ligularias, which combine spectacular blossoms in radiant shades of golden-yellow and apricot-orange with foliage that is equally bold.

But there's a hitch. All these plants require moist shade, or at least strongly prefer it. My garden, to put it gently, is very well drained, being no more than five inches of sandy loam (and more sand than loam) right on top of a layer of fine gravel extending down to kingdom come. For years I've perversely tried to grow aruncus and cimicifuga and similarly thirsty perennials. With copious daily watering during the summer (when I remember), they have survived, but only barely. The astilbes and the meadow rues are weak and sick-looking, mere shadows of what they ought to be. As for the ligularias, I know of no other plant that shows so quickly the stress of insufficient moisture. When the soil becomes the least bit dry, its leaves collapse to the ground in an alarming way suggesting that the plant is done for. Water—even a heavy dew—will revive them by the next morning to a surprising perkiness, but a collapsed ligularia is still painful to behold, enough to make any gardener wonder if he really ought to garden.

A friend told me a couple of years ago that the solution lay in an old bathtub. People around here are always throwing them away, he said. All I had to do was to wait for one to turn up on a curb on one of the streets in the neighborhood on trash day, then haul it home, bury it in the ground, and fill it with a mixture of half soil, half peat moss that could be watered by flooding deeply every week or so and that would retain moisture that otherwise would seep right down into that layer of gravel. I kept my eye out for bathtubs, but none appeared. It also occurred to me that burying a bathtub, even in sandy soil, was quite a chore. Last fall, a stone sink appeared on the curb of a house a block away. Perfect, I thought, and smaller than a bathtub, but by the time I drove home and persuaded my one son living here to go scavenging with me for discarded bathroom fixtures the sink had disappeared, probably cadged by someone else in town who was chagrined by the sorry sight of his thirsty ligularias.

This story—which I realize gardeners who live on marshy ground or struggle with heavy clay won't appreciate at all—has a happy ending, thanks to advice somewhat reminiscent of that which Dustin Hoffman received in *The Graduate* when someone sidled up to him at a party and intoned the magic incantation:

"Plastics!" I got it from a different friend than the one who recommended bathtubs, but she gave me, a few days after I had lost out on that stone sink, a formula that's much the same, if much simpler. Dig a pit two or three feet deep. Line it with heavy-duty plastic mulching film lightly perforated to provide a modicum of drainage. Fill the pit almost to the rim with soil and dampened peat, in equal parts, saturate the area with water, and then relocate the ligularias and astilbes and everything else into the instant marsh thus created, an artificial oasis in the sandy soil I work. In essence, in a single afternoon's work, I built a small bog for those perennials that mope when their feet get dry.

As early as last spring, it was clear that the idea was sound. All those moisture-loving perennials looked a thousand percent healthier than ever before—too healthy, in fact. They jostled up against one another in a way that testified clearly that they were planted too closely together. There are more pits to dig. But I don't have to scour the neighborhood any more for old bathtubs.

Tubs and Flue Pipes, Yes—
Tires, No

I have never been a great admirer of the aesthetic result of whitewashing old automobile or tractor tires and planting petunias or marigolds in them, generally in pairs on either side of the driveway or the front steps; not even of the modification of this practice whereby the tires—through some technique I don't profess at all to understand—are scalloped and fluted upward and outward to form the twentieth-century rubber equivalent of the terra-cotta urns that were so widely used in the terrace gardens of the Italian Renaissance. But the basic principle behind using worn-out tires as planters strikes me as sound, for two reasons. First, gardening in containers is highly practical and satisfying. Plants can be grown under controlled conditions in places—such as city rooftops or balconies—where a garden would otherwise be impossible. (Linda Yang's handy guide *The Terrace Gardener's Handbook* explores the subject very thoroughly.) A sterilized soil mix cuts down on the need for weeding, as well as on diseases transmitted by soil-borne microorganisms. Competition for nutrients from the roots of maples and other greedy feeders is eliminated. Plants with very choosy habits, such as rock-garden alpines with their need for scrupulous drainage or bog lovers which must have their feet wet at all times, can be accommodated, right alongside one another. In fact, by using containers it's possible to have water lilies and papyrus, a collection of alpine lewisias and saxifrages, and a few cacti growing cheek by jowl on the same deck or patio.

Containers, unless they're extremely large and heavy, can be moved around at will, giving the kind of person who's addicted to moving furniture around inside the house the same option al fresco. Flowering plants may be replaced according to the season, so that the same tub can hold pansies in the spring, petunias in the summer, and chrysanthemums in early fall. Obviously, containers offer those gardeners who use them options and opportunities not open to their brethren who simply dig in the earth. But my second reason for respecting at least the motives of those whose eyes light up when they spot an old tire and immediately rush to get some whitewash concerns two facts that anyone will know if he's spent five minutes looking around the nearest garden center: things sold specifically to be used as plant containers are certain to be expensive and quite likely to be homely as well. At the center I patronize, dinky window boxes start at $29.95—an almost minuscule sum compared with the prices asked for garden containers in those specialized catalogs for horticultural accoutrements which arrive, unsought, in the mailboxes of anyone who has ever subscribed to a garden magazine.

But gardeners are on the whole an imaginative tribe, with a keen eye for putting objects meant for other purposes into their own service. My wife, for example, is both an avid tender of houseplants and a nurse on the medical-surgical floor of our local hospital. About ten years ago, she suddenly looked at the disposable interlocking metal rods used to hang plastic bags for transfusion of plasma or saline solution and realized they were equally suitable for attaching—at various heights, depending on the number used—hanging baskets to the ceiling. Every window in our house now supports a jungle.

A short walk around my deck shows a similar proliferation of containers. I have an old whiskey barrel cut in half, planted this year in blue ageratum, white petunias, and a volunteer Russian sunflower from a nearby bird feeder. I may get a second; my friend Barbara Ellis of the American Horticulture Society tells me they're dandy for water lilies. There's a wooden nail keg spilling over with ivy geraniums, and I'm painfully sorry that nails don't come in kegs any longer, for I'd love to have more. What looks like a window box at one edge of the deck is an enormously heavy cast-iron pig trough, rescued from an old barn in upstate New York fifteen years ago. By drilling a few holes in the bottom for drainage, I turned it into a quite serviceable planter for summer annuals, generally portulaca, which reseeds prolifically from one year to the next. And right next to the door from the house to the deck sit six immense pots of both blue and white plumbago, neatly housed in three rectangular stainless-steel containers with handles on either end, their sides perforated at regular intervals an inch apart; these originally were used to hold silverware in a dishwashing machine at the old Traymore Hotel in Atlantic City, and we snatched them up at an auction there just before that noble edifice was blown to smithereens and the era of high rollers began.

Just below the deck, there's further evidence of my wife's keen eye. Last summer a few days after she was horrified at having to pay ten dollars for a fairly ordinary clay pot of medium dimension, she stopped by a brickyard that also sells sand, concrete, and other building materials. There she spotted out back a wide assortment of clay chimney flues of various dimensions. For under twenty-five dollars she brought back eight, each a different height and width. They look just fine, massed together and planted in blue ageratum and pink geraniums. I'm now toying with the idea of putting in a small pool for aquatic plants and a few goldfish. Twenty or so chimney flues, of various heights and planted with perennials, would make a splendid and inexpensive backdrop—and a square one, resting on its side in front of the pond, strikes me as a fine place to sit and contemplate the fish on a lazy August day.

Spectators at a Feast
for Other Creatures

Throughout our history, the human race has conducted an intense love affair with flowers, whose beauties have been sung by poets, celebrated by artists, and simply appreciated by most of us. Simple appreciation, after all, comes easy, whether it be something droll like a whiskered pansy, something crisp and pure like a plump stalk of white snapdragons, or something elegant like the green-and-purple blossoms of a lady's slipper orchid. Some plants delight the nose as well as the eye. Little can match walking into a room in January when it's filled with the delicate scent of freesias. I have seen people plunge their faces into the huge white blossoms, like chalices, of Southern magnolia, breathe deeply of its lemony fragrance, and assume an expression of ecstasy reminiscent of Bernini's *Santa Teresa*.

Our aesthetic responses to flowers are so strong that we are generally tempted to believe that they somehow exist for our benefit. No one has expressed this attitude more baldly than the British romantic poet Thomas Gray, in his "Elegy Written in a Country Churchyard":

> *Full many a flower is born to blush unseen,*
> *And waste its fragrance on the desert air.*

Gray had it wrong, of course. So did our nineteenth-century Victorian ancestors, who contrived to believe that flowers speak to us in a human language, in such a way that azaleas signify

[*228*]

"ephemeral passion," jonquils "violent sympathy," and sage "domestic virtues." So do those who more recently have bandied about the sentimental nonsense that plants have emotional lives in tune with our own, that the African violets on our windowsills thrive when we speak kindly to them and wither before our scorn. The plain fact is that no matter how much we may relish the fragrance of orange blossoms and jasmines, the opulent texture of rose or lotus petals, or the bold colors of tulips or dahlias, flowering plants play to an audience other than ourselves. Although in the dead of winter we may stand transfixed in a florist shop, paralyzed at having to choose between anemones the color of sapphires and white lilacs that evoke thoughts of May, nature never intended the flowers for us. We are chance observers of a spectacle meant not only for eyes other than our own but also for eyes much different from our own. We cannot fathom how flowers appear to the worker of the common honeybee, whose set of five eyes—three simple, two compound, for a total of 12,000-plus lenses—perceive ultraviolet light and the colors blue, green, and yellow, but not red.

Considered unsentimentally, a flower is a sexual device, a means of securing reproduction in a form of life that is rooted in the earth, unable to move about, and incapable of selecting its own mate. Some flowers—those of grasses and conifers, for example—are so inconspicuous that we hardly recognize them as such. Relying on currents of air to carry pollen, often in enormous quantity and over many miles, from male to female parts, they need neither colorful advertisement nor inveiglements of fragrant nectar. But the flowers we delight in—splashy hibiscus, sunflowers in their golden gleam—are enticements to creatures other than ourselves, lures to enlist their aid as intermediaries in the plants' deadly serious business of reproducing themselves. Flowering plants first emerged on the earth some 135 million years ago, long before *Homo sapiens* arrived. They have evolved along with a variety of accommodating sexual helpers. A myriad of species of bees are the most significant pollinators, but the list also includes wasps, moths, flies, mosquitoes, midges, beetles, ants, birds, bats, mice, and lemurs. In time, human beings learned to pollinate plants for their own purposes, but the Luther Burbanks of this world are still raw newcomers.

Flowers announce, by their colors, forms, and odors, that they are available for fertilization and that they have the benefit of nectar to offer. Bee-pollinated plants signal bees where to land and where the nectar is. (Flowers that appear solid yellow to the human eye often have markings that reflect ultraviolet light, visible to bees.) Plants that depend on being pollinated at night by moths are usually light in color, frequently white. A good example is the yucca plant, whose chief pollinator is the female of the moth *Pronuba yuccasella*, which mates in one creamy white blossom, gathers there a sizable ball of pollen, flies to another blossom, deposits her load of pollen on its pistil, and then lays a small number of eggs in its ovary, which will feed on its seeds upon hatching. (Too few eggs are laid to destroy the whole crop.)

If a plant bears trumpet-shaped or tubular blossoms that are red or orange, there will generally be hummingbirds flitting on iridescent wings from one flower to the next, sipping nectar and transporting pollen. But in the world of flowering plants, not everything is pleasant to consider. The blossom of the stapelia, which is the size and shape of a starfish and is colored an odd shade of brownish-purple, like an old bruise, produces a ghastly odor, like rotting flesh, to lure its pollinator, the carrion fly. The carrion fly, however, is deceived. Like the yucca moth, it lays its eggs in the flower it pollinates, mistaking it for the carrion it generally finds, but the stapelia lacks the nourishment its foul smell promises, and the fly's maggots die from starvation. Considerably kinder despite its name is the cruel plant (*Araujia sericifera*), a vine native to southern Brazil which is sometimes grown as a houseplant. It traps moths overnight in its fragrant, sticky white blossoms but releases them the next morning after their struggles have spread pollen inside.

Unquestionably the strangest exhibition of plant behavior is to be found among several species of the genus of orchids known as bee orchids or *Ophrys*; their hairy pouches at the bottom of each blossom resemble the bodies of female bees, enough so that the males are deceived and attempt copulation. Before the bee gives up its attempt at reproducing its kind, at least with this particular blossom, pollen sticks to its head—pollen that then will fertilize the next blossom with which he tries to mate. Incidentally, the bee orchid's successful strategy of achieving pollination by means of sexual impersonation is not an isolated example; other orchids mimic female flies and mosquitoes in the same way. Many human beings may also find orchids seductive, but in a far less literal sense.

We treat flowers as if they are ours. We use flowers artistically as the subjects of still lifes. We grow them and tend them. We pick them for our buttonholes. Winter and summer we bedeck our houses with them. We regard them as means to our ends. When the blossoms in our gardens fade and wither, we say that they have died, even though "spent" is the more fitting word, since nestled within these desiccated blossoms are the elements of their next generation.

We're fundamentally mistaken in seeing flowers as existing within and for our system of purposes, but there's a virtue in the mistake. The virtue lies in finding beauty and joy in things that are alien and apart from us and then incorporating them into our lives. Flowers have nothing to say to us, although we may speak of them with deep affection. They speak directly and most persuasively to bees and wasps and flies and midges, to hummingbirds, to bats and mice, all creatures that emerged on this planet long before us. Some flowers, of course, merely listen to the wind (to speak anthropomorphically), making no bright advertisement of themselves, depending on the breeze to lift their pollen grains high and scatter them far, one more step in a process whose outcome is the seed and thus life ongoing.

Confessions of
a Magpie Gardener

Classic Garden Design, The Education of a Gardener, The Principles of Gardening, The Garden Planner—all these books and more, most of them oversized and handsomely illustrated, sit in rough proximity to one another on the shelf of horticultural books in my study, as well as a cutesy little British import recently published here called *The Flower Garden Planner*. I call it *Ken and Barbie's Garden Book,* for it has several almost blank pages showing an empty perennial border, plus 140 press-out pictures of assorted flowering plants, the idea being that you can move these floral paper dolls around to see how *Liatris spicata* and *Crocosmia masoniorum* will look together before you decide to make them real neighbors in a real border. I also have every book ever published by Christopher Lloyd, as well as most of the things written by William Robinson, Gertrude Jekyll, and Vita Sackville-West, that trio of British garden writers who are well on their way to being canonized on both sides of the Atlantic.

Anyone who looks round my library might conclude that I must have some knowledge of the elementary principles of garden design. Maybe I do. I know that there should be vistas, focal points, inviting pathways, and an occasional nice surprise when a visitor turns a corner. I know that before a single plant goes in the ground there should be prudent forethought, that gardeners whose rash enthusiasms may mislead them into horticultural chaos should hire professional landscape architects to save them from nasty embarrassments later on. But knowing the good doesn't necessarily lead to doing it. On this point, I stand solidly with St. Augustine in his quarrel with Plato. It doesn't surprise me in the least, therefore, that if considered according to its overall design, my garden's a mess. No vistas. No inviting pathways with pleasing surprises at their turnings. No focal points—or better said, everything is a focal point, for in my garden the focus is on individual plants, mostly perennials. I have a friend who has described my style of gardening as the ongoing attempt to cram yet one more plant into my limited patch of earth. She's right. I am a magpie gardener, a collector of any plants that interest me, even if only momentarily.

I have an abstract knowledge of the virtues of restraint, and I understand the merits of massing several specimens—the minimal sacred number is three—of the same plant together. It's better to have ten clumps of the same daylily—Stella D'Oro, to name just one that is truly remarkable for its diminutive elegance and its recurrent bloom throughout the season—than to have ten different daylilies in the same space. I grow over one hundred different daylilies, one clump each, no massed effects, and when the space gets tight I divide them to share with friends and neighbors. My garden—and sometimes I say "yard," so as to make no false pretenses—is a living record of my successive enthusiasms, of which daylilies happen to be the most constant and enduring, a love affair that's lasted forty years now and that will probably still be going on when I'm collecting social security. But new passions always come along. I've already written about many—hardy fuchsias, hostas, sempervivums, to name a few. No doubt there will be more, as some new sort of plant sneaks into my affections, plunging me into the problem of finding a place for it. My garden has come into being entirely through happenstance, a series of accidents.

To any discriminating eye, it probably looks that way. But does it really matter very much? It pleases me, and I think of it as the embodiment of a principle of gardening that is seldom discussed in all those solemn garden books on my shelf, which if I took them seriously would wrack me with guilt. I don't believe that there's any place for guilt in a gardener's life. "Do what pleases you—even if it turns out to be a bad idea" strikes me as a fundamental rule of gardening, if it's to be any fun. Personally,

I'm what Frederick McGourty once called, in a terribly funny piece on plant snobs in a 1980 issue of *American Horticulturist,* a "monogenericphobe," someone who "can't stand particular kinds of plants." I'm probably a charter member of the imaginary organization he describes, the Anti-Salvia League of America, Inc. I detest salvias: the red annual ones, that is, not the blue perennial ones that may be the next plants to worm their way into my heart. But if my neighbor likes them, that's okay, too— so long as he plants them because he really likes them and not because he would, for some incomprehensible reason, feel guilty if he didn't. I'm willing to suffer other gardeners to have their vistas and focal points so long as they permit me to be a magpie.

Magpie gardening may be happenstance and accidental and random. But it still has its occasions of serendipity, when happenstance brings forth something so lovely to behold that it seems to have been planned with full knowledge of the outcome. Here's a single example. Last year, in a corner of a brand-new bed, I planted several miscanthuses and other ornamental grasses next to six yuccas massed together (the rules of magpie gardening permit exception), with a single specimen of dusty miller, something I've never used before, in front. In midwinter, when there was snow on the ground, this group of plants was unusually harmonious and handsome together. The grasses turned a pale, pale tan. The sharply pointed leaves of yucca turned so dark a green as to seem almost black. The dusty miller retained its silvery-gray color, but at the first hard freeze it went somewhat limp, looking somewhat like a small frozen waterfall. A dozen times at least, this group of plants, planted next to one another by pure coincidence, lured me out of the house to contemplate their harmony and rightness together. To those who garden more consciously and no doubt more correctly, I say: make neighbors of miscanthus, yucca, and dusty miller. All gardeners with good taste and a discerning sense of design know that they were made for one another.

Blossoms Beneath the Ice

It happened in 1946, when my family was living out in the country just west of Irving, Texas, so the memory is forty years old
and half a continent away from the place I now live, but it remains as vivid as the experience itself—perhaps even more
vivid, memory being the trickster that it is. It was late March,
and our orchard of thirty peach trees was in full bloom. The day
previous it had been full of bees, a testimony to spring, but that
night winter made its closing statement: the temperature dropped
into the upper twenties, and there was a slow and steady freezing
rain. The morning dawned still and brilliant with sunshine beneath a sky so deep a blue that "azure" was not enough to name
it.

Our orchard was far from the house, hidden from sight by
some ramshackle chickenhouses and a pretense of a barn, really
little more than a shed, where we kept a pony and a few bales of
hay. I do not remember walking toward the orchard, only being
there, dumfounded by the beauty and the surprise of seeing
thousands upon thousands of peach blossoms glowing a radiant
pink within a casing of glistening ice. The sun was warm on my
cheeks. The ice had started to melt, but it was still thick enough
that when a breeze arose the whole orchard rustled with a
tinkling sound unlike anything I'd ever heard before. As they
had the day before, bees buzzed in the air, but that morning they
had to wait until the warm sunlight released the blossoms from
their lovely captivity.

I cannot fully explain the beauty of this experience, nor why it has stayed so long in memory, when so much else has been forgotten. I suspect it has something to do with paradox, a word I learned much later to name those things that seem absurd or unthinkable but nevertheless confront us with the force of fact. Spring means bees and flowers and the renewal of life. Winter means frost and ice and if not exactly death then at least a halt in growth, a resting point. There is, however, that turning point, that time when winter isn't quite over, despite the signs of spring. There may be flowers, but on one surprising morning they may glisten in a silvery radiance, through the strange marriage of ice with sunshine.

Now I have a story that exceeds this childhood memory in its power over my imagination. My nurseryman friend Allen Bush told it to me in the bar of the University Hilton in Columbus, Ohio, where we were attending a conference on perennial plants. Most of the lectures and presentations we were treated to dealt with such practicalities as the uses of computers in running a mail-order nursery or how much treated sewage sludge to use in a soil-less planting medium for raising hemerocallis in one-gallon plastic pots. The high point of the conference had been a very personal, almost confessional, talk by Alan Bloom, who at eighty is Great Britain's leading plantsman, the founder of Bressingham Nurseries. Bloom has given gardeners on both sides of the Atlantic a wealth of choice new perennials, including an improbable thing called a solidaster, which is a cross between a goldenrod and an aster. He had talked about his horticultural successes, but he had also recited a history of the failures and false starts that had dogged his life until he was well into his forties—and he had also pointed out that the land he worked at Bressingham offered as many challenges as opportunities, much of it being marshy, part of it a fen.

Allen Bush and Alan Bloom—two marvelous names for nurserymen, incidentally!—had a friend in common, another plantsman, Will Ingwerson. Bush told me the barest outline of a story Ingwerson told him, about a visit he paid to Bressingham Nurseries one winter's day. There were hellebores in flower— Christmas and Lenten roses, which aren't roses at all of course, but a wonderful genus of garden plants with handsome somber-green foliage and single, long-lasting, five-petaled blossoms in pastel colors of cream and pink and mauve that are mottled with dusty tinges of green or brown or gray. Because different species and strains of hellebores flower at different times from winter to early spring, their season is long, and they are especially welcome for blooming at the slack time of the year, when not much else is going on in the garden.

Some of the hellebores at Bressingham, the story has it, grow in a fen. Bloom and his family have long been avid ice-skaters, and it is their custom in the winter to flood the fen—or perhaps it simply floods naturally. When the water freezes solid, they skate there, and they invite visiting friends to join them. Will Ingwerson told Allen Bush, who then told me, that when he skated on the frozen waters covering the fen, he saw hellebores blooming beneath the ice.

I have no more of the story than that. I don't know how many hellebores there were. Perhaps there were only a few. I don't know how large the fen was, or how much of it was covered in ice. I have only the barest facts: someone I don't know once went skating over a sheet of ice with some hellebores below its surface. Here, unfettered by more information than what little I have, my imagination has full rein—and reign—and I dream my way into the story Allen Bush told me in that bar in Columbus. That flooded fen covers twelve acres, all planted in Christmas and Lenten roses, as thickly as in a floral tapestry. The ice gleams in the sun. There are scores and scores of skaters, and the air is full of the sounds of their blades against the ice. I've never ice-skated before (it doesn't generally come with a childhood in Texas), but I put on skates and join the others. I am lost in wonder as I glide across the ice, with the hellebores blooming below my feet, as still as flowers made of glass, as lovely as those icy peach blossoms in Texas one morning a long, long time ago.

VI. SAVING
WHAT WE CAN

The Wild Cyclamens
of Montrose

Hillsborough, N.C.
Bellevue, Heartsease, Pilgrim's Rest, Seven Hearths—such pleasing names identify the houses dating from the eighteenth and early nineteenth centuries in this charming, somewhat sleepy Southern town. No one has ever gotten round to putting a historical marker at the driveway leading up from St. Mary's Road to the huge white house called Montrose. But a marker really belongs there. The house itself dates back only to the late nineteenth century, but it's built on land where Lord Cornwallis camped in 1781 during his war against the rebellious colonists. And some original outbuildings remain, including a barn, a smokehouse still used until a few years ago, and the simple but capacious and appealing one-story wooden frame building that William A. Graham—who was governor of North Carolina, Secretary of the Navy under Millard Fillmore, and an unsuccessful candidate for the Vice Presidency of the United States—put up in 1842 to serve as his law offices.

Montrose is named after the Graham family's ancestral home in Scotland, and here Nancy Goodwin, a very soft-spoken but highly determined woman, wages a crusade to save as many species of cyclamens as she can from extinction in Turkey, Greece, and elsewhere around the Mediterranean Basin, where they are being collected in the wild and shipped, quite illegally, to gardeners in Great Britain and the United States. Many of us who have bought cyclamens in the past don't realize that far, far too often the bulbs have been collected rather than seed-grown, that extremely rare sorts often are misidentified as commoner ones, and that in our entirely understandable yearning to grow these tiny but charming wildflowers we contribute to their extermination in their native habitats. The World Wildlife Fund and other conservation organizations have recently called attention to the plight of wild cyclamens, but word on such matters spreads much more slowly than juicy pieces of gossip about politicians and rock musicians. And in the meantime a devoted gardener and cyclamen lover in Hillsborough is doing everything she can to assure that we can have these things growing on our own piece of earth without aiding their destruction where they originated.

Before we begin to talk about the reasons that wild cyclamens are endangered and her crusade on their behalf, Nancy Goodwin takes me on a tour of the grounds at Montrose, occasionally stopping to bend down and pull up a stray weed that has invaded the immaculately tended flower beds surrounding the house and William A. Graham's old law office, now a studio where she gives piano lessons. We admire the splendor of a cardiocrinum, a lily-like plant with greenish white buds and blossoms like trumpets that rises so high above a boxwood hedge that it would take a stepladder to find out if it's as fragrant as it looks. On our way to the vegetable garden where her husband, Craufurd, an economist who is dean of the graduate school of arts and sciences at Duke University, grows his corn and tomatoes, we pause to admire a sprawling colony of *Clematis integrifolia*. This low, nonvining sort has lovely nodding blossoms the color of sapphires, and twisted silvery seed heads as handsome as any flower. We amble through an immense cutting garden radiant with yellow and ivory anthemis to some rows of raspberries ripe for the picking—a pleasant place to stand and talk, meanwhile eating some handfuls of berries.

I ask Nancy Goodwin about her career as a gardener. It's a lifelong thing—"probably hereditary." One grandmother had a wonderful rock garden in middle Tennessee. Another, in Georgia, grew old-fashioned plants like larkspur, poppies, and love-in-a-mist—all of which are abundantly in evidence at Montrose. Her mother was never happier than when the lady's slippers came into bloom in her shady garden in Durham, and her father, who recently retired as a professor of Victorian literature at Duke University, has long been locally celebrated for his success at raising vegetables.

"My first experience with gardening was a dismal failure," she explains, "but then disappointment is hardly a stranger to gardeners. My parents gave me an iris to tend, cautioning me to keep the soil off the top of the rhizome. The thing never bloomed, not even once. Then I started gardening in earnest in 1963, when Craufurd and I bought a house in Durham. That summer we went to England, where I saw my first wild cyclamen, which simply enchanted me. I ordered some tubers that fall, and then began to raise them from seed. Before long, I was totally consumed by a passionate interest in horticulture. I planted an herb garden. I joined the American Horticultural Society. I looked up the botanical names of everything I grew, determined to master the basic terminology."

When the Goodwins bought Montrose in 1977 from the great-grandsons of its original owner, there was no garden to speak of, merely some fine old boxwood hedges and shrub borders, a rock garden dating back to the nineteenth century that may be one of the earliest examples of Oriental influence on American horticulture (during William A. Graham's service as Secretary of the Navy, Commodore Perry sailed to Japan to open it to the West), and some venerable oaks and other native trees. "I hated to leave that garden in Durham, but I must admit that it meant leaving behind some bad mistakes in judgment, especially about color. I had put things that were separately wonderful right next to each other, where they clashed—red monarda with big hot gloriosa daisies, to name a particularly dreadful combination."

On this unusually sultry June morning, we have walked down a grassy path leading to a good-sized pond, fit for both swimmers and turtles, its creek- and spring-fed waters eventually tumbling over some small waterfalls to the Eno River, one of the nation's least celebrated watercourses. Here, after crossing through the stubble of a new-mown field and entering the welcome shade of a woodland strewn with boulders, the co-owner of Montrose cries out in warning: "Watch out!" There's no snake, just a small plant of *Cyclamen hederifolium* I'm about to trample underfoot. Nancy Goodwin is fiercely protective of cyclamens wherever they grow, at Montrose and elsewhere.

This woodland, recently cleared of poison ivy and brambles, was once farmed. Signs of plowing still remain, in the form of curving terraces against erosion. The forest litter of decaying leaves is deep, and everywhere there are cyclamens, which Nancy Goodwin identifies on sight—*C. cilicium, C. coum, C. graecum, C. pseudibericum, C. trochopteranthum,* and a varietal form of *C. hederifolium* with extraordinarily complicated leaf markings which the noted British garden writer E. A. Bowles named Apollo. Much of this planting is only one year old. With time—and continuing vigilance against the inroads of poison ivy —it should become one of the glories of Hillsborough. Every year the tubers will grow fatter, the blossoms more abundant, until each plant produces up to one hundred delicate blooms during its season.

We are back in the house William A. Graham's son built in 1898, a commodious place with enormous rooms and ceilings so high that air-conditioning isn't always needed against the fierce summer heat of the Carolina piedmont. Nancy Goodwin fixes tall glasses of iced tea with lemon slices and crushed leaves of spearmint, and we slip into the greenhouse. There thousands of little cyclamens grow in the plastic pots they will be shipped in, to cut down on the disturbance to the plants' root systems. Summer isn't really their season, so the bloom in the greenhouse is scanty, but the leaves look healthy and each plant has formed a tuber, either on top of the soil or beneath its surface, depending on the species. (*C. coum,* for example, stays high and dry; *C. repandum* buries itself all the way to the bottom of the pot.)

Nancy Goodwin speaks with genuine horror about mail-order nurseries which sell collected tubers—which can generally be distinguished from seed-grown ones. Those grown in cultivation from seed are smooth and rounded. Those taken from the wild are shriveled, indicating a long, hot journey from the eastern Mediterranean; they are, furthermore, gnarled and irregular in shape, and pocked with marks from the poor and stony soil of their native habitat. These tubers, some of them of species almost vanishingly rare, are greedily stripped from the wild, held for a year or two by several bulb dealers in Western Europe, and then, usually in poor condition and misidentified, placed on the retail market. Goodwin was already raising as many different species of cyclamen from seed as she could lay hands on—seed she got from plant societies, seed exchanges, botanical gardens, and other gardeners in the U.S. and abroad, as well as commercial sources —when she came to realize the full truth about the origins of most of the cyclamen tubers sold retail. Seeing a need for reliably named, seed-grown cyclamens for American gardeners, she stepped up her program of propagation, germinating seed from her own rapidly enlarging collection in her basement and on the windowsills of her piano studio and then raising them in pots on a screened porch until last year, when she put in a greenhouse. The result is Montrose Nursery, which issued in 1984 its first slender catalog, enlarged the following year to list many additional species and to include a great deal of practical cultural information based on Goodwin's keen and close observation of her favorite genus of flowering plants. (The catalog also lists a few other choice perennials, including primulas selected for their resistance to summer heat.)

Nancy Goodwin makes no claim that she's a lone voice crying in the wilderness. Some other nurseries, including We-Du Nursery in Marion, N.C., and Russell Graham in Salem, Oregon, also sell seed-raised cyclamens. But Goodwin is doing her part.

year-old tractor that still works and some wooden shovels and pitchforks. In another building, which is filled to the ceiling with wooden bushel baskets, he points out the redwood fermenting tanks, which held sixty bushels of grapes, a ton and a half at a time. People have tried to buy them from him to use as hot tubs on their back-yard decks or patios, but he has refused the offer. He has a sense of history. He remembers clearly the time, not so many years ago, when the early-autumn air had a yeasty, fruity tang that permeated the entire neighborhood. His son and his daughter used to swim in these tanks every spring when he hauled them outside for their annual washing.

"I was born here," Krumm tells me, "delivered by a midwife, right on the second floor of this building." We are standing at the entrance to the winery. It could stand a coat of paint, but it's a sturdy structure, one that will outlast many of the suburban dwellings in the neighborhood—unless, of course, the farm, a prime piece of real estate by any reckoning, falls into the hands of developers. Just across Central Avenue, a busy road that runs along the northern edge of David Krumm's farm, which is concealed from view by a row of apple trees and a juniper hedge, there's an undeveloped tract of 14.3 acres of former farmland now grown over with scrubby woodland. The bulldozers are coming. Plans have just been announced for a 208-unit apartment complex for senior citizens.

Krumm's farm has already been nibbled at, bit by bit, by the encroaching pressures of development. In 1946, he had forty acres of fertile sandy loam, stretching from the railroad tracks to the east to the Patcong, a tidal creek to the west. It was a self-sufficient truck farm. Like his father and his grandfather before him, he raised a bit of everything for market—string beans and limas, tomatoes, beets, carrots, squash, sweet potatoes, and corn. The grapes and the wine were a sideline. Now the farm is down to just seven acres, part of which is taken up by his house and the adjacent houses of his son and his daughter. There's a large vegetable garden to provide for his family's needs, but the only commercial crops are the grapes he raises and sells for table use, and some Christmas trees planted outside the vineyard.

The small sign above the door to the winery, whose windows

are heavily barred to conform with federal regulations, reads "Krumm's Winery 120—Bonded." Krumm explains that his wine business was a small one, not like the big operations in California and New York. At its peak, he produced no more than four thousand gallons a year, working with little or no outside labor. Some of his wine went to the resort hotels in Atlantic Ctiy, but most of his trade was retail sales to private customers who came to his door, often bringing their own jugs.

The winery's history goes back to Krumm's grandfather, but there was a thirteen-year interruption during America's experiment with Prohibition from 1920 to 1933. The vineyard continued to produce grapes, but the winery was rented out to a somewhat mysterious gentleman from Rochester, New York, who made something called "health wine," as well as salted wine for cooking and a number of wine jellies flavored to taste like rum and other forbidden substances. Not everything would seem to have been on the up-and-up. There was a copper kettle with a condensing coil on top, presumably to remove the alcohol from the wine jelly. It also produced alcoholic spirits, of course. David Krumm still remembers the fellow who used to drive over in his fancy Buick from Atlantic City, and the banging and clatter he made as he filled up his car with five-gallon metal cans filled with something that probably was neither water nor grape juice. The gentleman from Rochester disappeared rather suddenly the year before Prohibition ended, and the winery stood empty until 1938, when David Krumm turned twenty-one and was eligible to apply for a federal license to return to the wine-making that had been traditional in his family.

"Here was the real center of things," Krumm tells me. We have walked down a steep course of stone stairs into the quiet coolness of the vast cellar, which is dominated by a quadruple row of huge casks of corded oak. Some of the barrels are oval, and held 440 gallons of wine. They were made sometime in the 1880s by his grandfather's cooper. Others, cylindrical ones with a capacity of 750 gallons, were made in Spain, used to transport wine in bulk to New York City, where his father bought them from the shipping line sometime before the advent of Prohibition. The cellar, Krumm tells me, was built in 1912. Its walls, eighteen inches thick, are made of a red stone, quarried near Trenton, which was brought to Linwood in freight cars and then hauled to the farm by horse and wagon.

Krumm finds a peculiar-looking metal tool, used, he says, to scrape the barrels after they were empty, to remove the residue of oak partially dissolved by the chemistry of the wine they had contained. And he shows me the astonishingly small orifice which he had to use to enter the cask, to carry out a labor not meant for anyone with even a trace of claustrophobia. It was such work, combined with a period of ill health, that led him to close the winery down.

David Krumm and his son, Dave, Jr., still make their wines, purely for family use. A table in the cellar holds a number of dusty, cobweb-covered demijohns, Linwood Rieslings and other vintages. Wine will continue to be made here—for a time at least . . .

It has been a good day. I have met the last farmer in Linwood, and he seems a happy man. He is also a lucky man in at least one respect. The laws of New Jersey, which still calls itself the Garden State, try to protect farmers who work holdings of five acres or larger from the staggering tax rates levied on residential communities. Taxes are still high, but Krumm has managed, partly by selling some of his property over the years. He's been a farmer all his life, never worked at anything else. But his vision of the future is realistic and his outlook is resigned and philosophical. "You can't farm in the city any more," he tells me. "It's funny—people move into the country to be in the country, to breathe the good country air, but then when they get there they won't put up with the things that make the country country. They complain if a farmer gets up at dawn and makes a little noise plowing with his tractor. They don't want their neighbors to keep chickens, let alone pigs. They want the farmers' land to make a quick profit for themselves, and pretty soon the only crop in sight is all those lawns to mow."

I hope that vineyard stays here for a considerable time to come. Linwood still has its places of historical interest, its links with a past unsuspected by most people who live here, who, like

myself, came from someplace else. There's an old Quaker ceme-
tery down by the salt marsh. A block of houses on Maple Street,
which runs from the post office for a mile or two until it meets
Bog Road, now Oak Avenue, goes back to the early nineteenth
century, as does my own house a mile to the south, where Oak
dead-ends at Bellhaven. The rafters of my house are pegged
together, not nailed, and some old-timers hereabouts still call it
the old Barrett homeplace, after a family of farmers who passed
it down from one generation to another between 1853 and 1947.
The bicycle and jogging path that cuts through town occupies the
former right-of-way of the railroad that used to haul Linwood
(then Leedsville) produce to market in Philadelphia and Camden
and bring summer tourists from Pennsylvania to Cape May and
the other resort towns of the Jersey Shore. That day will be sad
when it's no longer possible to revel in the heady, indescribable
fragrance of grapes that have ripened in the Linwood sun, promising the wine that's to come.

Elwood Fisher:
Comfort Him with
Heirloom Apples

High on the slopes of Headformes Mountain in Virginia's Bed-
ford County, a few miles east of the Blue Ridge Parkway, Elwood
Fisher, a professor of biology at James Madison University, shakes
his head in disappointment. "We're about fifteen years too late,"
he announces. His companion, S. R. "Bobby" Parks, Jr., removes
his baseball cap and commiserates. "I'm just real sorry about that,"
he says.

Now belonging to the U.S. government and part of the
George Washington National Forest, the land the two men stand
on was once an orchard on the farm where Parks's mother grew
up. Bobby Parks, in his mid-fifties, distinctly remembers coming
here as a boy late every fall to pick a very special apple, the
Cannon Pearmain, a variety much praised by nineteenth-century
orchardists for its superb flavor and excellent keeping qualities.

Elwood Fisher, whose ruling passion lies in searching out and
preserving for posterity the heirloom varieties of fruits Americans
raised in colonial times and in the early days of the Republic,
came here today with high hopes that Parks, who owns a pros-
perous dairy farm a few miles away from Headformes Mountain,
could lead him to a surviving Cannon Pearmain. He wanted to
gather scions to graft onto understock in his back-yard orchard
in Harrisonburg. But it's too late. This old orchard has now re-
verted to a forest so deep it seems almost primeval. In what dim
light filters down through the dense canopy of the tall poplar
trees above, the remains of fallen apple trees lie among the un-

dergrowth of Christmas ferns and ebony spleenworts. Their gnarled trunks blackened with rot and covered with bracket fungi, they seem like ancient shipwrecks, hostage to time and decay.

Leading the way out of the forest to the car, Bobby Parks cautions Fisher to keep a sharp eye out for snakes. Rattlers and copperheads abound on this mountain, as the wilderness reclaims itself. Bears and bobcats are not uncommon, and mountain lions are persistently rumored.

There's one more chance that Fisher can find the Cannon Pearmain this midsummer's day. Parks remembers one tree that grew in the barnyard of a farm just down the mountain and over a ridge. The farm has been for sale for quite some time, but the tree might still be alive.

"There it is," he says a few minutes later when they arrive, pointing to one of two old apple trees just beyond a waist-high stand of meadow grass. The tree has its best days behind it. Only one main branch is still healthy, but that's enough. Fisher takes his budding knife from the scabbard at his belt, cuts twenty scions from the supple new growth in the crown of the tree, strips away their leaves, packs them in moist paper towels, wraps the bundle in plastic film, and sticks the object of today's quest in an ice chest. He explains to Bobby Parks that when he gets back to Harrisonburg he will graft buds from the scions onto branches of other trees in his orchard, carefully labeling each with a metal tag. In two or three years, when they bear fruit, he will check it against the descriptions of the Cannon Pearmain in his extensive collection of nineteenth-century books on pomology. It should have the pale yellow skin, the gray dots and crimson mottling, and the rich, brisk flavor that characterize this historic apple, which probably originated in Virginia in the early 1800s.

On the way back to his farm, Parks mentions that he's got another old apple growing in his own pasture. "It's not much good for eating right out of the hand," he says, "but it's a real fine one for cooking. Probably it isn't at all rare, like you say the Cannon is. They call it the Catshead apple."

Caught by surprise, Fisher smiles broadly and says, "I'd very much appreciate getting some budwood of that apple of yours, Bobby, if you don't mind." Early settlers brought the Catshead, an English variety of considerable antiquity, to Tidewater and Piedmont Virginia. It may have grown in Thomas Jefferson's orchard at Monticello. Fisher has been looking for it for over fourteen years, ever since he started collecting heirloom fruits. That tree in Bobby Parks's orchard might just be one of the last surviving Catsheads in America.

It's been a very lucky day for rescuing old apples.

Although it overtook him in his early forties, Elwood Fisher traces his passionate love for old apples and other heirloom fruits to his earliest childhood, which he spent on a farm outside Elkins, West Virginia. One of his grandfathers grew over eighty different kinds of apples in an orchard long since felled, and Fisher believes that all of them were superior to the Red Delicious, which he scorns as "looking about a thousand per cent better than it is," although it's the one apple modern Americans have come to think of, when they think apples. Besides the Red Delicious, the list of apples that dominate today's supermarket is short—Grimes Golden, Macintosh, Stayman, Winesap, and a few others—but Fisher's childhood taught him that the world of apples is far richer and more complex than the produce managers of current grocery stores would have us believe. He grew up knowing, for example, that although Ben Davis and Bentley's Sweet were both good keepers, Bentley's Sweet had a decided edge in flavor. He knew even as a boy that the same apple soemtimes had many aliases, so that there's not a penny's worth of difference between the Albemarle Pippin and the Newtown Pippin.

Some fifteen years ago, when Fisher built his house in Harrisonburg, on a hillside lot slightly larger than an acre, with a spectacular view eastward across the Shenandoah Valley toward Massanutten Mountain and the more distant ranges of the Blue Ridge, he remembered his grandfather's orchard and decided to grow as many of the kinds of apples from there as he could find. He knew, of course, that in his limited space he couldn't have standard or full-sized trees but would have to grow ones that had been dwarfed by grafting them onto special rootstocks which inhibit top growth.

Fisher discovered quickly that planting an orchard of living,

edible antiques was more easily said than done. Were he starting out today, his path would be smoother, for recent years have
been marked by increasingly broad interest in heirloom plants,
vegetables as well as fruits. Both private individuals and institutions, including universities and government agricultural agen-
cies have come to recognize the urgent need to maintain genetic
diversity in our major food crops by preserving the varieties our
great-grandparents grew. The members of the Seed Savers Exchange in Decorah, Iowa, grow old varieties of beans and other
vegetables to keep them from disappearing forever. Some of the
larger mail-order nurseries, such as J. E. Miller of Canandaigua,
New York, now offer a limited number of heirloom apples such
as Westfield-Seek-No-Further, and there are smaller nurseries
specializing almost entirely in heirloom fruits, such as Southmeadow Gardens in Lakeside, Michigan. But when he started out,
Elwood Fisher had to go it alone, actively seeking out the old
and the rare rather than merely passively ordering from a catalog.

Harrisonburg was a good base. It calls itself the turkey capital of the world, and it's home to some major printing companies,
but the poultry and printing industries are new. This has always
been apple country. The hills of surrounding Rockingham County
are richly blessed with cider mills, packing sheds, and vast commercial orchards planted with Staymans and Winesaps. More sig-
nificantly, the coves and ridges of the Appalachian backcountry
are dotted with small farms, many now abandoned, where some
of the old apples Fisher wanted still grow. (Unlike such stone
fruits as peaches and plums, apple trees enjoy great longevity
and can survive decades of neglect—provided they're not en-
gulfed by a poplar forest.)

"If the apple trees weren't going to come to me through the
U.S. mails," Fisher recalls, "then I'd just have to get in my car
and go to the apple trees." For the last fourteen years he has gone
to the apple trees at every chance, making hundreds of expeditions to the smallest hamlets in Virginia and to ancestral farms in
the hills and hollows. He's well practiced in his art—largely a
matter of stopping off at gas stations or country stores miles from
the nearest Interstate, making polite conversation about the
weather or the crops, then getting down to business and asking

ent from the ones you're familiar with. Far too many people in temperate areas just don't understand this difference. For one thing, tropical soils are very poor in organic matter and in nutrients, and what little organic material and nutrients they contain are destroyed when the forests they support are clear-cut and the soil exposed. For another thing, the seeds of many tropical plants are large and fleshy and viable only briefly. When a tropical forest is cleared over a vast acreage, you may get a scrub forest there as its successor. Or you may get a virtual desert. But you won't get anything like what was there originally. You should go down to El Salvador and see the appalling biological degradation that's taken place there."

He continues by telling me that the tropical timberlands are being felled not only by farmers, but also by large lumber companies in the United States, Japan, and Western Europe. And in Brazil, vast areas of forest—80,000 square kilometers between 1966 and 1982—have been converted into pasture for raising beef to meet the world's demand for a cheap hamburger: a dubious enterprise carried out for very short-term profit. This pasture land becomes utterly useless for any purpose, including cattle raising, in fewer than twenty years.

Worldwide, an amount of undisturbed tropical forest equivalent in area to the state of Delaware is lost, and lost for good, every week; in a year, an area roughly the size of Great Britain. Meanwhile, in that same year, a number of additional people equal to the population of Great Britain in 1985 is born in the tropics. There is an alarming disproportion between the population and its means of subsistence.

Raven shows little patience for the Pollyannas who can remain cheerful about the future by refusing to consider a problem that is already with us, not just on the horizon. "Frankly," he says, "when world population is at 4.8 billion, and when a number of people equal to the entire population of the world in the 1930s . . . when that number of people is being added within the next twenty years, and when 1.9 billion of these two billion people will be born in the tropics—where nearly half the population already lives in what the World Bank calls absolute poverty—

well, the notion that we can have business as usual is really wishful thinking of the most extreme kind.

"Record numbers of people are assaulting the tropics in an unprecedented way, and we're really not making any serious effort to look for a solution. I estimate that the worldwide expenditure for research in tropical biology in 1979, a typical year, was only $30 million—only $30 million devoted to studying the basic factors in the livelihood of a rapidly growing majority of the human race! Furthermore, we've only got fifteen hundred people in the entire world at present who are competent to identify even a single group of tropical organisms, and that with at least three million kinds of plants and animals and microorganisms there to study. That's the kind of work we ought to be doing right away, while there's still some tropical forest to study."

Raven recites numbers and statistics as easily as some people tell you their home addresses, but his figures become especially daunting when he touches the awesome theme of the extinction of whole species of tropical plants which is already taking place at a rapidly escalating pace. A forest, he points out, is always more than the sum of its trees. "Forests support an intricate web of mutually dependent forms of life, and especially so in the tropics. The destruction of their habitat and of the conditions necessary for their existence will mean that roughly one quarter of all the kinds of living things now found in the world—something approaching a million species—will become extinct within the next thirty to forty years. Only a tiny fraction of these species have even been given scientific names, much less studied in any systematic way. Would you like more coffee?"

While Raven is in the next room brewing a fresh pot, I brood about the rain forests, to which, to be frank, I'd never given much thought. I grew up calling them jungles, and what I thought I knew about them was a distillation from Tarzan movies and comic books. Jungles, in my mind, teemed with strange and hostile creatures; the rivers swarmed with horrid leeches and piranhas that could strip a person down to bare bones in forty seconds. Jungles, of course, were extraordinarily dense with vegetation—clear a jungle, and it will spring back immediately, almost overnight. Jungles were vast and gloomy, primeval and almost infinite, perennially luxuriant and eternally there, beyond all human capacity to destroy or even dominate.

It was an admittedly naïve vision.

The first tropical forest I saw was on a recent trip, from the window of a 747 jetliner high over Belize in Central America. Sipping a martini, I stared down at the featureless mass of deep green relieved by the occasional muddy ocher of a meandering river, and nothing suggested that the tropical forests were endangered. Now, having heard Raven's thesis, I am prepared to believe that they are being destroyed, but I can't help wondering what difference it will make.

Bringing the coffee, Raven resumes where he left off, but I interrupt him with this question: "Will widespread plant extinction affect the livelihood of anyone besides the botanists?"

He has a ready answer. "Of these vast number of endangered species, we know virtually nothing, including their possible contribution to human well-being. If we don't make the effort to learn about them in the next few years, our failure will have direct and tragic consequences in the lives of our children, certainly of our grandchildren. Take medicine, for example. About four out of ten prescriptions written in the U.S. today contain at least one product from a plant. Quinine, digitalis, reserpine, belladonna, codeine, morphine, aspirin—the world's pharmacies are filled with medicines derived directly from plants or using so-called molecules of interest first found in plants and then synthesized and modified in such a way as to retain their desirable medical properties but lessen their unwanted side effects. Twenty years ago, Hodgkin's disease was fatal nine times out of ten; now there's a recovery rate of four out of five cases, thanks specifically to a couple of chemicals derived from the Madagascar periwinkle, *Catharanthus roseus*, which a great many Americans grow under the old name of *Vinca rosea*. There's an almost extinct species of trumpet creeper which is now known to have properties that might aid treatment of some forms of cancer. It has recently been discovered that the ordinary Oriental poppy contains a chemical known as thebaine, which is easily converted into codeine but almost impossible to turn into heroin, thus making it an ideal replacement for the opium poppies that have brought with them so much for ill as well as for good. Contraceptive pills have their origin in research with yams that grow wild in Mexico. In the last ten years, the seeds of the evening primrose, which when I began studying it at the outset of my career was considered to be only a weed or wildflower of no particular use, have been discovered to contain an oil that's one of only two known sources of gamma-linolenic acid, an extremely important fatty acid that may be useful in treating several diseases, including arthritis and coronary disease. Considering that only about ten percent of the world's plants have ever been examined for their potential medicinal properties, I find it impossible to believe that of all those that now face extinction there aren't a good many which might someday have been used to relieve pain and to cure disease."

I think of my mother, who is still alive but a victim of Alzheimer's disease, an incurable malady that relentlessly strips away layer after layer of memory, so that consciousness and personality die long before the body is laid to rest. Perhaps this terrible disease may one day be prevented or treated by a drug using some molecule of interest produced by a tropical plant that hasn't been named yet.

"Or take food," Raven continues. "Some eighty-five percent of all food consumed by humans, either directly or indirectly through animal produce, comes from only twenty kinds of plants —twenty out of hundreds of thousands. And these twenty were all brought under cultivation by Stone Age peoples who had their Stone Age reasons, which are absolutely irrelevant today. It's irrelevant whether women sitting around in camp can harvest them easily while the men are out hunting. We need desperately to consider the question of our basic foodstuffs and to carry out research that may lead us to additional sources of nutrition in plants that may be on the verge of extinction."

Raven disappears for a moment to get some copies of monographs and articles he has written about the degradation of the tropical forests, as well as some literature about the extensive program of research in tropical botany sponsored by the Missouri Botanical Garden. The garden maintains a herbarium of some

3.4 million dried and pressed specimens, most from the tropics, and employs twenty-eight biologists, in St. Louis and in the field. As he gives me a thick envelope filled with printed matter, I ask him how a botanical garden a long, long way from the Equator came to be one of the world's leading institutions for tropical research. He tells me that, like most things, it just happened. In the 1920s, field researchers from St. Louis bought a collection of Central American orchids from a retired postman in Panama and maintained it there for study. Other researchers gradually began collecting herbarium specimens. In the 1940s, the Missouri Botanical Garden published a systematic account of the flora of Panama, then expanded its work northward into Costa Rica and Nicaragua and southward into Colombia. Today, projects are under way in Cameroon and Madagascar in addition to those in Central and South America. If its director has his way, the institution he leads will do everything it can to learn what the forests in these places contain, to save what it can from the approaching apocalypse.

After we have shaken hands and said our goodbyes, Peter Raven keeps me at his office door for a moment, summarizing. "Here's the main point. People in this country are increasingly aware that tropical forests are disappearing. But the number of them who realize that cutting them down is very different from cutting down a forest in the temperate zone is, well, let's say that the number is vanishingly small. That's the key. If cutting a forest in the Amazonian Basin in Brazil were like cutting one in the Ohio Valley, and if it gave rise to permanent cultivated fields where vast monocultures of corn or soybeans could be raised, who could object? I'm not a sentimentalist, after all, and I don't consider myself to be a strict preservationist. If there could be permanent fields in Brazil—and there can't because the soil there loses all fertility in a very few years—there would still be a great loss of species, including plants with useful though unrecognized properties of benefit to human beings. This loss, although a sad one, would merely be the high price necessary to achieve the goal of feeding people and supporting them. But cutting a tropical forest *isn't* like cutting one in Ohio. It means using it up, using it on a one-shot basis only, like oil or other hydrocarbons. Once cut down, it's over, finished, utterly done with, and we're one more step toward creating a world in which we cannot live."

The pathway down the hill from the building where Peter Raven has his office passes by two purple-martin houses, a sight that momentarily banishes from my mind the prospect of a million species disappearing from this earth within a couple of generations. Surely the martins will always be with us, ridding the air of mosquitoes and other bothersome insects in their swift flight, as will many other species of insect-eating birds that do highly beneficial work in the grain fields of the Midwest. But the martins, like many other birds, come here only to raise their young. Eight months of the year, they live in the forests of Central and South America. If the rain forests are imperiled, everything on this planet is threatened, too. There is no separate Eden.

Appendix

MAIL-ORDER SEEDS AND PLANTS

Except for those who live in big cities where horticultural enthusiasms run exceedingly high and the supply of out-of-the-ordinary plants is correspondingly great, most American gardeners will turn to mail-order seed companies and nurseries for many plants. Although there are a few unscrupulous companies that combine high promise with poor deliverance, the standards of the mail-order horticultural trade in the United States are very high. Here are some firms with which I have had good dealings over the years or else know by unimpeachably good hearsay to sell good merchandise at a fair price. (Prices for the catalogs are subject to change, and many nurseries permit a deduction of the catalog price from any order actually placed.)

Kurt Bluemel, 2543 Hess Rd., Fallston, MD 21047. Catalog $.50. Perennials, groundcovers, and a vast list of ornamental grasses.

Burpee, 2544 Burpee Bldg., Warminister, PA 18974. Catalog free. Primarily vegetable and flower seeds.

Busse Gardens, Rt. 2, Box 13, Cokato, MN 55321. Catalog $1.50. A fairly new nursery, Busse Gardens sells an extraordinary variety of fine perennials, including over a hundred hostas at the best prices I've seen.

Capability Books, P.O. Box 114, Highway 46, Deer Park, WI 54007. No plants or seeds here, just books on gardening. If it's in print and if it's any good, you'll probably find it here.

Carroll Gardens, 444 E. Main St., Westminster, MD 21157. Catalog $1. Perennials, herbs, shrubs, evergreens.

Appendix

Daffodil Haven, P.O. Box 218, Hubbard, OR 97032. Catalog $2.50. Superb American-bred daffodils.

The Daffodil Mart, Rt. 3, Box 208R, Gloucester, VA 23061. Catalog free. Large list of daffodils.

Russell Graham, 4030 Eagle Crest Rd. N.W., Salem, OR 97304. Catalog $1. General list of perennials, many native plants.

Greenlife Greenhouses, Griffin, GA 30233. Catalog $1. Christmas cactus, orchid cactus, small crape myrtles.

Joseph Harris Company, Moreton Farm, Rochester, NY 14692. Catalog free. Vegetable and flower seed.

Holbrook Farm, Rt. 2, Box 223 B, Fletcher, NC 28732. Catalog is $1 and is written with chatty charm. Perennials, some native plants, including *Gaura lindheimeri*. This nursery near the Asheville airport is small but choice and well worth visiting. Its owner, Allen Bush, follows the unusual policy of staying by his phone from 5 to 6 p.m. to answer calls—but no collect ones, please—from customers with questions.

Peter de Jager Bulb Co., 188 Asbury St., P.O. Box 2010, So. Hamilton, MA 01982. Catalog free. Dutch bulbs.

Klehm Nursery, 2 East Algonquin Rd., Arlington Heights, IL 60005. Catalog $1.50. Daylilies, hostas, iris, peonies.

Lamb Nurseries, E. 101 Sharp Ave., Spokane, WA 99202. Catalog $1. Many rock-garden plants, unusual perennials, hardy fuchsias.

Logee's Greenhouses, 55 North St., Danielson, CT 06239. Catalog $2.50. Exotic houseplants.

Louisiana Nursery, Rt. 7, Box 43, Opelousas, LA 70570. Catalog $1. Unusual range of perennials.

McClure and Zimmerman, 1422 W. Thorndale, Chicago, IL 60660. Catalog free. Sells good selection of bulbs in bulk quantities.

Milaeger's Gardens, 4838 Douglas Ave., Racine, WI 53402. Catalog $1. Attractive list of perennials.

J. E. Miller Nurseries, Canandaigua, NY 14424. Catalog free. Berries and fruit trees, including quinces and a limited number of heirloom varieties of apples.

Montrose Nursery, Box 957, Hillsborough, NC 27278. Catalog $1. Some perennials, a large and growing list of accurately named, seed-grown cyclamens not collected illegally in the wild.

Geo. W. Park Seed Company, Greenwood, SC 29647. Catalog free. Vegetable and flower seeds, bulbs, some perennials.

Pine Tree Garden Seeds, New Gloucester, ME 04260. Catalog $1. Flower and vegetable seeds, including heirlooms such as the Jenny Lind melon, and a good selection of books on gardening.

Rex Bulb Farms, P.O. Box 774, Port Townsend, WA 98368. Catalog $1. Hybrid lilies.

Rocknoll Nurseries, U.S. 50, Hillsboro, OH 451331. Catalog $1.

Anthony J. Skittone, 2271 31st Ave., San Francisco, CA 94116. Catalog $1. The best list of rare and unusual bulbs I've seen.

Southmeadow Gardens, Lakeside, MI 49116. Catalog $8. Heirloom fruit, including 239 kinds of apples.

Thompson & Morgan, P.O. Box 1308, Jackson, NJ 08527. Catalog free.

Tranquil Lake Nursery, 45 River St., Rehoboth, MA 02769. Catalog $.50. Siberian iris and a good assortment of hemerocallis both new and old.

Andre Viette Farm and Nursery, Rt. 1, Box 16, Fishersville, VA 22939. No-frills catalog listing many daylilies, hostas, iris, Oriental poppies, peonies, and other fine perennials, $1.50. A large nursery with extensive herbaceous borders where customers can see plants growing in a garden setting, Viette's is well worth a visit. A dividend is splendid scenery and views of the Blue Ridge Mountains. More plants in my own garden come from here than from any other nursery in the country.

Wayside Gardens, Hodges, SC 29695. Catalog $1. Always has some choice imports from Bressingham Nurseries in England and other overseas sources which cannot be obtained elsewhere. Wayside probably puts out the prettiest catalog in the world.

We-Du Nursery, Rt. 1, Box 724, Marion, NC 28752. Catalog $1.

White Flower Farm, Litchfield, CT 06759. Catalog services, $5. Choice perennials and bulbs. White Flower Farm puts out the most literate, even literary, catalog in the world, and it's handsomely illustrated.

Woodlanders, 1128 Colleton Ave., Aiken, SC 29801. Catalog $2. Specializes in native plants of the Southeast.

ORGANIZATIONS AND SOCIETIES

Gardeners work their patches alone, but they often feel the need to get together with like-minded people, especially to share their passions for particular sorts of plants. Thus it is that there exist a great many societies devoted to the culture and promotion of such beloved plants as daffodils and roses, as well as less common ones, such as actinidias and proteas. Other organizations promote horticulture in a more general way. Here is a list of the most recent addresses of a number of such societies and organizations, for the benefit of readers who may wish to write for more information. I am indebted to Barbara Ellis, the publications director of the American Horticultural Society, for supplying the information on which the list is based, but would also point out that the addresses of some of these organizations change fairly often.

Appendix

Pacific Horticultural Foundation, Box 485, Berkeley, CA 94701.
Palm Society, Box 368, Lawrence, KS 66044.
Pennsylvania Horticultural Society, 325 Walnut St., Philadelphia, PA 19106.
Peperomia Society, 100 Neil Ave., New Orleans, LA 70114.
Plumeria Society of America, 37 Stillforest, Houston, TX 77024.
Sempervivum Fanciers Association, 37 Ox Bow Lane, Randolph, MA 02368.
Sempervivum Society, 11 Wingle Tye Rd., Burgess Hill, West Sussex RH15 9HR, England.
Society for Louisiana Irises, Box 40175 USL, Lafayette, LA 70504.
Terrarium Association, 57 Wolfpit Ave., Norwalk, CT 06851.

FOR FURTHER READING

Barr, Claude. *Jewels of the Plains*. Minneapolis: The University of Minnesota Press, 1983.

Betts, Edwin Morris, ed. *Thomas Jefferson's Garden Book*. Philadelphia: The American Philosophical Society, 1944.

Earle, Alice Morse. *Old Time Gardens*. New York: Macmillan, 1901. Detroit: Singing Tree Press, 1968.

Fairchild, David. *The World Was My Garden*. New York: Scribner's, 1938. Miami: Banyan Books, 1982.

Harper, Pamela and Frederick McGourty. *Perennials: How to Select, Grow, and Enjoy*. Tucson: HP Books, 1985.

Haughton, Claire Shaver. *Green Immigrants: The Plants That Transformed America*. New York: Harcourt Brace Jovanovich, 1978.

Lawrence, Elizabeth. *The Little Bulbs: A Tale of Two Gardens*. Durham, N.C.: Duke University Press, 1986. (Reissue.)

Lees-Milne, Alvide and Rosemary Verey. *The Englishman's Garden*. Boston: Godine, 1983.

Lloyd, Christopher. *The Adventurous Gardener*. New York: Random House, 1984.

Loewer, Peter. *Peter Loewer's Month-by-Month Almanac for Indoor and Outdoor Gardening*. New York: Perigee Books, 1983.

Loughmiller, Campbell and Lynn Loughmiller. *Texas Wildflowers*. Austin: The University of Texas Press, 1984.

Mitchell, Henry. *The Essential Earthman*. New York: Farrar, Straus and Giroux, 1983. (Paperback ed.)

Perényi, Eleanor. *Green Thoughts: A Writer in the Garden*. New York: Random House, 1981.

Pizzetti, Ippolito and Henry Cocker. *Flowers: A Guide for Your Garden*, 2 vols. New York: Abrams, 1975.

Rix, Martin and Roger Phillips. *The Bulb Book*. London: Pan, 1981.

Appendix

Robinson, William. *The English Flower Garden.* New York: Sagapress, 1984. (Reprint of 1933 15th ed.)

White, Katharine S. *Onward and Upward in the Garden.* New York: Farrar, Straus and Giroux, 1979.

Whittle, Tyler. *The Plant Hunters.* Philadelphia: Chilton, 1970.

Yang, Linda. *The Terrace Gardener's Handbook.* Beaverton, OR: Timber Press, 1982.

Index

Index

Index

Index

Index

Index

Index